The National Security Council

Jackson Subcommittee Papers on Policy-Making at the Presidential Level

The National Security Council

Jackson Subcommittee Papers on Policy-Making at the Presidential Level

Edited by

Senator Henry M. Jackson

FREDERICK A. PRAEGER, *Publishers*

New York • Washington • London

Frederick A. Praeger, Publishers
111 Fourth Avenue, New York 3, N.Y., U.S.A.
77-79 Charlotte Street, London W.1, England

Published in the United States of America in 1965
by Frederick A. Praeger, Inc., Publishers

Introduction, © 1965, by Frederick A. Praeger, Inc.

Library of Congress Catalog Card Number: 65-15655

Printed in the United States of America

Contents

THREE: OFFICIAL DOCUMENTS

Introduction

SENATOR HENRY M. JACKSON

Free men are engaged in a bitter contest with powerful and resourceful adversaries. The responsibility of America is to defend vital national interests, promote the economic well-being of the nation, and use its power and influence with the good sense that marks a great nation. This is no easy task.

If our country is to stay the course until the world finds a way to assure peace with justice, then the Presidency, and the State and Defense departments, as well as other national security agencies, must measure up to the highest standards of competence. And members of Congress, too.

Americans have a healthy distrust of the concentration of power. I say "healthy" because it is so easy for a man to confuse his possession of power with the possession of wisdom. The tendency to this confusion is difficult to resist, as every parent knows. Wisely, the American people suspect claims to omniscience.

One of the great advantages of democratic government is that it rests on that old principle known as "turning the rascals out." If power must be concentrated—and some concentration is unavoidable—we want to concentrate it in the hands of men who can be turned out of office at the next election if we so decide. And not being wholly confident of the efficacy even of this principle, we have also built into our system a division of political authority, which we call the system of "checks and balances." Even within the executive branch, one department debates with and checks another, a technique originally devised to prevent any one department or group from becoming too dominant and now a major cause of procedural complications and delays in policy-making. Then, the three separate branches of government established by the Constitution check and balance each other: the executive branch initiates and prods; the independent legislature makes its own contribution to policy and watches over the executive; while an independent judiciary is alert to the abuse of power by the other two.

The President has considerable legislative and executive authority. But in our system, most of it may be checked by the authority granted to Congress. Constitutionally, the Presidency and the legislature are *separated* institutions *sharing* powers. And one of the powers shared by President and Congress is authority over executive departments. The President, as Chief Executive, appoints the department heads who together constitute the Cabinet. But the appointment of Cabinet members and other principal officers (Congress determines which officers are principal) are subject to confirmation by a majority vote of the Senate. The executive departments themselves are created by Acts of Congress; they receive their money annually from Congress; the programs they administer are authorized by Congress and changed by Congress. And Congress has the independent power to investigate the work of all departments.

Under our Constitution, therefore, the Secretaries of State and Defense and other department chiefs—granted public funds to expend and given government power to exercise—not only are politically responsible to the President, but are also accountable for the discharge of their duties to the Congress.

At the core of our system of government, then, is the principle and practice of Congressional surveillance and review—the duty of the legislature to cross-examine the temporary holders of executive power. I should add that with the greater and graver responsibilities held by the heads of our executive departments and by the President in our day, and with the increased concentration of power in their hands, Congress has an even greater responsibility to maintain surveillance—that is, to subject to *its* tests the performance of those in positions of authority in the executive branch, defending their performance when it believes they deserve to be defended and criticizing when it cannot honestly defend them.

One of the major purposes of this Congressional consideration of executive activities is an educational one. As long as we govern with the democratic system, the ultimate test of a government policy is its acceptance by the people. In the final analysis, the people must be persuaded of the effectiveness of the policy process and the wisdom of the policies and programs they are asked to support—and pay for. Congressional study and debate can be a vital element in this educational task.

With such considerations in mind, in 1959 I initiated a Senate study of the national security policy process. Authorized by resolution of the Senate, it was the first full-scale review since the discussion and debate preceding the creation of the National Security Council by Act of Congress in 1947.

The inquiry of the Subcommittee on National Policy Machinery —of the Senate Committee on Government Operations—was not directed to the substance of policy decisions. Rather, it was concerned with how the processes of government help or hamper prompt and effective action in national security affairs. The Subcommittee assumed that this was a national problem, transcending either political party or any particular administration.

President Eisenhower, and then President Kennedy, assured the cooperation of their staffs with the Subcommittee's work. Throughout, the study was conducted on a professional and nonpartisan basis.

The National Security Council, composed of the government's ranking officials in the fields of foreign and defense policy, was established to advise the President "with respect to the integration of domestic, foreign, and military policies relating to the national security." It can be of major assistance to a President as an accustomed place where he joins his top advisers in searching examination and debate of the "great choices" in foreign and defense policy. The Council and its subordinate committees and staffs were therefore a central subject of the Subcommittee's inquiry. Also receiving major attention were the roles and relations of the Secretaries of State and Defense, the Cabinet officials most concerned with the requirements of national safety, and the role of the Bureau of the Budget and the budgetary process itself in helping the President to plan and control national security policy.

The Subcommittee solicited the views of present and former government officials and students of the policy process. It held extensive hearings over a period of two years, during which time eminent witnesses gave generously of their counsel. The Subcommittee also issued a series of staff reports with detailed findings and suggestions for improvement. The studies found a wide audience in official Washington, in the academic community, and among private citizens. Upon the conclusion of the inquiry, in 1962, successor Subcommittees, which I have had the honor to chair, have continued to monitor the operations of the Executive Branch in national security affairs. Two statements from this subsequent record are included in this book—to provide up-to-date comment on the principles and procedures governing the work of the National Security Council under President Kennedy and President Johnson and to indicate the continuing problems in staffing a President in national security affairs.

Many difficulties in decision-taking and action brought to light in the testimony are deep-seated and are not amenable to quick or easy correction. The sheer size of the national security organization is one of the problems. It is too large for any one man to keep track of in its entirety. It is so large that unusual sensitivity and knowledge are necessary to draw on its resources when conducting national policy.

If every event had the clarity of Pearl Harbor, policy-making would be much easier than it is. But, as the citizens of Troy also discovered, appearances may be deceiving. It is for this reason that a certain amount of contention in the policy-making process becomes important. We need more than one intelligence office, more than one hierarchy of experts, if we are to get all the issues out on the table where they can be recognized. "Streamlining" and "unifying" can be carried to costly lengths; the life-and-death issues of national security are too important to sacrifice healthy competition in the name of efficiency.

In policy-making, of course, there is no substitute for sound judgment, and sound judgment depends not only on the relatively common quality of courage but also on the rarer quality of steadiness, on the capacity to consider in cool detachment the end of any road before starting out on it, on a sense of knowing when to act and when to be patient, and on skill in using advisers and expert help. Really sound judgment seems to depend upon experience. One reason, I think, why men who have distinguished themselves in the law or in investment banking have so often also distinguished themselves in the government is that success in law and banking is closely correlated with skill and shrewdness in judging the competence of advisers, in sensing when to have confidence in expert testimony and when not to. It is a skill that comes from dealing with people, rather than with numbers or things or production lines.

In the best of circumstances, it is difficult for a powerful executive to escape the "Yes-man hazard." One of an executive's major tasks is to create a climate in which dissent is encouraged and welcomed, even though the dissenter's recommendation is rejected. The clear-eyed executive will understand that he should be concerned about the possibility that he may, with the best of intentions, misuse his power—through some lack of sophistication, mistake in judgment, or shading of the truth to protect his personal reputation—and that the right of his advisers to differ among themselves and with him, and to give him their honest views, is a healthy restraint on his exercise of the powers entrusted to him. An executive needs, therefore, scrupulously to avoid retaliatory or vindictive measures against subordinates who disagree with him. He should be loyal to his staff and advisers if he expects loyalty of them.

Each President struggles afresh to make the agencies and staff units around him work in ways that meet his conception of his needs. By the same token, it would appear that no President leaves office thinking he has fully accomplished what he wanted to do. Quite naturally, Mr. Truman, Mr. Eisenhower, Mr. Kennedy, and Mr. Johnson—men of different backgrounds and temperament— approached their staffing and operations problems differently. Distinct Presidential styles of leadership and modes of doing business are revealed in the papers included in this book.

As these papers also make clear, there emerged from this Senate inquiry information and analysis that proved useful to the Administration of President Kennedy—and to the Administration of President Johnson. It is perhaps of particular interest that the Subcommittee's staff report on the National Security Council (December 12, 1960) served, in effect, as a task-force study for President-elect Kennedy. On January 1, 1961, in announcing from Palm Beach the appointment of McGeorge Bundy as his Special Assistant for National Security Affairs, the President-elect stated:

> I have been much impressed with the constructive criticism contained in the recent staff report by Senator Jackson's Subcommittee on National Policy Machinery. The Subcommittee's study provides a useful starting point for the work that Mr. Bundy will undertake in helping me to strengthen and to simplify the operations of the National Security Council.

Trends in administrative philosophy influenced by the Subcommittee's study include: support of the principle that each President needs freedom to adapt his Executive Office and policy procedures to suit his own style; resistance to proposals for super-Cabinet officers and super-staffs that clog the established line of authority from the President to executive department heads; emphasis on the authority of the individual executive who takes the oath of office—giving him responsibility, expecting him to use it, and holding him accountable for the use of it; upholding of the Secretary of

State's right and responsibility to be the President's chief adviser on national security affairs; acceptance of the principle that no government is better than the men and women it can develop through career service or attract from private occupations; and recognition that the criterion for appointment to a top national security post should be ability to do the job—regardless of party.

Actual reforms carried out in government operations that were sparked by the Subcommittee's study include: a simplification of the operations of the National Security Council and elimination of many interdepartmental coordinating committees; removal of certain nonessential staff activities from the immediate White House office; devolution to individual department heads, and to identifiable subordinates, of the responsibility for recommending policy and for overseeing the execution of decisions; improved coordination between the State and Defense departments, including the successful State-Defense Officer Exchange Program; the deliberate use of the Budget Bureau as a prime management tool of the President; reducing the rate of turnover of ranking executive officers by adopting the practice that candidates for national security posts give advance assurances that they intend to serve at the pleasure of the President and their department chiefs; renewal of the fight against overstaffing in the national security departments and agencies; and long overdue federal pay-raise legislation.

Many Congressional inquiries gain public attention without having much practical effect. But the changes in the policy process influenced by this Senate study continue to have a substantial effect on the course of this nation's affairs. I believe three special factors contribute to this outcome: At the first public hearing of the Subcommittee, on February 23, 1960, a great American, former Secretary of Defense Robert A. Lovett, provided brilliant and discerning guidance and a major theme for the study—"the authority of the individual executive must be restored"; throughout the inquiry, it was the good fortune of the Subcommittee to have the gifted service of an astute and sure-footed staff; lastly, in terms of technique and presentation, the unusual brevity, clarity, and good sense of the staff reports gained attention where it counted most —among responsible officials in Washington.

A special word of appreciation is due to all the distinguished witnesses who gave their testimony and encouragement. The papers included in this book are selected from the full record of published hearings and documents of the Subcommittees.

As far as possible, the staff reports and basic statements of contributors taken from the record of the Subcommittees are presented intact in this book. Only minor omissions have been made where condensation was necessary and possible without altering the meaning. In the editing of the material from the question-and-answer periods of the hearings, where some selection and compression was necessary, a special effort has been made to preserve the emphasis of the original record and the flavor of the exchange. Other testimony and the staff reports from the record of the Subcommittee on National Security Staffing and Operations have previously been published in book form by Frederick A. Praeger under the title *The Secretary of State and the Ambassador*.

I am profoundly grateful to Dorothy Fosdick, staff director of the successor Subcommittees, for her indispensable help in every phase of the work since 1959 and for her skilled assistance in directing the assembly and ordering of the material upon which this book is based.

I also want to mention particularly J. K. Mansfield, staff director of the Subcommittee on National Policy Machinery. He brought a very special combination of talent and experience to his task, and for his invaluable assistance I am deeply indebted.

I should like to acknowledge with sincere gratitude the contributions made to the inquiry by these other members of the staff of the Subcommittee on National Policy Machinery: Robert W. Tufts, chief consultant, Richard E. Neustadt, special consultant, and Judith J. Spahr, secretary—each of whom contributed during all phases of the study; Grenville Garside, Brewster C. Denny, and Howard E. Haugerud, professional members, and Edmund E. Pendleton, Jr. and William O. Farber, counsels to the minority—each of whom served during a portion of the study.

To my Senate colleagues in this undertaking, I am greatly indebted for their steadfast respect for a nonpartisan approach, and for their personal contributions—their candor and their judgment on problems that should be of concern to all those who strive to preserve their security and their liberty.

Finally, it is my lively hope that the publication of these papers in a form suitable for use in colleges and universities, as well as for a wider public, will help to make many able young Americans aware of the challenging, demanding, and deeply rewarding opportunities for public service. As Robert Lovett told the Subcommittee: "We can do whatever we have to do in order to survive and to meet any form of economic or political competition we are likely to face. All this we can do with one proviso: we must be willing to do our best." And to do our best, we need to draw into government service—in Congress and in the executive branch—the best Americans.

ONE:

ANALYSIS AND FINDINGS

Major Issues[*]

The Problem

In the years since the end of World War II, the traditional distinction between peace and war has been obliterated by a contest that knows no boundaries and no limits except those imposed on world Communism by expediency. The competition is total—it is military, economic, scientific, political, diplomatic, cultural, and moral.

Conflict, whether it be hot or cold, is a great simplifier, reducing issues to their fundamentals. And the essence of the present contest is the age-old struggle between freedom and tyranny. Free men are once again called to unite their strength to outperform tyranny.

The need, on this as on all other occasions when free men have been challenged, is for a unifying purpose and a plan of action, for the vision to see the threat as an opportunity and for the will to persevere. Free men must defend the boundaries of freedom and at the same time work for an enduring world community of peace with justice.

Good leadership in this cause is indispensable. But standing by itself, it is not enough. The cold war also confronts us with a critically important and enormously difficult problem of government organization. The policy road between Washington and an embassy officer in Laos, a military field commander in Germany, an information officer in Panama, a technical-assistance worker in India, or a scientist in a top-secret weapons laboratory is tortuous and long. Elaborate and complicated mechanisms and processes are inevitably needed to translate the national will into coherent and effective plans and programs.

The National Security Act of 1947, which created the Department of Defense and the National Security Council, and which called for "the establishment of integrated policies and procedures . . . relating to national security," represents the most recent major revision of our national security policy-making machinery. In

[*] From the *Interim Report of the Subcommittee on National Policy Machinery*, January 12, 1960.

essence, it codified the experience and lessons of World War II.

Momentous years have elapsed, however, since the passage of this act. These years have seen the cold war become the dominant fact of international life. They have seen the obliteration of time-honored distinctions between foreign and domestic policy. They have witnessed a multiplication of the resources required for national security. They have created many new demands on our intellectual resources as on our material wealth. They have seen science and technology move to the very center of policy-making.

The Subcommittee's goal is to review the effectiveness of existing policy-making organizations and methods against the background of the changed perspectives and problems of these last years, and to make appropriate recommendations for improvement of the policy process.

A wise and courageous President, top executive branch officials effectively discharging their responsibilities, a Civil Service correctly interpreting and properly executing our policies, a Congress affirmatively and constructively playing its crucial role in the national security policy process, a citzenry alert to the great challenges of the time and willing to make the sacrifices needed to meet them—these are the prerequisites for a strategy equal to the challenge. Lacking them, the organizational forms of policy-making will be ineffective—no matter how closely they may conform to the principles of sound management.

But to say this is not to subscribe to the mistaken notions that "Leadership is all that matters" or "All we need is ten more bright people in Washington." This study is based on the assumption that good national security policy requires both good policy-makers and good policy machinery. One cannot be divorced from the other.

The agencies and departments of the government involved in the national security process deal with a total annual budget of almost $50 billion. They call upon the direct or indirect assistance of millions of people. They work through literally thousands of interdepartmental and interagency committees. Daily, they must make and coordinate hundreds of different decisions having an important bearing on national security. Obviously, good organization helps the policy process, and poor organization hinders it.

Certain points seem fundamental in seeking ways and means to improve the national security policy process.

First, "paper changes" in organization do not necessarily bring corresponding changes in policy. It is easy, on paper, to draw organizational charts that have the virtue of symmetry and that conform to management textbooks. It is much more difficult to propose changes that will help policy-makers in fact.

Second, one should not impose rigid or doctrinaire organizational patterns upon the policy process. The principles of sound organization are constant, but they can be applied in many ways of equal effectiveness. Policy machinery should be adaptable to the style and work habits of individual planners and decision-makers.

Third, proposals for change should build upon existing organizational patterns and existing institutions wherever possible. The potential benefit of possible reforms must be measured against the potential harm of disrupting established practices.

POLICY-MAKING AT THE SUMMIT

The New Presidency

In our system of government, the President has the pivotal role in matters of national security. He is responsible for the conduct of foreign affairs; he is Commander in Chief; he makes the great decisions on the budget. Increasingly, his choices involve complex scientific and technological questions. The range of matters on which he must not only be informed but also provide leadership extends from agriculture to the zodiac.

The integration of national policy—domestic, foreign, and military—must take place, first of all, in the President's mind. The consensus needed to support national policy largely depends on his powers of leadership and persuasion. The organization of the executive branch for making and carrying out national policy should therefore be designed above all to help the President with the heavy tasks that world leadership has thrust upon him. The new demands and dimensions of the office make it a new Presidency, significantly different from what it was in more quiet times.

Each President will have his own style of doing business—the product of his nature and experience. Each President therefore needs great freedom to adapt his office and procedures to suit the peculiarities of his style.

The Need for Policy Integration

Almost every leading civilian and military officer who served in World War II concluded that the machinery then existing for the formulation of over-all national security policy was inadequate. The National Security Council, created by Act of Congress in 1947, was one of the answers to the complaints and frustrations of World War II policy-makers.

The Council is charged with advising the President—

> with respect to the integration of domestic, foreign, and military policies relating to the national security so as to enable the military services and the other departments and agencies of the Government to cooperate more effectively in matters involving the national security.

Although the National Security Council was created by statute and although there are certain statutory members on it, it is an adaptable institution, which different Presidents have used in different ways.

Under the Administration of President Eisenhower, the National Security Council meets more often and more regularly than before. The Administration created the NSC Planning Board, chaired by a Presidential Special Assistant for National Security Affairs and consisting of representatives of Assistant Secretary rank from the departments represented on the Council. It also created the Operations Coordinating Board by Executive Order— "in order to assist in the effective coordination among certain agencies of certain functions relating to the national security and to provide for the integrated implementation of national security policies by said agencies."

In addition, both a larger number and a wider variety of policy questions now go on the NSC agenda than previously. Indeed, the President determined that—

> he will . . . (1) not assign an area of national security policy formulation permanently as the responsibility of a department, agency, or individual outside the NSC mechanism; (2) make decisions on national security policy—except in special cases of urgency—within the framework of the Council.

The style of operation has also changed. The burden of drafting and redrafting policy papers falls more on the Planning Board and less on the departments and agencies. The format of the papers has been regularized, and meetings appear to be conducted on the basis of more precise agenda.

It is clear from the record that, while the NSC is a formal institution of government, it remains an institution for the President's use, and its mode of operation must therefore reflect the President's predilections.

Views on the NSC

There is a wide variety of opinion concerning the role actually played by the NSC in the policy process.

There is a general agreement that it serves certain useful functions:

It has been said, and not completely in jest, that "if there were no NSC, we would have to invent one." Few quarrel with the principle behind the establishment of the Council or with the necessity for some type of formal mechanism for coordinating and integrating departmental views at the highest level of the government.

The NSC also serves as a useful forum for discussion at top governmental levels. It gives the President an opportunity to meet, at one time and in one room, with the heads of the major national security departments and agencies. A two-way educational process between the President and his chief aides results.

The "debriefings" furnished by the participants after NSC meetings are reportedly very useful tools of communication between the President and the departments.

Many attach real importance to the existence of a written body of policy papers and a written record of decisions.

There is also general agreement that the NSC has certain limitations in its policy advisory role to the President:

The NSC confronts the same problems facing any interdepartmental committee with its built-in bias toward compromise.

It can never substitute for vigorous thinking and planning in the departments, especially the Department of State.

Many suggestions have been made to improve the NSC:

1. Some hold that the Council tries to deal with too many, and too wide a variety of policy problems. The argument goes that the Council would be of greater usefulness if it concentrated on a relatively small number of policy questions of overriding importance.

2. Another point of view is that the Council is not well equipped to resolve problems of great urgency and that it functions best when treating more routine matters.

3. Others maintain that, despite the efforts of the Special Assistant to the President for National Security Affairs, the emerging papers are still so compromised and general as not to furnish clear-cut guidance for action.

4. Others urge that the NSC process be more closely geared to the budgetary process. It is held that the two now go forward essentially independently of each other and that budgetary decisions taken outside the Council framework often negate or change the intent of NSC policy.

5. Still others propose various institutional reforms for improving the policy process. Among the suggestions made are these: giving more formal recognition in NSC deliberations to the primary role of the Secretary of State in national security policy formulation; encouraging debate on more sharply defined issues by giving departments or *ad hoc* task forces more opportunity to present policy drafts directly to the NSC; changing the composition of the NSC and the Planning Board to give greater weight to the views of the State and Defense Departments; making greater use of "discussion papers" to encourage wide-ranging and penetrating exploration of critical policy issues; substantially or modestly increasing the size of the NSC staff, with particular reference to broadening the base of scientific and military competence; and improving the monitoring function of the Operations Coordinating Board, by concentrating its activities on a narrower front of key problems.

Which criticisms, if any, are justified, and what form might remedial action take?

Policy-Making in the White House and Executive Office

Some observers favor shifting the "center of gravity" in national security policy-making from the departmental toward the White House level. In essence, they would have the White House or Executive Office staff play a larger part in the detailed formulation of policy. They argue that such a step is needed to overcome the parochial views of the departments and agencies.

One leading expression of this viewpoint takes the form of proposing a sizable national security planning staff at the Presidential level. Critics argue that such a staff would be too far removed from operating realities to produce realistic policies. They also warn of the danger of downgrading the prestige of the operating departments and reducing the vitality of intradepartmental planning.

However, even if moves to centralize national security planning at the Presidential level are rejected, Presidents, of course, still look to their staffs for help in national security matters. The increasing complexity and broadened scope of Presidential responsibilities in this field lead many to think that more staff assistance will be needed, not less.

Some favor loose and informal arrangements in this area. Others think it would be well to knit advisers together through formal organization arrangements in the Executive Office.

The following questions seem in order:

1. What are the merits and shortcomings of moves to shift the "center of gravity" in planning toward the Presidential level?

2. What observations are appropriate concerning the problem of organizational arrangements for staff assistance in the national security area?

The Key Departments: State and Defense

The Secretaries of State and Defense are the President's principal civilian advisers in the field of national security policy. In addition, they are responsible for running the two departments of the government that play the dominant roles in formulating and executing this policy. Any attempt to improve the policy process must therefore devote major attention to the roles and relationships of these two departments.

Should the Secretary of State Have More Responsibility?

The Secretary of State is the President's principal adviser on foreign policy; he is also the first officer of the Cabinet.

Just as we have a new Presidency, so also have circumstances conspired to create a new role and new responsibilities for the office of Secretary of State. Today's occupant of that office needs to be far more than a skillful practitioner of the arts of diplomacy. He needs a wide-ranging knowledge of the relations between military and foreign policies, of the uses and limitations of economic and military aid, of information, propaganda, and related programs, of the strengths and weaknesses of our adversaries, of the dangers and opportunities in countries around the world, and of the working of international institutions and of regional organizations.

Some would now have the Secretary of State assume still additional responsibilities in the formulation of national security policy. They reason as follows: Outside of the President, the Secretary of State is the official mainly responsible for formulating our national security goals. It is less and less possible, however, to divorce means and ends in security planning. The relationship between our political objectives and the military, economic, and other capabilities needed to achieve them is increasingly intertwined. Therefore, the Secretary of State should have a more dominant role in over-all national security planning.

Among the questions raised are these:

1. Are the responsibilities of the State and Defense departments in national security policy-making now correctly defined and divided? If not, what changes are needed?

2. Should the Secretary of State be formally charged with more responsibility in connection with our defense posture and the defense budget?

3. Should the Secretary of State be asked to testify in the Congress concerning foreign-policy implications of the defense budget?

4. Would it be desirable to create a "super Secretary of State" who would be responsible for the over-all direction of foreign affairs, and who might have under him additional Secretaries of Cabinet rank for such areas as diplomacy, information, and foreign economic matters?

Lightening the Negotiating Burdens of the Secretary of State

However the responsibilities of the Secretary of State may be defined, the problem of finding time to discharge them is formidable. A generation ago, when the other burdens of this office were far less onerous than today, a trip by a Secretary of State to an international conference occasioned headline news. But today, he is away from his desk for long periods of time, making it extremely difficult for him to shoulder his main responsibilities of advising the President and directing the work of his Department.

Questions frequently raised are:

1. Would it be desirable to create a Minister of Foreign Affairs of Cabinet rank, responsible to the Secretary of State,

who could represent the United States at foreign ministers' meetings?

2. Would any other arrangements help, such as appointments of ambassadors at large?

Better Planning in State and Defense

Even those who favor shifting the "center of gravity" in national security planning closer to the President would agree that the planning function of the departments and agencies is still vital. Many would go further and argue that the main burden of planning should and must fall upon the departments. They say there can be no substitute for the fullness of resources and the richness of operating experience found only at the departmental level.

One point seems beyond argument. Today, effective national security planning depends on intimate day-to-day contact between the diplomat, the soldier and his civilian colleagues, the scientist, the economist, and others.

Many believe that the planning process in State and Defense would be improved by enlisting the talents of officials experienced in a wider variety of fields than is now the case. They also seek ways of encouraging planning cross-fertilization through greater use of planning teams whose members represent diverse viewpoints and backgrounds.

These questions follow:

1. Should officials with more diverse backgrounds and experience be brought into the policy-planning process in State and Defense?

2. Is there need for a joint Planning Staff for the State Department, Defense Department, and Joint Chiefs of Staff?

3. Can greater use be made of *ad hoc* interdepartmental task forces on special issues of national security policy?

4. What is the proper relationship between State and the Joint Chiefs of Staff (and/or the Joint Staff of the JCS)? Should a representative of the Secretary of State participate in discussions of the JCS when appropriate?

A Joint Career Staff?

While stressing the importance of an integrated national security policy, many see the role of coordinating mechanisms in achieving this end as limited. They approach the problem through people, and seek ways to develop policy-makers with nonparochial viewpoints and wide breadth of experience.

One suggestion calls for a joint career service embracing a small and carefully selected number of military officers and senior career officials from the State and Defense departments and related national security agencies. Proposals for such a service, although varying in detail, have certain features in common. They advocate selection of candidates for such a service at roughly the level of colonel or its civilian equivalent. Those entering the service would serve tours of duty in a number of different departments or agencies. They would be required to address themselves to a wide variety of policy problems. They would be given special opportunities for advanced training.

These questions follow:

1. Is the proposed joint career service practical and worthwhile?

2. If so, how can it be administered so as to assure the selection of outstanding individuals and their assignment to areas where their skills can best be utilized?

3. What special problems might arise in integrating military officers into such a staff, and how might they be solved?

Resources for National Security

The past generation has seen a quantum jump in the demands that national security makes upon our national substance. The list of legitimate claimants for these resources grows ever longer.

The problem is twofold: to allocate existing resources wisely, and to generate additional resources where necessary.

The Budget

The budgetary process—the decisive resource-allocating instrument—lies at the very heart of national security planning and programing. Plans and policies without dollar signs attached are mere aspirations. It is the budgetary process that translates them into actual programs.

An enormous literature exists of comment on the budgetary process as it relates to national security. Recommendations for improvements of the process are as numerous and varied as criticisms of past and existing practices.

Major questions raised include the following:

1. Should the State and Defense Departments (and perhaps other agencies concerned with national security) participate fully in the initial establishment of budgetary guidelines for national security programs?

2. Does the present length of the budgetary cycle discourage timely initiation of important new programs and encourage the continuation of old programs after they have outlived their usefulness? If so, what might be done to shorten the cycle?

3. Should the budget be prepared in another form? Some maintain that in its present form the budget conceals policy alternatives rather than illuminating them. Such reforms as a functional budget for the armed services are proposed. Would this or similar changes be in order?

4. Should there be advance preparation of alternative budgets for all major national security programs? Some wish to see one proposed budget at x dollars; another at perhaps 10 per cent below this level; and still another at perhaps 10 per cent above. Such a procedure, they hold, would permit policy-makers to see more clearly, and sooner, what is sacrificed and what is gained at various expenditure levels. Can and should this be done?

5. Should the NSC process be more closely related to the budgetary process?

Economic Growth and National Security

The larger our gross national product, the greater is our ability to meet the various private and public demands on the economy. Many now argue for a closer relation between national security planning and economic growth.

Some say that our past and present long-term planning now fails to reflect fully enough our capacity for continuing a "normal" rate of economic growth. As a result, they contend, we sometimes deny ourselves the opportunity to undertake important programs that could be carried out without increasing the proportion of our gross national product devoted to national security.

Others go further. They say that national security planning based merely on a projection of existing growth rates into the future does not take full advantage of our potential ability to meet national security needs. They hold that long-term planning should be based upon our ability to accelerate the rate of economic growth through affirmative policies designed toward this end. Such forward planning, they believe, will enable us to fill such additional national security requirements as may arise, without endangering important domestic programs or imposing undue burdens on the private sector of the economy.

BETTER POLICY-MAKERS

In the making of national security policy, human talent is our most precious resource. Good people can often triumph over poor organization, but poor people will defeat the best organization.

Every person engaged in planning and executing national security policy has an indispensable contribution to make. The heaviest responsibility, however, falls upon three groups of people: (1) the political executive, (2) the senior career official, and (3) the younger official of exceptional ability and dedication.

The political executive—who may be a Secretary, an Under Secretary, an Assistant Secretary, or an official of comparable responsibility—represents the policy of the administration in office. The senior career official—who works at or near the top—provides the necessary continuity in policy-making and places at the service of the administration his long experience in his particular field. The younger official of unique talents brings freshness of view to the policy process while preparing himself for future leadership.

The problems are these: how to attract better officials, how to train them better, and how to retain them in government service.

Almost all authorities agree that inadequate compensation is a primary cause of our inability to secure and retain better government officials. Few propose that governmental salaries be brought to industrial levels, but almost all recommend a narrowing of the gap between the two. They note in passing that the gradual but steady rise in university salaries holds forth the prospect that the salaries of key government officials may soon compare unfavorably with top positions in the academic community.

What recommendations are appropriate to meet this problem?

It has often been argued that no corporation could prosper if its top officers were changed as rapidly as those of the national security departments and agencies. An example: Since the position of Secretary of Defense was established in 1947, it has been filled by six different men, each serving an average of two years. Eight men, each remaining in office an average of a little more than sixteen months, have served as Deputy Secretary of Defense since that post was authorized in 1949.

Those concerned with this problem point out that the period of education needed to familiarize top national security officials with their jobs is at least as long as that required to discharge correspondingly heavy responsibilities in industry. They also stress that this period of familiarization will grow steadily longer as the problems faced by governmental policy-makers increase in complexity.

What corrective action is in order? Could a contribution be made by a "sense of the Senate" resolution expressing concern with this problem?

THE CONGRESS

In the American system of government, the contribution of the legislative branch to national security policy is indispensable. It sets the broad framework for that policy; it votes the moneys needed to carry it out; it provides the most important forum for debate of national security issues. Just as the executive branch has in the past adapted its organization to new policy challenges, so also have congressional mechanisms evolved to meet changing circumstances. This will no doubt be true of the future also.

An immense body of recommendations exists concerning possible improvements in the organization of Congress as it relates to national security. Most commonly, concern is felt over the fragmentation of Congress in its methods for dealing with national security matters. It is stated that Congress lacks mechanisms for dealing with national security issues "in the round," that, because of this, Congress misses an opportunity not only to clarify its own thoughts on the relationships among political, military, and economic factors, but also to help guide its constituency on these problems.

Numerous suggestions for improvement have been made. They range from proposals for more frequent joint meetings of the Foreign Relations and Armed Services Committees, to proposals for establishing permanent National Security Committees in each House, or else for creating a Joint Congressional Committee on National Security. A variant proposal calls for a Joint Committee on the State of the Union, which would meet for only a few weeks at the beginning of each session to consider the President's major first-of-the-year reports to the Congress.

Many of those who favor some additional Presidential report on national security to the Congress, such as a Report on Requirements and Resources, draw an analogy with the Joint Economic Committee and favor establishing a nonlegislative joint committee to receive, study, and debate the report.

Some say that Congress should now take the initiative in reforming its existing procedures and structure for dealing with national security problems. Others point out, however, that past changes in congressional structure and practice have often tended to parallel corresponding changes in the executive branch. They cite the instances of the Joint Committee on Atomic Energy and the Joint Economic Committee. They note also that the establishment of the Department of Defense was followed by the creation of the Armed Services Committees in the Senate and the House.

Super-Cabinet Officers and Super-Staffs*

Introduction

This study will be appearing at a time when a new President is preparing to take over the reins of our government. There is widespread agreement that the executive branch of our government is not giving the President all the support he needs in meeting his responsibilities in foreign and defense affairs. This unsatisfactory situation has been clearly brought out in the testimony given this Subcommittee and in comments by other competent authorities.

The magnitude and the apparent intractability of many of these difficulties have led some to believe that the problems can be solved only by radical organizational changes. The changes proposed would tend to shift the center of gravity in policy development and coordination away from the great departments of the government and closer toward the Presidential level. The proposals have in common the creation of "super-Cabinet" officers or "super-Cabinet" staffs.

This report has a limited aim. Its purpose is to examine the merit of these proposals and to provide a background for such suggestions for improvement of the policy process as are appropriate.

The Besetting Problem

By law and practice, the President is responsible for the conduct of foreign relations. He is Commander in Chief of the Armed Forces. He directs the departments and agencies. He makes the key decisions on the executive budget. He cannot delegate these great tasks to any council or committee. The responsibility is his, and his alone.

New dimensions of national security make the proper exercise of the President's responsibility more difficult than ever before in our history. The line between foreign and domestic policy, never clear

* A *Staff Report of the Subcommittee on National Policy Machinery,* November 16, 1960.

to begin with, has now been almost erased. Indeed, foreign policy and military policy have become virtually inseparable. The tools of foreign policy have multiplied to include economic aid, information, technical assistance, scientific help, educational and cultural exchange, and foreign military assistance.

Historically, a President has looked to the Department of State for his principal help in developing and executing foreign policy. But, today, the sphere of the State Department is far narrower than the full range of contemporary foreign relations. As an organization, the State Department can now claim no greater concern in certain aspects of foreign policy than the Defense Department. The interest of Treasury and Agriculture in some areas of international affairs is almost equal to that of State.

Indeed, today, almost every executive department and some eighteen independent agencies are involved with national security policy. Four government agencies and six international financial organizations work in the field of foreign economic aid alone. The net result is this: the planning and execution of national security policy cut across the jurisdiction of many departments and agencies. This situation imposes a heavy burden upon the President. A host of responsible protagonists urge divergent advice upon him. He must resolve these conflicting approaches, select his own course of action, and see to its faithful and efficient execution by the very officials whose advice he may have rejected.

Presidents have in the past employed the budgetary process as an instrument for policy and program review and coordination. The budgetary process, in other words, has been traditionally much more than an exercise in accountancy, in the sense of merely keeping ledgers on the cost of ongoing and contemplated programs. Recent years, however, have seen a decline in the use of the budgetary process as a prime tool of the President in program evaluation and integration. The process has become more and more limited to an overly narrow concern for the fiscal aspects of foreign policy and defense programs.

Throughout the past decade, increasingly elaborate and complicated interdepartmental mechanisms have been created to assist the President in policy development, coordination, and execution. The best known of these bodies is the National Security Council and its subordinate organs, the Planning Board and the Operations Coordinating Board. At last count, there were some 160 other formal interdepartmental and interagency committees in the field of international affairs alone. This interdepartmental machinery has certain inherent limitations in assisting the President.

Committees, including the National Security Council, are primarily coordinating mechanisms. But they can coordinate and integrate only what their members bring to them; they cannot originate national security policy. The role of a committee in policy formulation is essentially critical and cautionary, not creative. The prime source of policy innovations is the contribution of a responsible individual who wrestles day in and day out with the problems of national security. Given imaginative proposals from such individuals, a committee may be helpful in criticizing, countering, or embroidering them.

If interdepartmental committees have limitations in policy initiation, they also have inherent shortcomings in policy coordination. The heads of the great departments and major agencies have been unwilling for the most part to concede to interagency committees the authority in policy development and execution which they regard as their right or the President's.

When policy stakes are high and differences in outlook sharp, department heads traditionally have sought to bypass coordinating committees while keeping them busy with secondary matters. Where this has not been possible, they have traditionally tried to keep the product of coordination from binding them tightly or specifically to undesired courses of action. The net result has tended to be "coordination" on the lowest common denominator of agreement, which is often tantamount to no coordination at all.

The President has been left in an unenviable position. He has found it necessary to undertake an endless round of negotiations with his own department heads or else he has been confronted at a very late date by crisis situations that resulted from a lack of adequate coordination at an earlier stage. The burdens of the President have increased correspondingly, and after-the-fact improvisation has too often substituted for forward planning.

A FIRST SECRETARY OF THE GOVERNMENT?

Contemplating the problems now faced by a President, some have concluded that he requires the assistance of a new "super-Cabinet" official who would deal across the board with national security problems. The idea is not new. In 1955, former President Hoover suggested having two appointed Vice Presidents, one responsible for foreign and the other for domestic affairs. More recently, President Eisenhower's Advisory Committee on Government Organization studied variants of the concept of a "super-Cabinet" official. In July, 1960, Governor Nelson Rockefeller, former Chairman of the Advisory Committee, appeared before this Subcommittee and made a specific proposal for statutory creation of a "First Secretary" of the Government.*

This officer would be appointed by the President subject to Senate confirmation. In Governor Rockefeller's words, he would be "above the Cabinet" and exercise Presidential authority by delegation in all areas "of national security and international affairs." The First Secretary would be authorized "to act for the President . . . at the Prime Ministerial level." He would have statutory designation as "Executive Chairman of the NSC" and would have statutory authority by delegation from the President to appoint the heads of subordinate and related interdepartmental committees. The First Secretary would have a staff of his own, and would supervise the personnel of the National Security Council and the Operations Coordinating Board. He would also be "empowered to use and reorganize all of the interdepartmental planning machinery . . . in the area of national security and foreign affairs."

At first glance, the proposal may appear an answer to current difficulties in the operation of policy machinery. The First Secretary's perspective would be expected to encompass the whole range of national security problems. He would be charged with giving committee coordinating mechanisms the stiffening of authoritative direction. Theoretically, he would be no mere White House staff assistant but a super-Cabinet official, thus able to direct fellow Cabinet members in a way that ordinary Presidential aides cannot. Theoretically again, he would relieve a President of many burdens both within the government and in negotiations with other chiefs of government. Finally, he could act as a first adviser to the President on foreign policy in its full, modern context.

Careful analysis of the First Secretary proposal, however, reveals serious shortcomings and limitations. The proposal would fail to solve the problems it is meant to meet and would introduce grave new difficulties into the working of our national policy machinery.

This proposal raises two problems. One concerns the First Secretary's relationship with department heads.

* See below, pp. 167-76.

Giving a man the title of "First Secretary" does not thereby give him power. The Secretaries of State and Defense and other Cabinet officers would retain their present statutory functions and authority. They would continue to be accountable to the Congress for the proper performance of their statutory duties. They would equally continue to be responsible to the President.

Being responsible to the President, the Secretaries of State and Defense and other Cabinet officers would report directly to him. They would be bound to question the decisions of a First Secretary; his placement between them and the President would inevitably generate friction and resentment. The First Secretary could gain the power he needed only if the President consistently accepted his judgment over that of the department heads.

But if the President were consistently so deferential to his First Secretary, who then would be President? And who would then be willing to be Cabinet officers? The primacy of the First Secretary could conceivably be established by filling Cabinet offices with relatively submissive men who lacked strong convictions or much will of their own. But this is a period of history when our Government needs more—not less—vigor and drive in high positions. This end would not be served by choosing for Cabinet positions men who could acquiesce to the downgrading of the historic posts they are asked to occupy.

A second problem raised by this proposal involves the relations of the First Secretary to the President.

The historical record shows that Presidential assistants draw effective power from their demonstrated intimacy with the President. On numerous occasions in the past, a President has deputized an intimate adviser to take charge of certain plans or operations and to act for him in dealing with department heads. In varying degree, such men as House, Hopkins, Byrnes, and Adams have served effectively as Presidential deputies. But the positions of these men were very different from that proposed for the First Secretary. Past deputyships have been *ad hoc* assignments given temporarily, at the President's own pleasure, to persons in his confidence whose intimacy with him was matched by their complete dependence on him. At the height of their effectiveness in government, a Hopkins or an Adams drew power not from statutes, titles, staffs, or paper prerogatives of any sort, but solely from the President's evident confidence in them and reliance on them.

Yet the proposed First Secretary would be in a very poor position to sustain that intimate relationship even if he had it at the outset. His statutory position, his formal status in the government, his supervision of assorted staffs, his chairmanship of manifold committees, his attraction for the press, and his accountability to the Senate which confirmed him—all would militate against the maintenance of his close, confidential, personal relationship with the President.

It is most unlikely that a President would in fact give a First Secretary the consistent backing and support he would require to maintain his primacy over the other Cabinet members. To do so would be to risk the First Secretary's becoming an independent force, politically capable of rivaling the President himself. It would run the further risk of rousing combined opposition from departmental and congressional sources and from affected interest groups.

The likelihood of congressional opposition to domination of departments by a "super-Cabinet" officer rests on the fact that Congress is constitutionally the creator of departments, the source of their statutory mandates, and the steward of their operations. Congressional committees long associated with particular governmental agencies could be expected to side with those agencies in their efforts to assert independence of the First Secretary. He would enjoy no equivalent of the solicitude that congressional committees often show to the heads of departments and agencies within their jurisdiction.

It is essential that a President have full, frank, and frequent discussions with his department and agency chiefs. Fully to understand the meaning and consequences of alternative courses of action, he must expose himself directly to the clash of argument and counterargument among advocates of different policy courses. Papers, no matter how carefully staffed, can never convey the full meaning of the issues in question. To the degree a First Secretary insulated the President from day-to-day contact with key Cabinet officers, he would leave his chief less knowledgeable than ever about matters he alone had to decide.

Even if the President were to give the First Secretary substantial backing, the latter would still be unable to do the job expected of him. For the critical budgetary decisions on the allocation of resources between national security needs and other national needs would still be outside his jurisdiction. Only the President's responsibility is as wide as the nation's affairs. Only he can balance domestic, economic, and defense needs—and if anyone else were to be given the job, the President would become a kind of constitutional figurehead.

In summary: our governmental system has no place for a First Secretary. He is thought of as a mediator and a judge of the conflicting national security policies advocated by the major departments, the Congress and its committees, and private groups. But in the American system, only one official has the constitutional and political power required to assume that role and to maintain it. That official is the President of the United States. He cannot be relieved of his burdens by supplying him with a "deputy" to do what only he can do.

THE VICE PRESIDENT AND NATIONAL SECURITY AFFAIRS

A variation of the First Secretary plan would assign to the Vice President continuing duties in the national security area as a matter of discretionary delegation from the President. One proposal recommends that the President authorize the Vice President to "coordinate and direct the Secretary of State, the Secretary of the Treasury, and all of the other instruments of Government" in the general area of national security, excluding defense matters.

Such plans derive from the same dissatisfaction that gives rise to the First Secretary proposal. Yet assigning the Vice President this responsibility not only would create the same problems associated with a First Secretary—it would also produce still other problems.

The specific proposal in question would exclude defense problems from the surveillance of the Vice President. This means that his jurisdiction would end precisely at the wrong point—the point of coordination between diplomatic, economic, and information programs on the one hand and military programs on the other.

A "super-Cabinet" officer whose jurisdiction was confined to that of the most tradition-bound Secretaries of State could do little to integrate foreign and military policy. If anything, the plan would make integration more difficult than it now is. It would reduce the Secretary of State to the level of Vice President's Assistant and add one more set of relationships that could only be adjusted by the President himself.

A deputyship of this kind for an elected Vice President creates still another difficulty for the President. A modern Vice President is likely to be a person of importance in the President's own party. A broad grant of executive authority to the Vice President could invite eventual misunderstandings and embarrassments between the two highest officials of our Government. The President, it must be remembered, has no control over the Vice President's tenure of office.

Of course, the role of the Vice President need not be limited to his constitutional obligation to preside over the Senate. Many ways of helping the President can be worked out by mutual agreement. When proper occasions arise, these can include tasks in the field of foreign policy. For example, a Vice President can relieve the President of part of the protocol burden; he can undertake special missions abroad; he can from time to time make special studies. He may, of course, play a role of great importance in the relations between the legislative and executive branches. But any attempt to make the Vice President a kind of Deputy President for Foreign Affairs would be to give the wrong man the wrong job. It would impair the effectiveness of the responsible Cabinet officers, the Vice President, and the President himself.

There have been still more drastic proposals regarding the Vice President which would make him not merely the repository of delegated authority from the President but a full-fledged deputy in the executive branch, charged by statute with authority for direction and coordination. But the Vice President is constitutionally the presiding officer of the senior body in the legislative branch. Executive power is constitutionally vested in the President, who heads another branch of the government. At a minimum, any proposal to vest executive authority in an officer of the legislative branch by statute would raise serious questions involving both the spirit and letter of the Constitution.

A Super-Staff for National Security?

A "super-Cabinet" official charged with broad responsibilities for national security would, of course, require major staff assistance. Indeed, most proposals for a First Secretary assume he will have the help of a sizable staff.

Some who would stop short of the First Secretary concept would nonetheless establish major White House or Executive Office staffs for national security planning and coordination. A representative proposal of this type would replace the present National Security Council staff, the Planning Board, and the Operations Coordinating Board with a Presidential Staff Agency for National Security Affairs.

The appeal of such an above-the-department agency is readily apparent. Those associated with this agency could presumably view national security problems "in the round"; their horizons would not be limited to the more parochial perspectives of the departments. And not being burdened with day-to-day operating responsibilities, they could presumably do a better job of long-term planning than their harassed counterparts within the departments.

But how much assistance would such an agency give the President? Its plans would lack the coloration, the perspectives, and the realism which come from actual involvement in operating problems. It would be hard to avoid "ivory-tower" thinking. Beyond this, the agency would create a new layer of planning between the President and the departments and thus insulate and shield him from the full flavor of the planning of responsible operating officials.

Such an agency would also be a bureaucratic rival of the historic departments. It seems safe to say that the rivalry would be one-sided. The staff agency would confront the traditional unwillingness of the departments to surrender their own responsibilities for policy development and execution. Lacking the autonomy and fixed entrenchments of a departmental base, such an agency could not compete for long, on favorable terms, with State, Defense, or Treasury. The end result, in fact, might be the worst of two possible worlds, with the staff agency lacking the power to give the President effective assistance, but sufficiently powerful nonetheless to meddle in the affairs of the great departments.

A President will, of course, need some assistants who concern themselves primarily with national security policy. But such assistants would act as extensions of the President's eyes and ears in a confidential relationship, not as members of a large and highly institutionalized "super-staff."

CONCLUSION

This study has argued that "super-Cabinet" officers or above-the-department "super-staffs" would not ease the problems now faced by the President in setting and maintaining our national course. In fact, such additions to the policy process would make his burdens heavier.

Reforms, to be effective, must be made in terms of the real requirements and possibilities of the American governmental system. That system provides no alternative to relying upon the President as the judge and arbiter of the forward course of policy for his administration.

It provides no good alternative to reliance upon the great departments for the conduct of executive operations and for the initiation of most policy proposals relating to these operations. Departments possess the statutory authority, the knowledge and experience and the technical staffs needed to advise the President, and the line administrators who alone can implement executive decisions. They will always be the main wellsprings of policy ideas and innovations.

Finally, the American system provides no good alternative to reliance on the budget process as a means of reviewing the ongoing activities of the departments and raising periodically for Presidential decision issues of effectiveness in actual performance.

But to reject the radical solutions is not at the same time to dismiss the besetting problems in which they have their origin. The problems remain. They cannot be solved by maintaining the status quo.

The promising paths to reform lead in these general directions:

1. *There are better ways for the President to delegate more authority for decision-making to individual heads of departments and agencies.* There has been too much emphasis on coordination and too little on delegation. Policy-making has tended to be reduced to a group effort in which no single person has real authority to act and where no one individual can be rewarded for success or penalized for failure. In the words of Robert Lovett—

The authority of the individual executive must be restored: the derogation of the authority of the individual in government, and the exaltation of the anonymous mass, has resulted in a noticeable lack of decisiveness. Committees cannot effectively replace the decision-making power of the individual who takes the oath of office; nor can committees provide the essential qualities of leadership.

2. *There are better ways to make the National Security Council a forum for more meaningful debate on issues that the President alone can decide.* One should not ask the National Security Council to do what it is not really capable of doing. The Council is an inter-agency committee: it can inform, debate, review, adjust, and validate. But, as a collective body, the Council cannot develop bold new ideas or translate them into effective action.

Yet the Council can still be a very useful advisory mechanism to a President. The evidence strongly suggests that this role can best be discharged by a Council that has fewer rather than more participants in its meetings; concerns itself only with issues of central importance for Presidential decision; works through fewer, rather than more, institutionalized procedures; relates its activities more closely to the budgetary process; and gives the Secretary of State a greater role in the development of broad policy initiatives.

3. *There are better ways to enable the Secretary of State to serve the President as first adviser in national security problems.* The Secretary of State *is* the First Secretary of the Government. He should be able to advise the President on the full range of national security matters from the point of view of their relation to foreign problems and policies. The Secretary of State need not and should not have any legal or supervisory authority over other Cabinet officers. Any moves in this direction would have many of the disadvantages of the "super-Cabinet" officer proposal. The goal is not to give the Secretary of State greater command authority: it is to enlarge the scope of his guidance and influence.

If the President is to ask more and to get more from the Secretary of State, the Secretary must be better staffed to offer policy guidance and initiatives across the whole span of national security problems. This does not mean a larger State Department; it may well mean a smaller one. But it does mean a Department competently staffed with generalists, economists, and military and scientific experts to support the Secretary in understanding and following all fields within his broad concern.

4. *There are better ways to relate military power more closely to foreign-policy requirements.* The Secretary of Defense shares with the Secretary of State the main burden of advising the President on national security problems. A full and welcome partnership of the departments of State and Defense is the prerequisite for coherent political-strategic counsel for the President.

In viewing the Pentagon, one must guard against seeking organizational solutions for problems that are not really organizational in origin. Yet there are reforms that are promising of results. They point in the direction of more vigorous employment of the broad authority already vested in the Secretary of Defense; more active participation of the Secretary of Defense in the deliberations of the Joint Chiefs of Staff; increased reliance on the Joint Staff for planning; an acceleration of existing trends toward functional commands; a budgetary process more consonant with the requirements of modern weapons technology; a promotion system that encourages officers to become versed in the broad problems of national security; a Pentagon career service that does more to develop outstanding civilian officials; and selecting for top policy positions only candidates who are willing to remain well beyond the period of apprenticeship on their jobs.

5. *There are better ways to make the budgetary process a more effective instrument for reviewing and integrating programs and performance in the area of national security.* There is need to return to the earlier tradition that regarded the budgetary process as a key program-management tool of the President.

Budget targets should be regarded not primarily as fiscal instruments but as policy instruments. The investigative analyses needed to achieve and adjust these targets must begin and end with substantive concerns and not simply with considerations of administrative organization and financial management.

6. *There are better ways to organize the Presidency to intervene flexibly, imaginatively, and fast where gaps in policy development or execution threaten to upset the President's cardinal objectives.* This does not require new and elaborate staff offices or highly institutionalized interdepartmental committees. It calls rather for more discriminating use of able staff assistants right in the immediate office of the President himself who are alert to trouble spots and sensitive to the President's own information needs.

7. *There are better ways to attract and retain outstanding officials for both appointive and career posts in the national security departments and agencies.* Poor decisions often result less from poor organization than from poor policy-makers. The one thing that could do the most to improve national security policy would be to raise the standards of excellence among career and appointive officials.

The nation should be grateful for the skill and dedication of those who now man the posts of responsibility in foreign and defense policy. But there is still room for vast improvement in developing and using the rich resources of talent now found among our career officials.

There is room for equally great improvement in eliminating the legal and financial problems that now discourage highly qualified private citizens from serving governmental tours of duty.

And, above all, there is need to abandon the outmoded conventions that have often deprived an administration of the service of members of the opposite political party. The yardstick for making appointments to key national security posts must be ability to do the job, regardless of party.

The National Security Council[*]

INTRODUCTION

By law and practice, the President has the prime role in guarding the nation's safety. He is responsible for the conduct of foreign relations; he commands the armed forces; he has the initiative in budget-making. He, and he alone, must finally weigh all the factors —domestic, foreign, military—that affect our position in the world and by which we seek to influence the world environment.

The National Security Council was created by statute in 1947 to assist the President in fulfilling his responsibilities. The Council is charged with advising the President "with respect to the integration of domestic, foreign, and military policies relating to the national security so as to enable the military services and the other departments and agencies of the Government to cooperate more effectively in matters involving the national security."

The Council was one of the answers to the frustrations met by World War II policy-makers in trying to coordinate military and foreign policy. It is a descendant of such wartime groups as the State-War-Navy Coordinating Committee.

The Council is not a decision-making body; it does not itself make policy. It serves only in an *advisory* capacity to the President, helping him arrive at decisions that he alone may make.

Although the National Security Council was created by statute, each successive President has great latitude in deciding how he will employ it to meet his particular needs. He can use the Council as little, or as much, as he wishes. He is solely responsible for determining what policy matters will be handled within its framework, and how they will be handled. An important question facing a new President, therefore, is how he will use the Council to suit his own style of decision and action.

This study, drawing upon the experience of recent years, places at the service of the incoming administration certain observations

* A *Staff Report of the Subcommittee on National Policy Machinery*, December 12, 1960.

concerning the role of the Council in the formulation and execution of national security policy.

THE COUNCIL AND THE SYSTEM

When he takes office in January, the new President will find in being a *National Security Council* and an *NSC system*.

The Council itself is a forum where the President and his chief lieutenants can discuss and resolve problems of national security. It brings together as statutory members the President, the Vice President, the Secretaries of State and Defense, the Director of the Office of Civil and Defense Mobilization, and as statutory advisers the Director of Central Intelligence and the Chairman of the Joint Chiefs of Staff. The President can also ask other key aides to take part in Council deliberations. The Secretary of the Treasury, for example, has attended regularly by Presidential invitation.

But there is also today an NSC system, which has evolved since 1947. This system consists of highly institutionalized procedures and staff arrangements and a complex interdepartmental committee substructure intended to undergird the activities of the Council. Two interagency committees—the Planning Board and the Operations Coordinating Board—comprise the major pieces of this substructure. The former prepares so-called "policy papers" for consideration by the Council; the latter is expected to help follow through on the execution of Presidentially approved Council papers.

The new President will have to decide how he wishes to use the Council and the NSC system. His approach to the first meetings of the Council under his administration will be important, for these early sessions will set precedents. Action taken or not taken, assignments given or not given, invitations to attend extended or not extended, will make it subsequently easier or harder for the President to shape the Council and the system to his needs and work habits.

He faces questions like these: Which principals and advisers should be invited to attend the first Council meetings? What part should Presidential staff assistants play? What should the participants be told about the planned role and use of the NSC system? Who will prepare the agenda? What items will be placed on the agenda? Should the Council meet regularly or as need arises?

The New President's Choice

The new President can choose one of two broad approaches to the National Security Council:

1. He can use the Council as an intimate forum where he joins with his chief advisers in searching discussion and debate of a limited number of critical problems involving major long-term strategic choices or demanding immediate action. Robert Lovett has described this concept of the Council in terms of "a kind of 'Court of Domestic and Foreign Relations'":

The National Security Council process, as originally envisaged—perhaps "dreamed of" is more accurate—contemplated the devotion of whatever number of hours were necessary in order to exhaust a subject and not just exhaust the listeners. . . . The purpose was to insure that the President was in possession of all the available facts, that he got first-hand a chance to evaluate an alternative course of action disclosed by the dissenting views, and that all implications in either course of action were explored before he was asked to take the heavy responsibility of the final decision.

2. The President can view the Council as the apex of a comprehensive and highly institutionalized system for generating policy proposals and following through on Presidentially approved decisions. Seen in this light, the Council itself sits at the top of what has been called "Policy Hill." Policy papers are supposed to travel through interdepartmental committees up one side of the hill. They are considered in the Council. If approved by the President, they travel down the opposite side of the hill, through other interdepartmental mechanisms, to the operating departments and agencies.

The Council's Span of Concern

The voluminous record of meetings held and papers produced makes it clear that the Council and its subordinate machinery are now very busy and active. A long list of questions always awaits entry on the NSC agenda. Presidential orders now in force provide that all decisions on national security policy, except for special emergencies, will be made within the Council framework. In theory, the embrace of the NSC over such matters is total. Yet many of the most critical questions affecting national security are not really handled within the NSC framework.

The main work of the NSC has centered largely around the consideration of *foreign-policy* questions, rather than *national security* problems in their full contemporary sense. A high proportion of the Council's time has been devoted to the production and study of so-called "country papers"—statements of our national position toward this or that foreign nation.

The Council, indeed, appears to be only marginally involved in helping to resolve many of the most important problems that affect the future course of national security policy. For example, the Council seems to have only a peripheral or *pro forma* concern with such matters as the key decisions on the size and composition of the total national security budget, the strength and make-up of the armed services, the scale and scope of many major agency programs in such fields as foreign economic policy or atomic energy, the translation of policy goals into concrete plans and programs through the budgetary process, and many critical operational decisions with great long-term policy consequences.

The fact is that the departments and agencies often work actively and successfully to keep critical policy issues outside the NSC system. When the policy stakes are high and departmental differences deep, agency heads are loath to submit problems to the scrutiny of coordinating committees or councils. They aim in such cases to bypass the committees while keeping them occupied with less important matters. They try to settle important questions in dispute through "out of court" informal interagency negotiations, when they are doubtful of the President's position. Or else they try "end runs" to the President himself when they think this might be advantageous.

Despite the vigorous activity of the NSC system, it is not at all clear that the system now concerns itself with many of the most important questions determining our long-term national strategy or with many of the critical operational decisions that have fateful and enduring impact on future policy.

THE PLANNING BOARD

As the NSC system operates today, most of the matters that appear on the Council agenda are the product of a highly formalized and complex "policy paper production" system. The heart of this system is the NSC Planning Board, an interagency committee whose membership parallels that of the Council at the Assistant Secretary level. Initial drafts of policy papers are normally written by the departments and agencies, acting individually or in concert. But the Planning Board is responsible for the final content and language of most papers that reach the Council table. As Governor Rockefeller told the Subcommittee, "I think the public does not recognize the degree to which the Planning Board really does 95 per cent of the work. It is not very often that a paper is changed by the National Security Council."

The Planning Board is an interdepartmental committee, chaired by the Special Assistant to the President for National Security Affairs. Although formally appointed by the President, who has admonished them to act in their individual capacities in seeking "statesmanlike" solutions, the departmental members are oriented to the problems and perspectives of their own agencies. They can be expected to try to guard departmental interests.

From the outset, the drafting of a Planning Board paper is an involved process of negotiation, barter, offer, and counteroffer among the many departments involved. Governor Rockefeller has described the Planning Board process in these words:

> A major question is presented to the Planning Board, and the various interested parties—namely, the departments, each with its own role in relation to the area under discussion—work carefully with highly skilled representatives to get language into the position paper that, while it does not violate the objective, protects their own position and their own special responsibility—I don't say interest—in this field. . . . You get a watered-down version before it comes to the NSC and . . . permissive language that is not too obvious in the phraseology. This is quite an art, this business.

Many papers going from the Planning Board to the Council do indeed contain "splits"—statements of different departmental viewpoints.

But it is not at all clear that the "splits" actually help the Council understand the real policy alternatives and the true policy options available on some issue under debate. They may crystallize minor points of difference between competing agency views. The alternatives the "splits" normally reflect, in any case, represent differences in departmental or agency viewpoints. Such differences do not necessarily define or illuminate the real policy choices available. Moreover, "splits" are themselves a product of interagency bargaining. Their phrasing is adjusted to what the traffic can bear and shaped in the interest of winning allies for particular points of view.

Furthermore, the Planning Board papers are not "costed" except in the most general way. The budgetary consequences of proposed courses of action are set forth only in order-of-magnitude terms. As a result, Council members are little assisted in weighing the benefits of alternative policy courses against the costs.

Finally, by its very nature, the Planning Board is not a creative instrument for developing and bringing forward imaginative and sharply defined choices, particularly in uncharted areas of policy. Interagency committees of this kind have a built-in drive toward lowest-common-denominator solutions. They can comment, review, and adjust, but they are not good instruments of innovation.

The limitation of the Planning Board itself in developing new responses to new problems is in part demonstrated by the employment for this purpose of outside consultants and "distinguished citizens committees," such as the Killian and Gaither Committees on defense and the Draper Committee on military and economic assistance.

The main source of policy innovations is the contribution of an individual. He may be found outside, or anywhere within, the government. But normally he will be found working in a government department or agency, grappling day in and day out with some pressing national security problem. Given imaginative proposals from such individuals, interagency committees like the Planning Board can be helpful in criticizing and commenting. But if, in the interest of "agreed solutions," such committees blur the edges and destroy the coherence of these proposals, they do the President a disservice. There is strong reason to believe that this is now the case.

THE COUNCIL ITSELF

The National Security Council now holds regular weekly meetings, which vary in size. Sometimes, the President meets with only a handful of principals in conducting important business. On other occasions, thirty or forty people may attend. A typical session may have two dozen people present; some fifteen may sit at the Council table, with perhaps another ten looking on as observers and aides.

James Perkins has made this comment on the size of Council meetings:

I think that the more one uses the NSC as a system of interagency coordination and the legitimatizing of decisions already arrived at, the growth in numbers is inevitable, because people left out of it and not at the meetings whose concurrence is required have a *prima facie* case for attending.

But if one views the Council primarily as a Presidential advisory body, the point quickly comes when the sheer numbers of participants and observers limits the depth and dilutes the quality of the discussion. The present size of most Council meetings appears to have reached and passed this point.

There are different kinds of Council meetings. Some are briefing sessions designed to acquaint the participants with, for example, an important advance in weapons technology. Other meetings center around so-called "discussion papers," which aim not at proposing a solution to some policy problem but at clarifying its nature and outlining possible alternative courses of action.

The more typical Council session, however, follows a precise agenda and focuses upon the consideration of Planning Board policy papers. Robert Cutler has described them:

> For convenience, a routine format for policy statements was developed. Thus, the busy reader would always know where to find the covering letter, the general considerations, the objectives, the courses of action to carry out the objectives, the financial appendixes, the supporting staff study; for they invariably appeared in this sequence in the final document. . . . The standardization of these techniques made it possible for the Council to transact, week in and week out, an enormously heavy load of work.

The main work of the Council, thus, now consists of discussion and a search for consensus, centering around Planning Board papers.

The normal end product of Council discussion is a Presidentially approved paper setting forth the recommendations of the Planning Board paper, with amendments, if any, adopted after Council deliberations. This paper is transmitted through the Operations Coordinating Board to the operating departments and agencies.

But one point is fundamental: policy *papers* and actual *policy* are not necessarily the same. Pieces of paper are important only as steps in a process leading to action—as minutes of decisions to do or not to do certain things.

Papers that do not affect the course of governmental action are not policy: they are mere statements of aspiration. NSC papers are policy only if they result in *action*. They are policy only if they cause the government to adopt one course of conduct and to reject another, with one group of advocates "winning" and the other "losing."

It appears that many of the papers now emerging from the Council do not meet the test of policy in this sense.

THE OPERATIONS COORDINATING BOARD

The job of helping to follow through on policies emerging from the Council and approved by the President is entrusted to the Council's Operations Coordinating Board. In terms of the NSC system, the OCB is to policy follow-up what the Planning Board is to policy development. It is an interdepartmental committee at the Under Secretary level, chaired, like the Planning Board, by the Special Assistant to the President for National Security Affairs.

The OCB, assisted by an elaborate system of interagency working groups, prepares plans for carrying out the intent of NSC policies, transmits them to the departments and agencies, secures information on the status of programs under way, and reports back through the NSC to the President on progress.

In theory, the OCB does not *make* policy. Its mandate extends only to helping to *carry out* policy. But this limitation is not and cannot be observed in practice.

When it receives an NSC policy paper, the initial job of the OCB is to determine the real meaning of the document in hand. It must often translate general statements, susceptible of varying interpretations, into tangible objectives together with plans for achieving them.

Departmental aims and interests are at stake in this determination. The process of translating an NSC paper into an action-oriented program therefore involves the same kind of interagency bartering and negotiating that takes place earlier in the Planning Board.

The OCB is an interagency committee that lacks command authority. It can advise, but not direct, the operating agencies.

Many of the most important decisions affecting the course of programs under OCB surveillance are made outside the framework of the Board. Programmatic budgetary decisions are a notable example. Also, the departments often bypass the OCB, pursuing their own interpretations of policy or engaging in "bootleg" coordination through extramural means.

The formal machinery of the OCB includes a large number of working groups that turn out detailed follow-up studies and papers. The significance of much of this work has been strongly questioned. Secretary of State Christian A. Herter made this comment before the Subcommittee:

> I was Chairman of OCB for two years. The feeling of utility varied an awful lot. At times, you felt that you were being very useful. At other times, you felt you were fanning the air or spending a lot of time reviewing minutiae. . . . When you get into the formal sessions, you again apply yourself to paper-work. Sometimes you get yourself so bogged down in the editing of a word or a sentence that you say, "My God, why am I spending so much time on this?"

The nature of the danger seems clear. Actually, the OCB has little impact on the real coordination of policy execution. Yet, at the same time, the existence of this elaborate machinery creates a false sense of security by inviting the conclusion that the problem of teamwork in the execution of policy is well in hand.

Recently, the OCB has abandoned or relaxed many of the rigid reporting requirements that governed its work when it was established, and has focused its attention upon a smaller number of important problems rather than spreading its efforts across the board. These steps have reportedly been helpful. But there is a more fundamental question at issue: Can an interdepartmental committee like the OCB be counted on to discharge effectively major responsibilities for follow-through? The evidence points to the contrary.

NEW DIRECTIONS

Two main conclusions about the National Security Council emerge:

1. The real worth of the Council to a President lies in its being an accustomed forum where he and a small number of his top advisers can gain that intellectual intimacy and mutual understanding on which true coordination depends. Viewed thus, the Council is a place where the President can receive from his department and agency heads a full exposition of policy alternatives available to him, and, in turn, give them clear-cut guidance for action.

2. The effectiveness of the Council in this primary role has been diminished by the working of the NSC system. The root causes of difficulty are found in over-crowded agenda, overly elaborate and stylized procedures, excessive reliance on subordinate interdepartmental mechanisms, and the use of the NSC system for comprehensive coordinating and follow-through responsibilities it is ill suited to discharge.

The philosophy of the suggestions that follow can be summed up in this way—to "deinstitutionalize" and to "humanize" the NSC process.

The President's Instrument. The Council exists only to serve the President. It should meet when he wishes advice on some matter, or when his chief foreign and defense policy advisers require Presidential guidance on an issue that cannot be resolved without his intervention. There are disadvantages in regularly scheduled meetings. The necessity of having to present and to discuss something at such meetings may generate business not really demanding Presidential consideration. Council meetings and the Council agenda should never become ritualistic.

The Purpose of Council Discussion. The true goal of "completed staff work" is not to spare the President the necessity of choice. It is to make his choices more meaningful by defining the essential issues that he alone must decide and by sharpening the precise positions on the opposing sides. Meetings of the Council should be regarded as vehicles for clarifying the differences of view on major policy departures or new courses of action advocated by department heads or contemplated by the President himself. The aim of the discussion should be a full airing of divergent views, so that all the implications of possible courses of action stand out in bold relief. Even a major issue may not belong on the Council agenda if it is not yet ripe for sharp and informed discussion.

Attendance at Council Meetings. The Secretaries of State and Defense share the main responsibility of advising the President on national security problems. They are the key members of the Council. Whom the President invites to Council sessions will, of course, depend on the issue under discussion. However, mere "need to know," or marginal involvement with the matter at hand, should not justify attendance. Council meetings should be kept small. When the President turns for advice to his top foreign-policy and defense officials, he is concerned with what *they themselves* think. The meetings should, therefore, be considered gatherings of principals, not staff aides. Staff attendance should be tightly controlled. As a corollary to the strict limitation of attendance, a written record of decisions should be maintained and given necessary distribution.

The Planning Board. The NSC Planning Board now tends to overshadow in importance, though not in prestige, the Council itself. However, some group akin to the present Board, playing a rather different role than it now does, can be of continuing help to the Council in the future.

Such a Board would be used mainly to criticize and comment on policy initiatives developed by the departments or stimulated by the President. It would not be used as an instrument for negotiating "agreed positions" and securing departmental concurrences.

More reliance could also be placed on informal working groups. They could be profitably employed both to prepare matters for Council discussion and to study problems that the Council decides need further examination. The make-up and life of these groups would depend on the problem involved. So, too, intermittent outside consultants or "distinguished citizens committees," such as the Gaither Committee, could on occasion be highly useful in introducing fresh perspectives on critical problems.

The Secretary of State. The Secretary of State is crucial to the successful operation of the Council. Other officials, particularly the Secretary of Defense, play important parts. But the President must rely mainly upon the Secretary of State for the initial synthesis of the political, military, economic, and other elements that go into the making of a coherent national strategy. The Secretary must also be mainly responsible for bringing to the President proposals for major new departures in national policy. To do his job properly, he must draw upon the resources of a State Department staffed broadly and competently enough with generalists, economists, and military and scientific experts to assist him in all areas falling within his full concern. He and the President need unhurried opportunities to consider the basic directions of American policy.

The Operations Coordinating Board. The case for abolishing the OCB is strong. An interdepartmental committee like the OCB has inherent limitations as an instrument for assisting with the problem of policy follow-through. If formal interagency machinery is subsequently found to be needed, it can be established later.

Responsibility for implementation of policies cutting across departmental lines should, wherever possible, be assigned to a particular department or to a particular action officer, possibly assisted by an informal interdepartmental group. In addition, the President must continue to rely heavily on the budgetary process and on his own personal assistants in performance auditing.

Problems of Staff. The President should at all times have the help and protection of a small personal staff whose members work "outside the system," who are sensitive to the President's own information needs, and who can assist him in asking relevant questions of his departmental chiefs, in making suggestions for policy initiatives not emerging from the operating departments and agencies, and in spotting gaps in policy execution.

The Council will continue to require a staff of its own, including a key official in charge. This staff should consist of a limited number of able aides who can help to prepare the work of the Council, record its decisions, and troubleshoot on spot assignments.

The NSC system now contains several staff components. These might well be more closely integrated. Also, various special project staffs on foreign policy matters have been established in recent years at the White House. Consideration could be given to bringing them within the NSC framework.

A Special Problem. The National Security Act intended that one Council member regularly bring to the NSC perspectives on our domestic economy and domestic resources. The Director of the Office of Civil and Defense Mobilization is the present heir of that role. But the concern of the OCDM focuses on civil defense and mobilization problems of wartime emergencies. The Council of Economic Advisers, among other agencies, is now much more concerned than the OCDM with the kind of domestic perspectives relevant to the problems of a protracted conflict that stops short of major war. The new President and the Congress may therefore wish to ask whether the Director of OCDM should have continued statutory membership on the Council.

The NSC and the Budgetary Process. Today, there is often little resemblance between a policy statement emerging from the NSC and the programs finally carried out by the operating departments and agencies. The actual scale and scope of these programs is determined largely by budgetary decisions made outside the Council.

An attempt to use the Council for the details of resource allocation would be no more feasible than trying to use the Cabinet for this purpose. Yet the search for ways and means of relating the Council's advice more closely to the budget process must be pursued. The problem is not to make the Council the manager or czar of budget preparation. Rather it is to insure that the perspectives of the Secretaries of State and Defense are brought to bear on an ordering of national priorities at the target-setting stage of the annual budget preparation. The National Security Council is the appropriate body for helping the President define such priorities.

The Secretary of State
and the American System*

THE PRESIDENT'S PROBLEM

Traditionally, Presidents have turned to the Secretary of State for their principal help in initiating and executing foreign policy. However, the breadth and complexity of foreign policy today, together with departmental fragmentation of responsibility for dealing with it, have created certain new problems for the President and also for the Secretary.

The means for meeting our foreign-policy objectives now go far beyond those of traditional diplomacy. They embrace economic and military aid, scientific and technical assistance, information programs, surplus food programs, and educational and cultural exchange. They invoke work through alliances and international organizations—with all the attendant complications. We have mutual defense treaties with forty-two nations; we are members of four regional defense organizations and an active participant in a fifth; we belong to the United Nations and some two dozen other major international organizations.

Both in its making and execution, moreover, foreign policy has become interdepartmental. Not only the Department of State but the Department of Defense and the military services, Treasury, Commerce, Interior, Agriculture, the Atomic Energy Commission, the Federal Communications Commission, the Export-Import Bank, the Development Loan Fund, and more than a score of other agencies are all deeply involved in international activities.

This situation has provided fertile soil for the exuberant growth of interagency coordinating committees. These include the complex committee substructure of the National Security Council and the multitude of formal coordinating groups operating outside the NSC system. Rival claimants from different executive departments with different missions are introduced into the policy process, re-

* A *Staff Report of the Subcommittee on National Policy Machinery*, January 28, 1961.

quiring power to be shared even though responsibility may not be.

Robert Lovett calls this the "foul-up factor" in our methods. He told the Subcommittee, "The idea seems to have got around that just because some decision may affect your activities, you automatically have a right to take part in making it. . . . There is some reason to feel that the doctrine may be getting out of hand and that what was designed to act as a policeman may, in fact, become a jailor."

In operation, coordinating committee mechanisms have proved to have severe limitations, and they have exacted a heavy price in terms of loss of individual responsibility, excessive compromise, and general administrative sluggishness.

The magnitude and persistence of these difficulties have led many people to believe that the remedy lies in some radical organizational change—a grand council of "wise men," a new cold-war strategy board, a "super-Cabinet" First Secretary, or a "super-staff" agency in the White House. The appeal of a quick solution is understandable, if one could be found. But such novel additions to the policy process, far from reducing the President's burdens, would in all likelihood increase them. The President's best hope lies along another path—strengthening the traditional means of executive power.

In the American system, there is no satisfactory alternative to primary reliance on the great departments, and their vast resources of experience and talent, as instruments for policy development and execution. At the same time, there is no satisfactory substitute for the budgetary process and the staff work of Presidential aides in pulling departmental programs together into a truly Presidential program, prodding the departments when necessary, and checking on their performance.

The President's problem is to invigorate both sets of instruments of executive power, and a strong President will want strength in both.

The President and the Secretary of State

Sought-for improvements in the national security policy process must give major attention to the Secretary of State and his department.

In the American system of government, the Secretary occupies a unique position. He is the ranking member of the Cabinet for purposes of protocol, but he is also "first among equals" in a deeper sense.

Of the Cabinet officials, only the Secretary of State is primarily charged with looking at our nation as a whole in its relation to the outside world. His perspective, like that of the President's, is essentially political-strategic. Together with the President, the Secretary of State speaks and acts for the priority of national political policy over lesser considerations and goals. As Dean Acheson has said:

> Foreign policy is the whole of national policy looked at from the point of view of the exigencies created by "the vast external realm" beyond our borders. It is not a "jurisdiction." It is an orientation, a point of view, a measurement of values—today, perhaps, the most important one for national survival.

It is in the nature of foreign policy, today more so than ever before, that the Secretary must seek help from other parts of the government for most of the things he wants to accomplish. He needs the help of the President's own aides and his Cabinet colleagues from Defense, Treasury, Agriculture and the like. But the Secretary's authority to command—his power to direct, discipline and reward—is confined to his own department. In dealing with others, he can only request, and try to guide and influence.

The success of a Secretary in influencing his colleagues is directly related to the President's confidence in him and reliance on him. When the President confides his thoughts to him, seeks his counsel, and uses him, the Secretary can be strong and helpful in shaping the course of national policy as the President wishes it shaped. A Secretary who lacks this relationship is soon neglected by his Cabinet associates and cannot provide detailed, day-to-day guidance of national policy. Nor can the President—much less a White House aide—readily or fully assume the role that he has made impossible for the Secretary to perform for him.

The Secretary must, of course, be deserving of the President's confidence and show that he is the official best able to help the President on foreign-policy problems. Aided by his department, he must be ready and willing to assert his proper jurisdiction and to exercise full leadership across the whole front of national security matters as they relate to foreign policy. He must earn the role of first adviser by being the President's first helper.

The Secretary faces these major problems:

1. He must establish working relations with other parts of the government that fortify him as foreign-policy leader.

2. He must secure talent and resources necessary to deal with the problems of foreign policy in their full contemporary context.

3. He must take steps to assure that he is available in Washington to the President, the Congress, and his own department.

THE CENTRAL PARTNERSHIP—STATE AND DEFENSE

The Secretaries of State and Defense are the Cabinet officials most concerned with the government programs that must rank highest on any list of national priorities. They speak for the requirements of national safety and survival.

Today, perhaps the most important problems of national security are joint State-Defense problems, requiring joint action by the two departments for their solution—from the development and execution of military-aid programs, the negotiation of base rights, and arms-control planning, to the overriding problem of properly relating military means with foreign-policy ends.

Yet cooperation between State and Defense has not always been close. Typically, Defense lacks confidence in State's handling of military matters and feels it cannot get precise enough long-term political guidance. State, commonly, deplores the Pentagon's inability to speak with one voice on strategic doctrine. The diplomat may regard the soldier's approach to planning as mechanistic, while the soldier thinks the diplomat is an improviser and a hunch-player.

Despite the deep-seated differences of tradition and outlook which have stood between the Pentagon and Foggy Bottom, a full and sympathetic partnership between State and Defense is critical to achieving our national security goals.

Almost every day, the Secretary of State confronts some diplomatic problem requiring knowledge of our present military strength and its deployment. Also, in looking ahead, he must gear his political-strategic planning to the evolution of our own military forces, the prospective capabilities of our adversaries, and the broad direction of weapons developments in the offing. On the other hand, the planning of the Secretary of Defense and his military chiefs must reflect an appreciation of our foreign-policy problems, commitments, and goals.

The partnership of State and Defense must obtain at all levels. Nowhere is it more important than in the lower echelons, where the critical initial work on planning takes place. The need is for continuing staff work across the Potomac, between people who can think both in foreign-policy and military terms and relate each to the other. The partnership will be still-born unless the two Secretaries themselves set its tone and style. They need frequent and unhurried opportunities to talk together, think together, and plan together.

It is in the budgetary process that some of our most important goals are translated into concrete action-oriented decisions. The Secretary of State need not and should not concern himself with the budgetary details of the military establishment. Yet, at budget preparation time, the Pentagon should know his views on the underlying political-strategic assumptions and on the relationship of proposed force levels and weapons systems to foreign-policy problems.

Moreover, the counsel of the two Secretaries should be sought by the President at the target-setting stage in the annual budgetary cycle—before the initial over-all budgetary ceiling is established. And this consultation should be more than *pro forma*. Otherwise, the subsequent planning will fail to reflect their informed perspectives and best judgments on the magnitude and nature of emerging national security problems, and on the shape and size of the programs required to meet them.

THE SECRETARY AND INTERDEPARTMENTAL COMMITTEES

The Secretary's ability to exert foreign-policy leadership is closely related to the way that interdepartmental committees are organized and handled.

Interagency committees are the gray and bloodless ground of bureaucratic warfare—a warfare of position, not of decisive battles. The State Department commonly sees them as devices for including "outsiders" in matters it regards as its own, and it resists this encroachment. Other departments and agencies use them as instruments for "getting into the act."

"Control or divert" is the State Department's guiding strategic principle. When it cannot gain the upper hand, it tries to occupy committees with "busy work," while getting key decisions through informal bargaining with its adversaries or directly from the President. One clear illustration lies in the Operations Coordinating Board of the National Security Council. But the strategy has not been wholly successful, and over the years State has given ground. In some cases, the chairmanship of foreign-policy committees has gone to other agencies. The National Advisory Council on International Monetary and Financial Problems, for example, is chaired and staffed by Treasury—not State. Another example is the Trade Policy Committee, chaired by Commerce.

The State Department may sit on other committees as one among equals though it is mainly responsible for solving the issue in question. The price paid for committee agreement may be heavy in terms of policy compromised, time wasted, and decisions deferred. Filtered through committees, the Secretary's voice becomes muted, his words blurred. His responsibilities to the President remain, but his power and authority to exercise them diminish.

Committee Killing

A very high percentage of committees serve no useful purpose. Or, performing a necessary service in the beginning, they live on long after their reason for being has come to an end.

Averell Harriman has suggested the possibility of a "committee-killing outfit," regularly reviewing the need for the continued existence of particular committees and identifying those that merit extinction. The Bureau of the Budget might properly give this task high priority.

The Management of Committees

Where interdepartmental committees are necessary, the problem is how to manage them so that the political-strategic leadership of the Secretary of State on foreign-policy matters is strengthened, and how to administer them so that the legitimate concerns of other departments are brought to bear without excessive dilution and delay.

Certain administrative reforms can be helpful.

1. The State Department should in most cases chair interdepartmental committees working on problems with a heavy foreign-policy component. If jurisdiction is more or less evenly divided with other departments, the situation should be resolved in favor of State.

2. Committee chairmen should be given more responsibility for decision and action. Their possible suppression of opposing views is far less dangerous than the disappearance of any coherent view at all in a quicksand of generalities under the rule of *liberum veto*. Members of committees should serve in an ad-

visory capacity to the chairman, whose final conclusions and recommendations should be his own. Of course, the members should have full opportunity to present their points of view, and they should be free to file dissenting comment, if they so desire, or to appeal the chairman's recommendations to higher authority.

Committee chairmen and members should be in a direct line of responsibility to their department or agency chiefs, so that their recommendations and views can enter the mainstream of policy.

3. A single department, more often than not State, should be responsible for directing the execution of foreign-policy decisions, by delegation from the President, even if several departments must take part in their execution. Where joint action is required, it is almost always preferable to put one action officer, from one department, in charge, leaving the other agencies free to appeal his decisions.

4. Greater use should be made of informal joint working groups in the first stages of developing foreign-policy initiatives. These should normally be chaired by someone from the State Department. Such groups can be formed to deal with particular problems, and their members should be handpicked accordingly. When they serve as individuals rather than formal agency representatives, the participants are less bound by departmental party lines, and their recommendations are more likely to reflect fresh viewpoints and their own best estimate of desirable courses of action.

The Secretary and Key National Security Posts

As foreign policy leader, the Secretary of State requires the presence, both in his own department and other parts of the government, of more top-level officials who can deal with national security problems "in the round." Some of these officials will be citizens drawn from private life; others will come from the career services.

Today, those career services are not well designed to give senior officials the kind of training and job experiences needed for a broad grasp of national security problems. In terms of their own needs, the armed services have done far better. They have recognized the requirement for military generalists. The career patterns followed by promising officers expose them to the problems of their service as a whole. And today, attendance at the National War College or its equivalent, together with a tour of duty in a joint or international command, is virtually required of those reaching general officer rank. No comparable effort is now made—in State, Defense or elsewhere—to give civilian officials a correspondingly wide background of training and experience. The situation requires correction.

The typical civilian official spends almost his entire career working for one agency. Even then, he has few chances to see its problems as a whole. In contrast with the military services, civilian officials have only limited opportunities for advanced training. But many of the most effective senior officials in government today gained invaluable experience by serving in two or more departments and agencies during their careers. Yet personnel regulations do not encourage lateral transfers between agencies, even when such a transfer is clearly in the national interest. Personnel practices that inhibit such transfers need review and revision to meet present needs.

Another path of reform lies in exchange arrangements giving officials in one department opportunities to work in another. A pilot program has just been started for the exchange of outstanding civilian and military personnel between the departments of State and Defense. This program was outlined first before the Subcommittee last summer by the then Secretary of State Herter. Under it, State Department officials are given job assignments in Defense; in return, Pentagon civilians and military officers undertake tours of duty in State.

Two more steps seem desirable at an early date: the enrollment of more officials in this exchange program, and the broadening of its scope to include the Central Intelligence Agency, the Treasury, the Atomic Energy Commission, and the Bureau of the Budget, among others.

This exchange program should also be used as a testing laboratory for studying the practicality and desirability of a more formal "joint career service" in the area of national security. The members of such a service, composed of a limited number of civilian officials and military officers of outstanding ability, would follow career patterns specifically designed to acquaint them with a wide range of national security problems. They would receive critical job assignments and training opportunities which would sharpen their skills to the utmost.

A program for exchange of personnel among agencies should be accompanied by more aggressive efforts to give greater numbers of civilian officials advanced training in government-sponsored schools and in universities. Robert Bowie told the Subcommittee: "In a world that is moving as fast as ours, an opportunity to get away from the day-to-day work and try to get perspective on the problems is absolutely indispensable for the top policy jobs."

The need can be met in part by increased enrollment of first-rate civilians from Defense, State, and other agencies in the National War College and the other service schools. Conversely, larger numbers of military officers might attend the Foreign Service Institute of the Department of State. The Foreign Service Institute, however, was long a poor relation of the Department of State, and it is not yet funded, supported, or staffed on a basis comparable to the military service schools. Its programs and curricula need prompt review aimed at setting high standards for the students and expecting high performance.

To perform their jobs properly, increasing numbers of civilian officials must become masters in depth of specialized problem areas. This need can be met by sending more officials of outstanding promise to universities and other study centers.

The Secretary and His Staff

To take the lead in developing and executing foreign policy, the Secretary of State needs a department with staff resources that span the full range of his problems.

Today, the Secretary's staff is built around the diplomat—whose skills and perspectives are indispensable. But the skills the Secretary must draw on today, like his problems, go far beyond those traditionally associated with the practice of diplomacy—representation, negotiating, and reporting. His need for stronger staff and line assistance is most pronounced in these areas:

Executive Managers. Too few State Department officials now possess the background and experience required for executive tasks. Increasingly, the administration of foreign policy is "big business," and it must be run by skillful administrators. This is especially true for today's ambassadors, who may lead "country teams" composed of hundreds of representatives from numerous agencies and the armed services. The needed management abilities can be found both among able and experienced men from private life and among career officials from the Foreign Service and the other career services.

Specialists. The integration of the departmental and foreign services, undertaken in 1954, desirable though it may have been in some respects, made the State Department a less congenial home for specialists.

The State Department does not require large staffs of "house technicians" in each narrow specialty bearing upon foreign policy. But the Secretary does need, in his own family, more first-rate experts in economics, science and technology, intelligence, and military matters who can interpret their specialties in terms of his needs.

Career management patterns should permit specialists to pursue long-term careers within their own fields, and give them greater incentives and rewards for excellence than they now enjoy.

Military and Technical Competence. The State Department's need for broadened staff competence is perhaps most acute in the area of military and scientific-technical problems. Close at hand, at the top level of the Department, the Secretary needs a small number of civilians charged with bridging his problems and those of the Pentagon and able to give him expert counsel on political-military problems.

The Department also must move fast to reach a higher level of technical competence to deal with the problems of arms control, space, and other questions with complex political-technical relationships.

The Policy Planning Staff. A better planning effort is needed in the State Department. What Dean Acheson has called "the thundering present" necessarily occupies the department's main energies, but "the true problem lies in determining the emerging future and the policy appropriate to it."

The creation of the Policy Planning Staff by General Marshall in 1947 was an important and long overdue step to provide the Secretary with advice on long-range trends. In a department as large as State, there is surely room for a few experienced persons to reflect on the direction of existing policy, question assumptions, raise a critical voice, and recommend new departures. If competently manned to take into account the entire range of the problems of our foreign relations, the Planning Staff can give the Secretary continuing counsel on basic strategic policy not likely to be provided by other parts of the department.

Help from the Outside. The Secretary of State needs study in depth of a kind difficult to secure even from a strengthened and broadened departmental staff, particularly in the case of long-range problems only now appearing on the horizon. The time has come for him to get more help from the outside.

There are a number of ways of "contracting out" for this help—closer and fuller relations between State and such organizations as the Institute for Defense Analyses; creating a "State Department RAND"; establishing a new organization to conduct policy research for State and other parts of the government; or strengthening and making greater use of research centers and universities throughout the nation.

The question of how the State Department can best meet its need on a long-term basis deserves early attention. In the meanwhile, however, the Department can revitalize its own Bureau of Intelligence and Research and take fuller advantage of universities and existing study and research centers.

THE SECRETARY'S AVAILABILITY IN WASHINGTON

Much of the effectiveness of the Secretary of State depends upon his being in Washington, on hand to advise the President, lead his department, and consult with the Congress. Recent Secretaries of State have been away from their home base much of the time, attending international meetings abroad. The trend toward frequent high-level meetings, the formation of the United Nations and regional defense organizations, protracted negotiations like those on arms control—all have exerted upon the Secretary of State a magnetic pull away from his desk.

Ways must be found to relieve the Secretary of State of part of these travel and negotiating burdens. The stage has been set for improvement by Secretary Rusk's statement that it is the President's intention and his, "to use freely the diplomatic channel for informal as well as formal discussions and consultations with other governments."

Ambassadors at large and Special Representatives. One promising step lies in greater use of ambassadors at large, who can represent the President and the Secretary at high-level international meetings. One such official has already been named by the new administration; others may well be needed.

Another useful instrument would be a reserve of special representatives who possess particular competence in specialized problems of emerging international importance. Arms control is one example; space is another. Distinguished citizens who have represented our nation in past negotiations can serve as the cadre of such a reserve. The reserve should be large enough and seasoned enough to permit quick and flexible employment as problems arise.

The standing of such representatives is all-important; their professional reputations must command respect at home and abroad, and
they should obviously enjoy the trust of the President and the
Secretary.

An International Protocol Conference. The protocol of present-
day diplomacy, established at the Congress of Vienna 150 years
ago, contributes to drawing the Secretary away from Washington
and to involving him in time-consuming ceremonial duties. Existing protocol practice requires that the Secretary of State himself
represent our nation at many international meetings; it also burdens him with many official social obligations—giving and attending receptions, greeting foreign visitors, and the like. Lightening
this load requires international action, with nations subscribing to
a new set of protocol rules. Robert Lovett proposed to the Subcommittee that an international conference be held to bring protocol regulations up to date, especially those regarding the level of
representation required at international meetings. Former Secretary of State Herter later made a similar proposal.*

Out of such a conference might come an agreement that Under
Secretaries and Assistant Secretaries of State, ambassadors at large,
or special representatives, together with their foreign counterparts,
could play larger roles in representing their nations at high-level
meetings. Similarly, the conference might agree on rules to reduce
protocol-type entertaining when high government officials travel
abroad.

* See below, pp. 89, 148-49.

The Bureau of the Budget and the Budgetary Process*

THE PROBLEM

The struggle with world Communism is broadening, deepening, and quickening. Our rivals are pledged to see their system triumph over the free way of life. They think, plan, and act in terms of the long haul. The task confronting us is harshly plain—to outthink, outplan, outperform, and outlast our foes. Our answer to the challenge cannot consist of mere responses to Communist thrusts and probes. A policy of simply reacting to the initiatives of Moscow and Peking can lead only to the eventual defeat of freedom.

We need a forward and affirmative national strategy—a clear and widely shared understanding of where we aim to go in the world and how we propose to get there. The President's key problem is to create such a strategy and to establish an order of national priorities on its behalf. His task is to map a course of action that puts first things first, that separates the necessary from the merely desirable, and that distinguishes between what must be done today and what can wait until tomorrow.

The President must grapple with formidable questions: How much of our national substance should be devoted to the requirements of national security? What is the right level of foreign aid? What is the best division between military and economic aid? What is the proper balance between conventional and nuclear military forces? What should be the relative emphasis on offensive and defensive armaments? Will prospective revenues cover the cost of needed programs? If not, how should we meet the bill?

In answering these questions, a President requires and seeks help from many quarters. He turns to the National Security Council, the State and Defense departments, his own aides, other departments and agencies concerned with national security matters, and interagency committees and task forces. In addition, a President

* A *Staff Report of the Subcommittee on National Policy Machinery*, October 16, 1961.

can secure major help from the Bureau of the Budget and the budgetary process.

The need is this: to make sure that the Bureau of the Budget and our government's use of the budgetary process keep pace with the spiraling complexity of foreign and defense policy, toward the end of giving the President and the Congress maximum assistance in a world of Berlin and the ballistic missile.

THE BUREAU OF THE BUDGET AND NATIONAL SECURITY

The Budget Bureau will never win a bureaucratic popularity contest. The total program requests of the operating departments always far exceed any budget a President can prudently approve. The Bureau must often be a nay-sayer and help the Chief Executive to trim agency programs to fit the Presidential cloth. Hence its reputation, even if undeserved, as the villain of the executive branch.

Each President must decide how he wants to use the Budget Bureau.

A President can employ the Bureau mainly to keep a lid on expenditures. In such cases, the Bureau is told to "hold the line"—but may be given little guidance concerning the Chief Executive's priorities and program goals. In coordinating and auditing executive-branch performance, reliance is placed less on the Bureau and more on interdepartmental coordinating mechanisms or White House aides. Used thus, the Bureau becomes a kind of "Certified Presidential Accounting" office.

A President can, however, employ the Bureau differently. He can use it as his "lengthened shadow" across the whole front of fiscal policy and program management. The Director of this kind of Budget Bureau sits in the innermost policy councils of the Presidency. Program planning and budgeting are seen as but different aspects of one process, which starts with the formulation of policy objectives and ends with costed and time-phased programs for action. Here, the President will regard the Bureau as his strong right arm in executive management.

A President will do well to use the Bureau of the Budget in this way. The budgetary process can be the President's most powerful instrument in establishing a scale of national priorities and marshaling through the Congress the resources required on their behalf.

The budget pulls together, into one comprehensive reckoning, information on all the competing claims of national policy, foreign and domestic. It offers the President unique help in ranking rival claims on the basis of a system of priorities, and allocating resources accordingly. David Bell, Director of the Bureau of the Budget, put it this way: "The budget operates as an extremely effective element of discipline on the President and the executive branch because it requires that each proposed use of resources—for defense, science, natural resources, or whatever—be tested against others and against the total size of the budget."

Employed with sophistication, the budgetary process can also be the President's most discriminating and effective tool in controlling the executive branch. It reaches deep into the activities of the great departments; it is the one Presidential management device common to all of them; it works on that most sensitive pressure point —the pocketbook nerve.

The Bureau of the Budget helps the President in other major ways. On his behalf, it reviews all legislative proposals originating in the departments or agencies or the Congress to see whether they conform to his program, and it continually reviews the organization of the Federal establishment and makes recommendations for improving its effectiveness.

The Bureau is uniquely equipped to serve the President well. Aside from the President himself, the Budget Director has the most comprehensive view of the policies and programs of the Government. As an "above-the-department" Presidential staff unit in the Executive Office, the Bureau is exempt from the shortcomings of interdepartmental committees. Its permanent professional staff of almost 300 members dwarfs any other found at the Presidential level and is seasoned and outstandingly able.

Certain things follow if the Bureau is to be the President's true "lengthened shadow."

The Budget Director and his colleagues should never be left in the dark about the President's scale of priorities and his policy aims. Not only should the Director be privy to the inner councils of the Chief Executive, but the Presidential word must get down the line to the junior officials of the Bureau. Unless, from top to bottom, the Bureau has a clear and current understanding of the President's aims, its predilections may come to substitute for the President's pleasure. The Bureau then becomes an independent agency, a rival both of the departments and of its chief. The stronger the Bureau, the more the need for clear Presidential direction and strong Presidential control.

The Bureau should preserve an arm's-length relationship with the departments and agencies. In working with agency program and budgetary officers, the danger is always present that Bureau members may themselves become committed to particular agency budgets and end as departmental protagonists. The Bureau members must remain the President's men.

The Bureau should on occasion be a prodder and a yea-sayer. New programs important for the President's goals may lack a natural departmental home, an effective lobby. Or programs with low agency priority may have high Presidential priority. The Bureau should then be prepared to recommend that we do more and go faster.

One point above all: The Bureau should be staffed more broadly and richly with officials who have a substantive understanding of the issues crossing their desks. The Bureau need not have technical experts in every specialized field, but its members should be able to comprehend the significance of programs in terms of the President's over-all policy objectives. Nowhere is this more important than in the area of national security, where the price paid for poor counsel is highest.

MODERNIZING BUDGET-MAKING

Over the past forty years, each administration has made improvements in the budgetary process. Distinguished private citizens, like the members of the Brownlow Committee and the first and second Hoover Commissions, have helped in this task. But budgetary reform, particularly in the area of national security, has not kept pace with the changing and growing challenges to our nation. The budget sent to the Congress last January retains the essential format of the first budget President Harding submitted to the Congress. To a too great degree, its appropriations categories, its emphases, and its balance of detailed information among programs remain unchanged.

Over the years, the budget has increased in size and complexity. It is now a massive document about the size of a big-city telephone directory, and it takes over two years to prepare. The budget has developed its own vocabulary, comprehensible in large measure only to budgetary specialists. It distinguishes, for example, between "direct obligations," "new obligational authority," "reimbursable obligations," "obligations incurred," "recoveries of prior year obligations," and "total obligations." The budget, moreover, carries an overly heavy burden of legacies from the past. Matters of little contemporary importance are treated in exhaustive and exhausting detail—while information on far more important programs is meager or nonexistent. A President, a top agency official, a Senator, or a Congressman must now run an obstacle course through obscure funding concepts, archaic appropriations categories, and fiscal jargon in using the budget to help make policy and program decisions.

The time is at hand for a determined effort to make the budget shorter, simpler, and easier to read and understand. The main problem, however, goes deeper. Despite substantial progress in budgetary reform, our government has been slow to take full advantage of the contributions the budget process can make to planning and executive management.

Federal budget-making has concentrated in the main on developing information that is useful for the day-to-day administration of the departments and agencies. Not nearly as much attention has been paid to preparing budgets so as to make them more useful in establishing priorities, in forward planning, in choosing between programs, and in measuring expenditures against meaningful performance yardsticks.

This is in strong contrast to the contemporary budgetary practices of progressive private organizations—business firms, banks, and universities. A modern corporation uses the budgetary process for much more than checking costs and controlling expenditures. It employs it as a main tool in planning its corporate future—to help to decide on capital expenditures and to establish product lines, to spot management weaknesses, and, most important, as an early warning system of problems and opportunities coming up on the corporate horizon. Programs and budgets extending several years into the future have become the rule. The job of making the Federal budgetary process a more versatile and useful tool of the President badly needs doing.

Two problems rank highest: how to make the budget more helpful in forward planning; and how to make it more useful in illuminating program choices and measuring program performance.

Extending the Budgetary Time Horizon

Particularly in the area of national security, our government needs to extend its budgetary time horizons further into the future.

We need to know where the cost of present plans and activities may take us, not simply through the next fiscal year, but for several years ahead.

A twelve-month budget reveals only the tip of the fiscal iceberg. The initial outlays for the man-to-the-moon program will result in billions of dollars spent during the remainder of this decade. The development of major weapons systems and foreign-aid programs are other obvious cases in point. To be meaningful, cost estimates must be based on the full expected lifetime of programs.

Longer-term budgetary projections do not imply a change in the present system of presenting a budget to the Congress each year and of voting appropriations on an annual basis. Nor is the aim to make in 1962 decisions that can only be made in 1966. It is to take greater account of the consequences in 1966 of the budgetary decisions that must be made in 1962. Maurice Stans, who served as President Eisenhower's last Budget Director, made this comment before the Subcommittee: "I would not agree that we should appropriate for defense purposes for more than one year in advance, but I think it is very important that the Congress and all concerned know the implications of the beginning of a program in one year on the budget requirements of future years."

Budgetary projections grow less accurate, of course, as they extend into the future. It is easier, also, to project spending for military hardware than for foreign policy, where the unpredictable and the uncontrollable loom so great. Alternative projections, based on different assumptions about the future, may be necessary. In any event, the projections must be revised as necessary and kept up to date.

The previous administration published in its final days a pioneering ten-year projection of the Federal budget for the period 1960-1970, with high, medium, and low estimates of Federal expenditures.

Under the new administration, the Bureau of the Budget is now testing the feasibility of developing comprehensive five-year program and budgetary projections. It is at the same time encouraging the departments and agencies to plan, program, and budget on a longer time scale. Last spring, a set of alternative projections compiled by the Bureau were considered by the President in establishing guidelines for the 1963 Federal budget.

The Department of Defense has been in the vanguard of this effort. Beginning in fiscal year 1963, it aims to have available at all times a projection of requirements and tentatively approved programs with dollar signs attached, extending at least five years into the future. As Secretary of Defense McNamara told the Subcommittee, "We . . . propose to maintain that plan or budget up to date with monthly revisions to it so that at any particular time when a budget for a special period, such as the fiscal year, is required, it can be abstracted from the continually modified and continually adjusted military program."

Forward budgeting can be no better than the forward planning that underlies it. Many departments and agencies have had little experience with long-range programing—or with relating it to budgeting. Departmental planning staffs have only occasionally viewed themselves as co-workers with the budgetary officers. The problems of developing the necessary planning skills and of creating a productive partnership between the planner and the budget officer are vexing ones. Their solution deserves and will require sustained effort.

This applies particularly to the Department of State. The Secretary of State's concern, like the President's, is political-strategic. He speaks for the primacy of national policy over lesser aims. A President can find no effective substitute for the Secretary and his Department in helping him to define the basic direction and broad priorities of national security policy. The Department of State should be staffed to do more forward planning—and it should be asked to do more.

Economic Projections

The relationship between the budget on the one hand and the economy and the Government's tax receipts on the other is critical. Can prospective program costs over the next several years be met within the present tax structure? Or will they require deficit financing, new taxes, or other measures to stimulate Federal revenues?

Revenue estimates for the current fiscal year are of only limited help in answering this question. Treasury receipts may be abnormally high or unusually low, depending on the stage of the business cycle.

In making program and budgetary decisions, a President should therefore have projections of national income and associated tax receipts for several years ahead, based on differing assumptions about the factors that will influence the level of economic activity.

The Bureau of the Budget, the Treasury, and the Council of Economic Advisers are now cooperating in preparing longer-term economic projections.

Projections of economic activity and tax revenues for a particular future year are subject to notoriously large margins of error. Projections can shed helpful light on broad trends, however. They should be regarded as helpful informational aids, not as predictions or forecasts of future economic performance.

BETTER WAYS OF FEDERAL BUDGETING

No one form of budget preparation and presentation is the best for all purposes. Modern corporations know this. A progressive company may work with three or four budgets at the same time, each serving a different purpose—checking plant efficiency, planning capital expenditures, measuring the contributions of different products to the profits of the enterprise.

The appropriations categories of today's Federal budget, oriented as they are toward the administrative surveillance of department and agency programs, serve one useful purpose. But the budgetary process can also provide other ways of "walking around the elephant." Different ways of packaging and presenting budgetary information lead to insights that are not otherwise obtainable.

The new administration, building upon the efforts of its predecessors to present budgetary information in more useful forms, is moving along three fronts.

Program packaging. In its traditional form, the Defense budget is prepared and presented in terms of the requirements of the individual services and certain expenditure categories like "military personnel," "operation and maintenance," and "procurement." While useful for many purposes, this way of presenting budgetary information does not relate defense spending to military missions or tasks—defending the North American continent against attack, moving troops to crisis areas, or the like. It is important that the Defense budget be made a more useful informational tool for comparing the cost and worth of alternative programs in terms of functions or missions to be performed. Although it has been possible to assemble such information for special requirements, the financial management system in the past has not been designed to do this on a continuing basis.

The Department of Defense is now undertaking a systematic and comprehensive effort to relate military spending to missions. It plans to supplement the traditional form of budget presentation with a series of program packages that will cut across the lines both of the services and the traditional expenditure categories. Some examples of these packages are "central war offensive forces," "central war defensive forces," and "sealift and airlift." These packages will try to project the costs of such end programs five or six years into the future.

By relating costs to jobs to be done, and by doing this on a longer time scale than heretofore, the program package approach should contribute to a better appraisal of program alternatives.

Country development programing. It is important that our aid to foreign governments be closely related to their self-help development programs and to assistance forthcoming from international agencies or other outside sources. Moreover, each part of the United States effort—economic or military aid, loans or grants, or Food for Peace sales—ought to be seen in the light of an over-all program.

In preparing foreign-aid budgets, the administration is now trying to relate our own assistance more closely to country development programs that look several years into the future. This step should help in deciding upon appropriate forms and levels of United States aid, and in making sure that all the types of aid we give a country make a maximum contribution to our true national interest there.

Coordinated forward budgets. Many important national security programs, particularly in research and development, are widely dispersed between departments and agencies. This year, a coordinated oceanographic research program involving seven different agencies was sent to the Congress. Such coordinated forward budgets make sense in numerous other areas. They pull related activities together; they make it easier for each agency to do its own planning in relationship to the plans of others; and they help the President and the Congress see programs "in the round."

The law of diminishing returns places obvious limitations on the number of ways in which budgetary information can usefully be pulled together. As Wilfred McNeil, former Comptroller of the Department of Defense, warned the Subcommittee, "An effort to be too accurate or too precise can get the real objective lost in the details."

The budgetmakers' task, however, has been made much easier by the development of computers and coding devices. Ideally, the financial management system should eventually be able to produce information on costs in terms of whatever program groupings are helpful to the President, his key lieutenants, and the Congress.

Performance Measurement

Private businesses have yardsticks for judging their effectiveness —profit and loss statements. Efficiently run private enterprises also hold their managers strictly accountable for results.

It is necessarily more difficult for our government to determine how well its national security programs are faring. By what criteria do we measure the success or failure of some assistance programs? How do we judge whether we are getting the most for our money?

Granted the difficulties, our Government pays insufficient attention to this problem of performance measurement. The whole field is almost unexplored. We cannot learn from our successes or our mistakes unless we can identify them. The Bureau of the Budget, working with the departments and agencies, ought to take the lead in developing better ways of measuring performance.

Concluding Statement[*]

Free men are locked in a struggle being waged on the earth's continents, in the depths of its seas, and in the reaches of space. Our Communist foes acknowledge no bounds except those imposed on them by expediency. They draw twenty-year plans portraying a Communist utopia in 1981, while they build walls around their unwilling subjects in 1961. In their pursuit of power, they debase language itself. In their lexicon, "democracy" becomes the rule of the few over the many; "peace" becomes the surrender of free men to Communist domination.

The question is this: Can free societies outplan, outperform, outlast—and if need be, outsacrifice—totalitarian systems? Can we recognize fresh problems in a changing world, and can we respond in time with new plans for meeting them?

The requirements of national security press ever more strongly on our resources. Can we establish a proper scale of priorities that separates the necessary from the not really essential? Program choice grows ever harder. Can we establish the right mix of military and economic aid? How are we to choose between competing multi-billion-dollar weapon systems?

Presidential control over foreign policy and defense programs becomes more difficult. How may the globe-girdling programs of the national security departments and agencies be harnessed on behalf of the Presidential purpose? How can we assure their efficient execution?

Standards of performance adequate for quieter times will no longer do. The Presidency, the State and Defense departments and the rest of our government must now meet new tests of excellence.

1. *We need a clearer understanding of where our vital national interests lie and what we must do to promote them.*

Faulty machinery is rarely the real culprit when our policies are inconsistent or lack sustained forward momentum. The underlying

* Statement by Senator Henry M. Jackson (Chairman), November 15, 1961.

cause is normally found elsewhere, in the absence of a clear sense of direction and coherence of policy at the top of the government.

Unless our top officials are in basic agreement about what is paramount for the national interest—what comes first and what comes second—there is bound to be drift and confusion below. This has been so under every administration.

In our system, two men bear the heaviest responsibility for giving our national security policy focus and structure. One is the President. The other is his first adviser, the Secretary of State.

A clear and reasoned formulation of national policy, and its effective communication downward, is the prerequisite of successful delegation and coordination.

There is still much to be done in defining our vital interests and developing a basic national policy which supports them.

2. *Radical additions to our existing policy machinery are unnecessary and undesirable.*

Our best hope lies in making our traditional policy machinery work better—not in trading it in for some new model.

The Subcommittee inquiry brought to light scores of plans for novel changes in the policy process. They include proposals for a so-called First Secretary of the Government, who would stand between the President and his Cabinet chiefs; large planning staffs attached to the White House or the National Security Council; cold-war strategy boards; and councils of wise men.

Such proposals have certain common weaknesses: they try to do at the Presidential level things that can better be done by the departments and agencies; they violate sound administrative practice by tending to interpose officials between the President and his key Cabinet officials; they rest on the mistaken assumption that the weaknesses of one organization can be cured by creating another.

In fact, any proposals for net additions to our present national policy machinery should be greeted with a basic skepticism.

This is particularly true of suggestions for new committees. Committee-killing, not creating more committees, remains the important job.

Properly managed, and chaired by officials with responsibility for decision and action, committees can be useful in helping to make sure that voices which ought to be heard are heard. But a very high percentage of committees exact a heavy toll by diluting the authority of individual executives, obscuring responsibility for getting things done, and generally slowing decision-making.

3. *The key problem of national security is not reorganization—it is getting our best people into key foreign-policy and defense posts.*

Good national security policy requires both good policy-makers and good policy machinery. But organizational changes cannot solve problems which are really not due to organizational weaknesses.

More often than not, poor decisions are traceable not to machinery but to people—to their inexperience, their failure to comprehend the full significance of information crossing their desks, their indecisiveness, or their lack of wisdom.

4. *There is serious overstaffing in the national security departments and agencies.*

The caliber of the national service is impressively high. But like so many large private organizations, our government faces the problem that people are engaged in work that does not really need doing. The size of the national security departments and agencies has swelled out of proportion even to the increased number and complexity of our problems.

The payroll costs, although formidable, are less important than the price paid in sluggishness of decision and action. Unnecessary people make for unnecessary layering, unnecessary clearances and concurrences, and unnecessary intrusions on the time of officials working on problems of real importance. Many offices have reached and passed the point where quantity of staff reduces quality of product.

Occasional swings of the personnel axe, accompanied by much fanfare, yield more in headlines than in lasting results. The fight against overstaffing must be waged each day anew.

5. *The career services should be made better training grounds for posts of national security leadership.*

Our career services are not producing enough officials with the large executive talents, breadth of experience, and width of perspective needed in top foreign-policy and defense posts.

A program for improvement should give officials of exceptional promise much greater flexibility and latitude in job assignments; it should stress movement of personnel among agencies; it should offer more opportunities for advanced training of the kind made available by our most efficient private corporations.

And above all, we need higher salaries at the top of the civil service and at the sub-Cabinet level. Present pay scales are dropping further and further behind those obtaining in private life—not only in business but also, increasingly, in the academic world. These inadequate salaries discourage too many able people from entering government service and encourage too many to leave it.

6. *We should reduce the needless barriers that stand in the way of private citizens called to national duty.*

Our system of government uniquely depends upon the contributions of distinguished citizens temporarily in high government posts, who come from and return to private life—the Stimsons, the Forrestals, and the Lovetts. In time of hot war, we let no obstacle stand in the way of getting our ablest people to work in the government. But in this cold war, whose outcome will be equally fateful for the nation, we tolerate pointless impediments to public service.

The present conflict-of-interest laws are a prime example. We will always need regulations to deter or penalize the rare official who tries to use his public office for private gain. But the laws now on the books are archaic—most of them go back to the Civil War. They are more responsive to the problems of the 1860's than the 1960's, and they often make it unduly hard for outstanding people to accept government posts. The job of updating these laws should be completed.

7. *Used properly, the National Security Council can be of great value as an advisory body to the President.*

The true worth of the Council lies in its being an accustomed place where the President can join with his chief advisers in searching examination and debate of the "great choices" of national security policy. These may be long-term strategic alternatives or crisis problems demanding immediate action. The Council provides a means of bringing the full implications of policy alternatives out on the table, and a vehicle through which the President can inform his lieutenants of his decisions and of the chain of reasoning behind them.

The pitfalls to be avoided are clearly marked: at one extreme, over-institutionalization of the NSC system—with overly elaborate procedures and over-production of routine papers; at the other extreme, excessive informality—with Council meetings tending in the direction of official bull sessions.

8. *No task is more urgent than improving the effectiveness of the Department of State.*

In our system, there can be no satisfactory substitute for a Secretary of State willing and able to exercise his leadership across the full range of national security matters as they relate to foreign policy. The Secretary, assisted by his Department, must bear the chief responsibility for bringing new policy initiatives to the President's desk, and for overseeing and coordinating our manifold foreign-policy activities on the President's behalf.

The State Department is not doing enough in asserting its leadership across the whole front of foreign policy. Neither is it doing enough in staffing itself for such leadership. State also needs more respect for comprehensive forward planning. The Department as a whole attaches too little importance to looking ahead in foreign policy and is too wedded to a philosophy of reacting to problems as they arise. The Policy Planning Council is not now in the mainstream of policy-making.

State needs more officials who are good executive managers and who are broadly experienced in dealing with the full range of national security problems that now engage the Department. The administration of foreign policy has become "big business." This places a high premium on the ability to manage large-scale enterprises—to make decisions promptly and decisively, to delegate, and to monitor.

This need for "take charge" men is particularly urgent down through the Assistant Secretary level and at our large missions abroad. Round pegs in square holes are a luxury we cannot afford.

9. *We need a stronger, not a weaker, Bureau of the Budget.*
Rich as we are, we cannot do all the things we would like to do to assure the national safety and provide for the general welfare.

The job of the President is to rank the competing claims on our resources in terms of their national importance—to distinguish between what cannot wait and what can wait. The budgetary process is the President's most helpful tool in establishing such an order of national priorities and in seeing to it that the departments and agencies' operating programs conform to these priorities. In this task, the President needs the help of a Bureau of the Budget staffed still more strongly than it now is with officials who can interpret agency programs in terms of their contributions to the President's over-all goals.

The danger is always present that Bureau members will become champions of their own, rather than the President's, program preferences. A strong Bureau requires strong Presidential control.

10. *The Congress should put its own house in better order.*

Although the Subcommittee inquiry was directed toward the executive branch, there is clearly much room for improvement on Capitol Hill.

One major problem is fragmentation. The Congress is hard put to deal with national security policy as a whole.

The difficulty starts with the executive branch. Except in the State of the Union and budget messages, it presents national security information and program requests to the Congress in bits and pieces. The present mode of operation of the Congressional system compounds the problem. The authorization process treats as separable matters that are not really separable. Foreign affairs, defense matters, space policies, and atomic energy programs are handled in different committees. It is the same with money matters. Income and outgo, and the relation of each to the economy, come under different jurisdictions.

There is no place in the Congress, short of the floors of the Senate and the House, where the requirements of national security and the resources needed on their behalf, are considered in their totality.

The need is to give the Congress, early in each session, better opportunities to review our national security programs as a whole. For its part, the executive branch can take the initiative by presenting our national security requirements "as a package," with dollar signs attached. To put these requirements in better perspective, the Secretaries of State and Defense and other ranking officials could make themselves available for joint appearances on the Hill.

The Congress should move in parallel. At the beginning of each session, it can encourage authorizing committees to meet jointly to take testimony on the full scope and thrust of our national security programs. A closer partnership can be urged upon the revenue and expenditure committees. And parent committees can undertake to secure more comprehensive briefings on programs before dividing them up among the subcommittees for detailed analysis.

One last point: too many people believe that the cards are stacked in favor of totalitarian systems in the cold war. Nothing could be more wrong. Democracies headline their difficulties and mistakes; dictatorships hide theirs. The archives of Nazi Germany told a story of indecision and ineptitude in policy-making on a scale never approached by our own nation.

The words spoken by Robert Lovett at the first hearing of the Subcommittee are still the right words:

> While the challenges of the moment are most serious in a policy-making sense, I see no reason for black despair or for defeatist doubts as to what our system of government or this country can do. We can do whatever we have to do in order to survive and to meet any form of economic or political competition we are likely to face. All this we can do with one proviso: we must be willing to do our best.

TWO:

SELECTED TESTIMONY

Perspective on the Policy Process[*]

ROBERT A. LOVETT

*Robert A. Lovett has a record of national service
going back more than forty-five years, when, as a
naval aviation pilot in World War I, he won the
Navy Cross. Named the first Assistant Secretary of
War for Air in World War II, he received the Distinguished Service Medal in 1945. His postwar
service has included duty in the Truman Administration as Under Secretary of State and as Deputy Secretary and Secretary of Defense, and thereafter
continuing responsibilities in an advisory capacity
under Presidents Eisenhower, Kennedy, and Johnson. In 1963, President Kennedy awarded him the
Presidential Medal of Freedom with distinction.
Mr. Lovett is a general partner in Brown Brothers
Harriman & Co., and is Chairman of the Executive
Committee of the Union Pacific Railroad.*

Mr. Chairman, your committee has invited me to appear before
it and to state, first, "my estimate of the broad challenge confronting the United States today and in the years ahead"; and second,
"to select the areas which, in my opinion, have special significance
to national security or survival," with particular emphasis on the
existing machinery, its adequacy, and its problems in making effective our foreign policy, and defense planning and operations.

A series of searching questions in your interim report were sent
me, covering a very wide range of subjects within the terms of the
Senate resolution authorizing your study. Many of these questions
lie in areas of government outside my experience. Therefore, if it
meets with your approval, I should like at the outset to limit my
comments to an attempt to identify a principal cause for the delays

[*] Testimony delivered to the Subcommittee on National Policy Machinery,
February 23, 1960.

and difficulties in the operation of policy-making machinery in our democracy; and, thereafter, to narrow my comments to the more specific questions dealing with the fields of government operations in which I served some years ago—the Department of State and the Department of Defense.

These comments are based for the most part on notes made some eight years ago—in connection with a report submitted in November, 1952, and not then used because of emphasis on procedures. Reflections on these subjects and brief periods of association with them during the subsequent years have not materially changed my opinion as to the desirability of having a hard look at some of the points raised for discussion. It should be clear, therefore, that none of these observations is intended to be critical of any individuals or of operational decisions.

Background Conditions

The operation of our governmental machinery today is complicated by a number of factors which we must not only comprehend but to which we must also readjust. We see in the world today a rate and variety of change that in our history has never been equaled. We have not only to face the challenge of bold new scientific and technological advances, but also to adjust to changing conditions created by the emergence of new and independent countries and a growing sense of nationalism in many parts of the world.

This would be difficult if government machinery were perfect and decisions on policy could be promptly translated into action. But our problem is magnified by the fact that our system of government and our way of life have come under direct and deadly challenge by an implacable, crafty and, of late, openly contemptuous enemy of both.

We need not waste much time in attempting to prove this point. If the public statement "We will bury you" does not carry the message to us, then words have lost their meaning. Attempts to explain away this blunt warning of intention by calling it jovial, or by saying that it really does not mean a big military funeral but just a little economic one is a form of jocularity too close to the jugular to lighten my heart.

If we are not prepared, after that statement and the evidence of the past several years, to admit that we are in a struggle for survival involving military power, economic productivity, and influence on the minds of men in political, scientific, and moral fields, then we have truly succumbed to the hard sell of the soft attitude.

For whether we like it or not, we are in the early stages of a ruthless and lengthy period of competition between our system of free men governed by their consent, in a society of reasonably free enterprise, and the communistic system, with the so-called advantages derived by a dictatorship endowed with coldblooded patience, continuity of determined effort, and openly declared singleness of purpose directed toward world domination.

As one observes the new and heightened tensions of the world today and adds them to the longstanding and unsolved problems we have been trying to settle for many years, it is not surprising to hear occasional doubts expressed about the inability of our governmental procedures to meet today's needs, magnified by the enormous compression of time and space, and the consequent requirement of prompt decisions leading to prompt action.

One of the questions most frequently asked, either profanely or with a sad whimper, is "Why does it take the Government so long to make up its mind?" or, in the more restrained language of this committee's questionnaire, "Can anything be done to speed up our Government policy-making machinery?"

In the search for an answer, I should like to explore briefly—and solely within the executive branch itself—a field responsible, I believe, for many of the procedures and methods of policy-making that cause bewilderment, seem redundant, and have, occasionally, even less attractive characteristics.

I do so because, if a fairly accurate identification can be made of one of the basic problems affecting government machinery and causing certain parts of it to malfunction, perhaps some corrective measures can be taken by the executive branch within its existing powers or with the help of the Congress.

I am not suggesting that a major cure in policy-making delay is in sight or that any real progress will come from something as appealing as "simplifying" or "streamlining." It is wholly unrealistic to talk of making government simple. We can aspire to make it manageable and effective, but its characteristics make simplicity of machinery impossible. This is the result of its vast size, its complexity, its multitude of activities, and particularly the wide divergence of interests it represents and the different needs of the various groups of citizens which it must reconcile.

It is this last requirement, I think, that we must focus on if we are to recognize one of the main reasons for the great amount of time consumed in the making and execution of national policy. The often forgotten fact is that our form of government, and its machinery, has had built into it a series of clashes of group needs. They appear to have been originally designed to protect the individual citizen and to keep any one group or department of government from becoming too dominant.

This device of inviting argument between conflicting interests— which we can call the "foul-up factor" in our equation of performance—was obviously the result of a deliberate decision to give up the doubtful efficiency of a dictatorship in return for a method of protection of individual freedom, rights, privileges, and immunities.

When government was small, the "foul-up" system must have worked very well; when government became large, it probably worked fairly well. But government has now become gigantic, at the very moment in history when time itself is not merely a measure, or a dimension, but perhaps the difference between life and death.

The Federal government is by far the largest and most complicated operation in this country. This huge organization would be hard enough to run if authority were given where responsibility was placed. Yet, that frequently is not the case.

The Constitutional principle of the separation of powers certainly sounds as though the intent was neatly to assign certain authorities and responsibilities to separate branches of government charged with executive, legislative, and judicial functions. But then, the necessity of putting limits on power had to be met, and it is at this point that we run head-first into the system of "checks and balances" as it applies to the executive departments.

We are interested here only in those overlaps occurring between departments, agencies, etc., within the executive branch. This is really a method of requiring power to be shared—even though responsibility may not be—and of introducing rival claimants from another department with a different mission into the policy-making or decision-taking process.

This is the "foul-up factor" in our methods, and it needs some careful examination because there is, I think, a discernible and constantly increasing tendency to try to expand the intent of the system to the point where mere curiosity on the part of someone or some agency, and not a "need to know" can be used as a ticket of admission to the merry-go-round of "concurrences." This doctrine, unless carefully and boldly policed, can become so fertile a spawner of committees as to blanket the whole executive branch with an embalmed atmosphere.

Whether or not this itch to get in the act is a form of status-seeking, the idea seems to have got around that just because some decision may affect your activities, you automatically have a right to take part in making it. In consequence, the general area of executive department checks and balances is the source of a broad stream of procedural complications that consume vast amounts of time and energy. It would be well to look into it, I believe, because there is some reason to feel that the doctrine may be getting out of hand and that what was designed to act as a policeman may, in fact, become a jailor.

May I now turn from the point just discussed as part of the general subject of "problem areas requiring possible remedial action" and try to respond to the questions asked in relation to the narrower limits of the Department of Defense and the Department of State.

As I understand them, the questions here asked fall into two rough categories:

1. Does the government machinery, as presently provided, give us adequate means for determining national security policy?

2. Can you identify "problem areas" and suggest "any constructive and practical reform"?

The Department of Defense

Taking the Department of Defense first, since it is freshest in my mind—I believe that adequate policy-making machinery in its special field is currently available; that proven operations machinery is in being; that it has, furthermore, the essential military attribute of close relationship between planning and operational responsibility; that it enjoys through the military services a fair amount of stability and continuity (though still inadequate, in my opinion); and that it can be staffed by specially trained personnel, giving whatever balance or mix is desired among military, civilian, scientific, and professional skills. While I have not seen at first hand the effects of the reorganization of 1958, I doubt whether anything in it materially reduced the availability of competent and specially trained military officers with which the Department has fortunately been endowed for some years.

But while we talk about policy as if it were the end product of a machine, we are, of course, really speaking about people in the military department and, fortunately for us, very good people, with a high percentage of them uniquely dedicated and skilled in their professions. These men are custodians of a great tradition of duty and honor that entitles them to our respect and to our understanding of the pride they must develop in their demanding service. They respond to a wide variety of stimuli, just as the rest of us do, and they function best under certain working conditions and in an orderly, disciplined atmosphere.

The military portion of the national policy-making machinery will, I believe, function with least difficulties and with the highest quality of output under certain conditions which are conducive to its best performance. These include the following:

1. The Department of Defense and its military establishments should be nonpolitical and nonpartisan: the great tradition that the military services are nonpolitical should, I am convinced, apply equally to the civilian heads of these departments. If this principle were not more persuasive on other grounds, the practical consideration of representing the needs of the nation as a whole before the Congress, and the nonpolitical operation of the draft law, ought to make the desirability of nonpartisanship in the military structure abundantly apparent. The only thing more dangerous than an external enemy is a group of home-grown military sycophants.

2. Military policy and strategic planning require a prior step—the determination of a national political policy: the military professionals should be contributors to and not makers of national political policies. They are trained to carry out such policy, not to originate it. They clearly cannot do their planning job until a higher level fixes national goals.

3. The number of committees in the Department of Defense and the military departments is still far too great. There is excessive staff layering. The constant increase in the number of committees —other than those statutorily created—has reached a point where they are no longer mere nuisances but have become positive menaces to the prompt and orderly conduct of business.

Some committees obviously are necessary—for example, certain interdepartmental ones—but I think it is fair to say that Dr. Parkinson's first law finds its best examples in this field. Committees reviewing other committees, or overlapping them, are one of the most productive sources of vacillating administration and wavering policies.

Of some importance also is the fact that the number of committees adds materially to the difficulty of protecting highly sensitive material and makes increasingly likely those leaks that are dangerous to the national security.

Excessive staff layering results, I think, in overstaffing in certain areas of the military departments and contributes much to delay and little to vigorous and imaginative planning. The visible results lie in unnecessary costs and in the number of initials on a paper. At some point, their quantity must inevitably reduce quality and increase porosity.

4. The authority of the individual executive must be restored: the derogation of the authority of the individual in government, and the exaltation of the anonymous mass, has resulted in a noticeable lack of decisiveness. Committees cannot effectively replace the decision-making power of the individual who takes the oath of office; nor can committees provide the essential qualities of leadership.

Committees occasionally serve those in authority as a device to postpone or avoid making decisions; others sometimes seem to spring into being because higher authority does not fully trust the judgment of the subordinate executive. But two heads are not always better than one, particularly if they are growing on the same body.

5. Civilian and military executives alike should stick to the fields in which they have special training and aptitudes: if they do, the chance of making the machinery work well is excellent. One of the few humans as exasperating as a civilian businessman who suddenly becomes an expert on military strategy and tactics is the military adviser who magically becomes an expert in some highly sophisticated production problem in which he has no background or experience.

6. Turnover of key civilian executive personnel: everyone is aware of this much discussed problem of government. In the Department of Defense, it has a special importance largely because continuity of planning and operations is of vital concern. It takes a long time for an able man, without previous military service of some importance and experience in government, to catch up with his job in this increasingly complex department. At a guess, I would say he could pay good dividends to the government in about two years. Meanwhile, of course, he is becoming a more valuable asset each day. To lose him before or just as he becomes productive is manifestly a serious waste of the effort that went into his training. How to hold him is a problem to which I do not know the an-

swer. But I have a feeling that, in many cases, the cause of his leaving lies in the conditions surrounding his entry into government and his terms of employment in the first instance. Reasons most commonly ascribed to the problem of hiring good men usually center about the so-called conflict-of-interest laws and their effect on the man who has built up, over a period of years, a right to a pension or other incentive benefits made important to him by some of the more grotesque provisions of our tax laws. Frequently, a sharp reduction in standard of living is another part of the problem.

But I think the order of magnitude of these difficulties can be reduced if we want to do it; and that sensible, even if only partial, answers can be found by applying realistic rules of reason through legislation which might take into account modern business' capital structure and its operation under present-day regulations.

7. "Split papers" from the Joint Chiefs of Staff should not be regarded as inherently objectionable; naturally, they need not be welcomed. But it is vitally important to a Secretary of Defense, as one of the advisers to the President, with a special responsibility, to know what the alternatives are to a course of action, or what serious obstacles to a proposed program are foreseen by a responsible Chief of Staff, so that, in reaching a decision, he will be possessed of all the facts available.

8. Need for constant, close, and sympathetic cooperation with the Department of State: national political policy includes foreign policy and defense policy—among others—and simply cannot be fragmentized. It should, of course, be integrated. Military power is today so intertwined with national foreign policy that the Department of State must be a full partner—and, above all, a welcome one—in all major decisions of planning and policy. While lateral liaison should be insisted upon and must take place at the lower levels that work on planning and policy papers at the first stages, the tone of the cooperation must be set by the two Secretaries.

The Department of State

Now we come to the Department of State. Because policy-making has historically been its main function, it is more difficult to isolate those elements of its machinery that have special importance to national security or that serve to complicate it.

This Department, furthermore, has a unique position in the executive branch because it draws its powers in part from those directly delegated to it by the President from his constitutional responsibilities for foreign affairs and in part from statutory sources.

The Secretary of State is the President's principal adviser on foreign policy and his agent when the President chooses to have him so act. He is the ranking Cabinet officer and heads a department that has been going through a period of violent transition in the last twenty years. Today, he must operate as an adviser and executive in a world that carries an open threat to our national security and one in which the easily distinguishable boundaries of the past, between domestic and foreign policies, have disappeared. And, still, the end of such complications is not in sight.

The Secretary has, therefore, to rely less on the broad powers of his Department and more on integrated planning with other members of the executive branch. As the interim report of this Subcommittee correctly says, "He needs a wide-ranging knowledge of the relations between military and foreign policies, of the uses and limitations of economic and military aid, of information, propaganda, and related programs, of the strengths and weaknesses of our adversaries, of the dangers and opportunities in countries around the world, and of the working of international institutions and of regional organizations."

This is enough responsibility to keep anyone fully occupied and the workload, not counting the necessary formal social functions of the office, is in my opinion already at the dangerous level. This feeling colors the answers I attempt to give below to certain of the specific questions asked.

1. "Is the Department's organization adequate for policy-making?"

The policy-making machinery and procedures in the Department seem to me, in general terms, to be adequate. Adjustments designed to accelerate decisions and provide guidelines for other departments would seem possible with certain changes in method of operation covered briefly below.

2. "Should the Secretary be given a more dominant role in overall national security planning?"

I think not. He already has more than he can do properly and his opinion can now carry whatever weight the President feels it deserves. Increasing the Secretary's role will not relieve the President from making the ultimate decision on foreign affairs which, as is pointed out earlier, is a necessary first step in national security planning.

3. "Are the responsibilities of the State and Defense Departments in national security policy-making now correctly defined and divided?"

I think they are adequately defined at present. The effectiveness of any such allocation depends on the intent and cooperation of the parties at interest. No organization chart is a substitute for a sense of common goals. Such charts are, I think, generally, proof that a picture of a lot of oblong boxes—especially when colored—can be more deceiving than a thousand words.

4. "Should some of State's functions in national security policy-making be shifted to a sizable planning staff at the White House level?"

I believe this would solve nothing, would increase organizational layering and promote overstaffing, and would prove wasteful in time, money, and manpower. It seems to me that if planning is removed too far from operating responsibility, a misleading lack of realism results. The President ought to be provided, I think, with the full flavor of the operational department's planning.

5. "In view of his formidable burdens of office, can the negotiating responsibilities of the Secretary of State be lightened?"

My answer is an emphatic "yes." As indicated in an earlier paragraph, the Secretary's duties are extremely heavy. His voice in council is of cardinal importance if delay and vacillation in policy and performance are to be avoided or substantially reduced. To have him dashing about all over the world to an increasing variety of meetings or negotiations makes very little sense to me.

Our system of government, with its checks and balances and other essential procedures, differs so materially from most of the others in the world that the argument "They can do it, why not we?" rings hollow and false. Actually, the ability to yank our Secretary out of his chair for some foreign ministers' meeting—and keep him out of the country for days or weeks—is a rather neat way to throw a monkeywrench in our policy-making machinery and in our method of consulting the Congress.

Among the most important attributes a Secretary of State must possess are, in my opinion, trustworthiness, reliability, and availability in Washington. One hears much of the first two virtues but little of the almost equally important third. The travel burden placed on the Secretary in the last ten years has steadily increased. If the trend keeps up, he will soon find that such time as is not spent in overseas meetings is barely enough to devote to the enforced neglect of his other duties.

A possible solution—and the only one with much appeal that I have heard of—is to continue to regard the Secretary of State as the first-ranking Cabinet member and Presidential adviser with responsibility for the conduct of the State Department. Then create a new Cabinet position, responsible to the Secretary of State and, through him, to the President, and have him devote full time to meetings and negotiations. He could be given such title as is needed to do the job—perhaps Minister of Foreign Affairs. The skills and special gifts needed for this work may prove more easily developed when not burdened with other executive responsibility.

6. On the budgetary process, "Should State and Defense (and perhaps other agencies concerned with national security) participate fully in the initial establishment of 'budgetary guidelines' for national security programs?"

I believe they should, since a sound budget can only be developed if both State and Defense—the latter in particular—go painfully through the steps of determining (*a*) what is necessary (and not merely desirable) for national security; (*b*) whether it is feasible from the point of view of national resources and production machinery; and (*c*) whether it is socially or politically acceptable to the people.

An added reason lies in the importance of having the budgetary goals determined from the outset by a great concern for a system of priority of national need and not have them too greatly influenced by the officials of the Bureau of the Budget itself.

Finally, national security depends, I believe, on something far more important than the machinery that is supposed to serve it. It depends on many things. Some of them, to be sure, are material, but the more important are matters of the national spirit. It depends on our belief in the future; it depends greatly on our sense of values; and it depends on our willingness to give up a little of today in order to have a tomorrow.

While the challenges of the moment are most serious in a policy-making sense, I see no reason for black despair or for defeatist doubts as to what our system of government or this country can do. We can do whatever we have to do in order to survive and to meet any form of economic or political competition we are likely to face. All this we can do with one proviso: we must be willing to do our best.

In brief summary, therefore, I suppose that there is nothing wrong with the machinery that cannot be corrected by the removal of some excess parts, the replacement of some worn-out ones, by lubricating generously with an understanding approach to the personnel problem involved, and by having a destination clearly in mind before we start out.

Is a Greater Effort Needed?

SENATOR JACKSON. I want to ask you, Mr. Lovett, whether in your judgment the threat now confronting our country is sufficiently serious to require a greater effort than we are now making.

MR. LOVETT. In general terms, Mr. Chairman, my answer to that would be yes. While I am not familiar with the details of the military requirements or the debates that have centered about them, it seems to me that the country's security lies also in fields that embrace things other than mere military end-products themselves, such as our position in the eyes of the world, or the psychological image we present to the world as a whole. I feel that we are doing something short of our best. I think our past performance may have raised the hopes of the world excessively high. But I still feel, sir, that we are doing something short of our best in several fields, excluding the military items with which I am not familiar.

SENATOR JACKSON. Mr. Lovett, it is sometimes said that we cannot afford to spend more on defense and other national security programs. What is your judgment on this?

MR. LOVETT. Well, sir, I must frankly say that, as I attempted to point out in my statement, I am personally confident that whatever needs to be done to promote our security in the world today and to assure our future can be done, in a financial sense and in an economic sense, without materially downgrading the position of this country.

SENATOR JACKSON. I believe you were in the Department of Defense when the budget was raised very substantially and very dramatically in a short period of time. Do you recall what that adjustment was in terms of national defense?

MR. LOVETT. Yes, sir. I have a very vivid recollection of certain aspects of it. When I came to Washington early in the fall of 1950, we were then going into the stages of supplemental budgets, the Korean war having broken out. The first full budget we submitted had requests, as I recall it, from the three military departments, for something over $100 billion. I think it was around $102 billion or $104 billion. Through the screening processes that were applied strenuously, it was reduced to the $60 billions. My impression is that we came up to the Congress with a budget of about $62 billion or $63 billion, and there were adjustments made in the congressional hearings that gave us something over $60 billion for fiscal 1952, I think it was.

SENATOR JACKSON. And that was from a level of about $14 billion?

MR. LOVETT. Perhaps a little higher than that, but it was in that order of magnitude.

The Individual Executive vs. Committees

SENATOR MANSFIELD. In your opinion, Mr. Lovett, do you think there are too many committees and too many commissions within the government?

MR. LOVETT. Yes, sir, I do.

SENATOR MANSFIELD. Do you think that in late years, under both Democratic and Republican administrations, one of the ways in which we have met our problems, or one of the ways we have swept our problems under the rug, is to create a committee or commission and then forget about it?

MR. LOVETT. I am afraid it has been used as such a device very frequently, sir.

SENATOR MANSFIELD. Would you say that that is generally true throughout the government?

MR. LOVETT. In my opinion it is, Senator Mansfield, very definitely.

SENATOR MANSFIELD. Would you say that it is increasing in late years?

MR. LOVETT. Well, I have no yardstick by which to measure it in more recent years. It was increasing in my time, and simply by the passage of time, since this is a self-multiplying affair, I would gather that the number has undoubtedly gone up.

One of the problems here, to be quite blunt about it, is, I believe, that the position of the individual in government is being constantly downgraded. You don't get much judgment from a committee. Usually the committees, of the sort we are speaking of now, are the result of some rather lonely, melancholy men who have been assigned a responsibility but haven't the authority to make the decisions at their levels, and so they tend to seek their own kind. They thereupon coagulate into a sort of glutinous mass and suddenly come out as a committee. When you have one of those things, you have real trouble.

Lightening the Secretary of State's Negotiating Burdens

SENATOR MUNDT. I was intrigued by your suggestion about a new sort of second Secretary of State, a Minister of Foreign Relations. You suggest a new Cabinet officer responsible to the Secretary of State and through him to the President, which is at least a different arrangement from what we have for other Cabinet officers. Could you not perhaps achieve that same desirable objective by having an Under Secretary of State selected because of his capacity as a negotiator, whose job it would be to handle these international negotiations?

MR. LOVETT. It might be a possibility, Senator Mundt. I doubt whether the Under Secretary or an additional Under Secretary would be wholly acceptable to our foreign counterparts at these meetings. They lay a great deal of emphasis on protocol and title. While they would deal with a man who had Cabinet rank, I think they would regard it as being somewhat downgrading to their own importance if they accepted someone of Under Secretary rank. We had that experience in my time, when we had an Under Secretary for Economic Affairs, Secretary Clayton, who was extremely competent in his field. Yet, in some of the meetings abroad, there was an indication that where he met with the foreign minister of a foreign country, that foreign minister expected someone of at least equal rank.

In other words, it is a matter very largely of protocol. It is a thing we run into in the military departments frequently. We have fought many wars quite successfully with a four-star rank. But when you run into field-marshal ranks in international meetings, then it is necessary to get the five-star rank for our men so as to make everybody feel comfortable about dealing with equals.

SENATOR JACKSON. Mr. Lovett, you served as Under Secretary of State and during that time I believe you had to serve as Acting Secretary of State for long periods of time. So you speak from some personal experience, too?

MR. LOVETT. Yes, I do, sir. I think the Acting Secretary is accepted with some generosity of spirit, depending on the country, but he is hardly as warmly welcomed as the established and appointed Secretary.

SENATOR MUNDT. Of course, it might require some education of our friends we negotiate with. But you run into that same difficulty, do you not, when you have to explain to these foreign negotiators that you still have the U. S. Senate, which has to approve any treaty. It is a little hard for them sometimes to accept that. Or if you are talking about a foreign-aid program, you say, "Yes, we will certainly take care of giving you X million dollars, provided that the Appropriations Committee comes through." There are a lot of things that are unique about our system that we have to explain as we work along with our friends overseas.

MR. LOVETT. That is true. I think most of the countries overseas have come to accept the U. S. Senate as an act of God.

As to this man who shall be especially assigned the job of familiarizing himself with the requirements of international negotiation, it seems to me that there is a very useful function that could be performed—now that we have fast aircraft and other means of immediate communication—by getting together with other nations and working out a system of rules for international meetings.

As I recall it, the Congress of Vienna, along about 1815, met specifically to work out a system of rules for international discussion and international cooperation in terms of those days. It is now 145 years later. I do not recall any meetings having occurred in the interim—at least not in my lifespan. I feel that it might be a very fruitful step, if you could get the major countries together to adopt a set of rules as to who would represent a country in certain areas of international problems.

The Secretaries of State and Defense and Partisan Politics

SENATOR MANSFIELD. My question has to do with your statement that the Department of Defense and its military establishments should be nonpolitical and nonpartisan. Do you think under a Democratic administration, let us say, that the members comprising the leadership in the Department of Defense should be allowed to go out to make Jefferson-Jackson Day addresses?

MR. LOVETT. Well, they were not allowed in my time, sir, which was in a Democratic administration. There may have been an individual who attended one and may have made a speech or something like that. But it was not either by direction of the Secretary of Defense or with his permission. General Marshall felt very strongly in those areas, as I do.

SENATOR MANSFIELD. During your time, did not both the Defense Department and the State Department usually keep their top officials out of anything that might be considered pertaining to politics?

MR. LOVETT. We had definite instructions from the President to keep ourselves out of politics, no matter from what source the request came. Requests frequently came from the national committees of both parties, and the matter was always referred to the White House for handling. We didn't have any trouble that I recall.

Certainly, one of the reasons in the Department of State would be manifest, as a bipartisan enterprise. The Congress was Republican and the administration was Democrat. So it would have been the height of something greater than folly to have gotten into the political field even if it hadn't made good solid sense to stay out of it altogether. That was the case in both departments.

The Budgetary Process

SENATOR MANSFIELD. Do you think, Mr. Lovett, that the Bureau of the Budget in this day and age has too much power allocated to it?

MR. LOVETT. I can speak to the question more accurately, Senator Mansfield, by relating it to my own time. I felt that it had too much power assigned to it then. The situation seems to me to be almost the reverse of what you run into in some of the operating departments, where you frequently find responsibility without authority. In the Budget Bureau, you very frequently find authority without responsibility. They are just about equally irritating forms of danger.

SENATOR JACKSON. I wonder if you think it might be desirable to bring the Secretaries of State and Defense into the budget process before the initial, over-all ceiling is established.

MR. LOVETT. I think that is terribly important, Mr. Chairman. Actually, the determination of size, it seems to me, is empty unless it takes into account the basic needs of the country, and the basic needs of the country obviously have at their head the ability to survive, in a national-security sense and in other aspects related to it. So I would say emphatically that they ought to be cut in on the discussion before the budget figure is determined.

SENATOR JACKSON. What improvements do you think we could make in the budgetary process insofar as it affects national security?

MR. LOVETT. Mr. Chairman, I think there are two fields about which I feel reasonably confident in expressing an opinion. The first is that I think that the one-year budget system is inadequate in many cases and in a sense is detrimental to both the congressional and executive branches in their attempt to make a policy effective.

I think that for any experimental development program involving research, and the awkward period during translation of research into an actual item, funding it for one year is unrealistic. I think we need to have something longer, in order not to have to reset sights and suffer the vacillation which ensues. One of the most painful things that an executive goes through in the Government departments is the change of program while you are right in the middle of it. You lose momentum and you delay the output. So I would say we need some form of budgeting for certainly half of the period of gestation of any new weapon, which used to be in the order of five, six, or seven years—about five years, to take the low side. That would mean two to three years, say, of funding for some approved experimental research-and-development purpose.

Another thing that seems to have become something of a habit —it started in my time and I observe that it has gone on since—is the so-called stretch-out. I am afraid that the Bureau of the Budget has forgotten what a stretch-out really can and cannot do.

If you have sound economic or social reasons for delaying the delivery of certain end products now currently in production, developed and in the line, then I think it is acceptable after appropriate investigation. But the moment you stretch out or attempt to stretch out an experimental and research project, particularly when it is an attempt to translate basic research into some experimental item, all you are doing is absolutely guaranteeing that you are going to get an obsolete or at best obsolescent item. That is the point at which you should try to compress time, not expand it.

Performance Audit by Congress

Senator Mundt. I was visiting with a high functionary in the Defense Department the other day who related to me the number of days and hours he spent on Capitol Hill, reporting first to one committee and then to another committee. I wish you would tell us whether or not this did prove to be time-consuming and whether we can streamline our machinery so that fewer committees can get the information and handle it.

Mr. Lovett. Senator Mundt, I think appearances before the congressional committees are a part, and a very important part, of the responsibility when you take your oath of office. It is a very time-consuming necessity. There is no question about that.

If you could appear before combined committees, as, for example, in the case of the Marshall Plan—there was the committee of the House and the committee of the Senate meeting in a joint hearing—that accelerates consideration very considerably.

I would not venture to express an opinion on its general applicability, because I am not familiar enough with congressional procedures. But I learned a very painful but useful lesson during the war when, having gotten rather beaten down by consistent appearances before various committees of the Congress, I suggested to Senator O'Mahoney, after one of the Appropriations Committee meetings of the Senate, that this was getting to be terribly time-consuming and exhausting, and it was very hard to keep up with, and couldn't something be done about it. He said, in effect, just breathe deeply and this will pass off in time; go back and do your job and do not worry about this aspect of it. Which I did.

I subsequently made an inspection trip to Germany, and in the process was presented with the information that had been collected by teams sent to question leading German industrialists and war production leaders. One of these was Dr. Albert Speer. It was his opinion, expressed to our examiners, that one of the reasons that the German economy collapsed and that the Wehrmacht was left inadequately supplied in the latter days was that, under a dictatorship, once a department head got the nod from Hitler, he went ahead as a little dictator and rode his particular hobby without criticism. There was no performance audit run on him as his program continued. The best example of that was their use of jet fighters. They were so impressed by our use of the fighter bomber that they tried to turn their interceptor jet fighter into a fighter bomber and, of course, failed, because of the difference in thrust on take-offs, as compared with propeller planes.

This impressed me so much as I went further into it that I found it necessary to come up and eat humble pie before Senator O'Mahoney. I said then that if I had to choose between having a congressional committee breathe on the back of my neck as a form of performance audit and getting in the position of a department executive riding some particular conviction or belief to the point of defeat, I would choose a congressional hearing. And I still feel that way about it. Appearing before committees is time-consuming, it is exhausting, it is sometimes terribly irritating, but on the whole, as long as we have our form of governmental system, I think it is a necessary part of it.

The time-consuming part is the duplication of hearings, of walking from one side of the Capitol to the other before committees interested in the same material.

SENATOR MUNDT. It was, of course, the duplication that I was concerned about. I do not want anybody to suggest that congressional hearings should be eliminated, but there are at least five, and possibly six, Senate committees that, during the course of the first few months of a year, will call the same high executive, perhaps the Secretary of Defense or the Secretary of State, to go through pretty much the same material.

It seems to me that if we could streamline that procedure or consolidate hearings, to have the person appear before committees meeting together, it would move in the direction of our target, and that is to streamline the activities and get good results faster.

SENATOR JACKSON. The Subcommittee has received a wide range of suggestions from various individuals and groups, including proposals for joint meetings of the Foreign Relations and Armed Services Committees, proposals for establishing a permanent national security committee in each House, or else a joint congressional committee on national security. I personally have a feeling that when the executive branch comes up with some consolidation in the national security area, corresponding changes will take place in congressional structure.

For instance, when the services were put together in the Department of Defense, the Naval Affairs Committee and the Military Affairs Committee were abolished, and one committee was created —the Committee on Armed Services in the House and the Senate. This is an example of one vast area in which you had this kind of consolidation.

The statute setting up the Atomic Energy Commission requires that the AEC keep the Congress currently informed. This has resulted in a diminution of the problem of executive privilege. The AEC does keep the Joint Committee on Atomic Energy currently informed, and it represents an innovation in our system of government, where the two branches work together in many areas. It has brought the executive and legislative branches closer together. A great body of tradition has grown up which represents a very fine example of what can be done if some of these things are tried out.

I believe that you are completely right in raising this issue, Mr. Lovett—of trying to simplify the procedures.

The National Security Council *

MR. LOVETT. Since the National Security Council was designed for the use of the President and was meant to be a help in determining an integrated national security policy, its organization clearly should conform to his wishes and meet his particular work habits.

In earlier testimony, however, during discussions of problems in the Department of Defense, I referred to the matter of so-called split papers, and, with your permission, I should like to complete that point.

Since perfectly legitimate and occasionally valuable differences of opinion develop in Joint Chiefs of Staff papers, so also do different points of view or emphasis cause disagreement between, say, State and Defense, on some proposed plan of action or policy.

In the early days of the National Security Council, as procedures were being worked out by the cut-and-try method, a basic purpose was to provide a kind of Court of Domestic and Foreign Relations before which, with the President presiding, both departments could present their views, debate the points, be subjected to cross-examination, and so on.

The purpose was to insure that the President was in possession of all the available facts, that he got first-hand a chance to evaluate an alternative course of action disclosed by the dissenting views, and that all implications in either course of action were explored before he was asked to take the heavy responsibility of the final decision.

The President has, I think, a better chance of getting these factors with a minimum of fuzzy compromise if he gets them fresh from the vigorous staffs of the departments charged directly with both planning and operations in these special areas of concern.

The relatively small number of officials attending the first meetings made it easier to handle such matters. Furthermore, both the Secretary of State and the Secretary of Defense were directed to bring before the National Security Council only matters of special importance, all others being handled in the two appointments reserved weekly for them or in the Cabinet meetings.

SENATOR JACKSON. Mr. Lovett, do you think the Security Council

* Testimony delivered to the Subcommittee on National Policy Machinery in executive session, February 23, 1960.

can operate effectively, as it was designed originally, if you have a large number of participants?

MR. LOVETT. I would have very grave doubts about its ability to operate in a mass atmosphere. I think it would inhibit frank discussion. I think it would be an embarrassment as regards the vigor with which a man might want to defend his position. I think it would limit the quality of the debate the President ought to hear. Quite apart from those considerations, which would be adequate in my mind, the more people you get into one of those things, the more chances of loose talk. I would not go so far as to say that it would create a leak, but certainly it does not promote security.

SENATOR JACKSON. And it is questionable whether it is really necessary.

MR. LOVETT. I doubt very much that it is necessary.

SENATOR JACKSON. Essentially, the National Security Council represented a codification of our wartime experience, did it not?

MR. LOVETT. Yes, sir; it did, and particularly it was an attempt to translate into our form of operation some of the benefits we saw in the British system.

SENATOR JACKSON. With that background, then, was it your understanding that the NSC should be rather limited in size in order to be effective?

MR. LOVETT. Yes, sir; it was. Secretary Forrestal was one of the leading spirits in attempting to do two things: (1) to get this form of "court," in effect, over which the President would preside, so that you could get a decision in the light of all the facts; and (2) a hope—which was implicit in the act as it came out of Congress, but quite explicit in the original recommendations—that it would promote staff continuity.

This group was to have in it, regardless of changes in the administration, a hard core of trained, continuous public servants who might assist in the presentation of the points of view of their particular departments.

SENATOR JACKSON. Now to turn to this question of the jurisdiction of the NSC: Do you think it should confine itself to a few important issues as opposed to having a lot of issues brought in?

MR. LOVETT. Yes, sir; I do. I think the fewer the better. The National Security Council process as originally envisaged—perhaps "dreamed of" is more accurate—contemplated the devotion of whatever number of hours were necessary in order to exhaust a subject and not just exhaust the listeners.

It was, I think, fairly productive in the early days. I recall with some sense of discomfort, because I usually was not as persuasive as I would like to have been, the debates in which I engaged with the Secretary of State at that time. They were hearty and covered the subject rather fully. Once the decision was made, Mr. Chairman, and I think this is an important point, the subject was dropped. That was that. You had your orders. You went out and did your job.

I think the only field in which the NSC permanent staff was called upon to act after the decision was really an extension of the White House function of following up. I believe that that particular function, if you will call it an audit of performance, is a very necessary and admirable thing in government, and, of course, as you know far better than I, it is one of the principal contributions an astute congressional committee can make to the executive branch.

SENATOR JACKSON. At the present time, the OCB apparently is the instrumentality that is supposed to implement the orders worked out in the NSC.

Do you think the National Security Council should be closely tied to the budgetary process? In other words, shouldn't the NSC have some part in the determination of the budget as it pertains to matters within its jurisdiction?

MR. LOVETT. As presently organized, Mr. Chairman, it seems to me to be a rather amorphous thing. It is a little bit too large to take the precise line which is needed in dealing with the budget. But insofar as it is a meeting place for the Department of State and the Department of Defense, it might offer an excellent vehicle, at least to get their points of view. Once you get the other agencies of government involved in it, I think it reduces the impact of both State and Defense on the expression of national needs.

SENATOR JACKSON. I take it from your statement that, based on your own experience, you believe in debate before the President in the NSC so that the President will have the opportunity to make a decision based on sharp, clear, and understandable alternatives.

MR. LOVETT. I think it is a real disservice to the President not to debate matters of some importance before him, because it denies him, in those circumstances, the possibility of seeing an alternative or an obstacle. Full debate forces him to look down the full length of the hard road and not simply the first few steps of it.

SENATOR JACKSON. In other words, the President has the constitutional responsibility as Commander in Chief and as head of the government to make decisions in the area of national security. You do not necessarily lighten the load of the President by bringing to him agreed-upon papers where no decision is involved, other than to say "We will go ahead with this." Don't you think there is confusion on this point, that there is a tendency to help the President, to lighten his load, by trying to do his constitutional work for him? Isn't this a danger?

MR. LOVETT. Yes, sir. I think the President, for his own protection, must insist on being informed and not merely protected by his aides. I think that is abundantly apparent in the desire of all of the younger assistants, myself once included in that area, to try to keep the bothersome problems away from your senior's desk. I think that is very unfair to him in many cases, and it is something that General Marshall simply would not tolerate. I think that is the only occasion that I recall in which he regularly got very vehement about things.

MR. PENDLETON. On the meeting of the National Security Council, do you believe it would be more advisable for the President to be present at those meetings and hear the debate or to receive, afterwards, the recommendations and findings of the National Security Council?

MR. LOVETT. I think he ought to be there, because so much of the feeling of the intensity of the support comes through when you sit and listen to it yourself. It is a little bit like your own legal profession, where it is much better to have the judge sitting up there and hearing the arguments with a chance to question than it is to have the cold, printed brief put before him and then to ask him to make up his mind.

SENATOR JACKSON. It is the ancient advantage of cross-examination to elicit the truth and to get facts out that might not otherwise appear in a unilateral presentation.

MR. LOVETT. Yes, sir.

MR. PENDLETON. Mr. Lovett, do you feel it would be helpful in this budget process, tying in the relationship of national security policy-making, to have the Director of the Bureau of the Budget be a statutory member of NSC? I believe at present he attends the meetings but is not a statutory member.

MR LOVETT. No, sir; I do not think he should be a statutory member. My conception of the budget process is colored perhaps by my civilian, nongovernmental background. It seems to me that the budget is a procedure. The budget is a device. It is one of the tools that the executive uses to maintain control, through controlling the purse strings. The second aspect of it is that it is a procedure to require forward planning, so that you think ahead and do not spend all of your money in the first six months and have none for the payroll in the last six months. So I think the financial officer normally should be a consultant and participant, but not a decision-maker.

The National Security Council under President Truman[*]

SIDNEY W. SOUERS

Sidney W. Souers was the first Executive Secretary of the National Security Council, from 1947 to 1950, and served as a special consultant to President Truman on foreign and military policies until January, 1953. For his contributions during World War II, he received the Legion of Merit and Distinguished Service Medal. In 1946-47, he was Director of Central Intelligence under the National Intelligence Authority. Admiral Souers is Chairman and Chief Executive Officer of the General American Life Insurance Company, St. Louis, Missouri.

Mr. Chairman and members of the committee, your invitation to me to appear here today to give my views on "how the National Security Council can best function as an advisory mechanism to the President" is appreciated.

When the National Security Council was brought into being by statute in 1947, I was appointed Executive Secretary and served in that capacity until 1950. At that time, my assistant, Mr. James Lay, succeeded me as Executive Secretary, and I was appointed special consultant to the President on national security matters. I continued in this capacity until January, 1953.

Mr. Lay is a loyal and devoted public servant who was selected because it was felt that he would be acceptable to subsequent administrations and would provide continuity in the staff work, which is so desirable.

My comments today are based solely on my own experience, and since I am not acquainted with present operations of the Council,

[*] Testimony delivered to the Subcommittee on National Policy Machinery in executive session, May 10, 1960.

my observations should not be considered as critical of anything that is being done today. I would like to make that very clear.

The National Security Council was a new mechanism injected into our governmental structure. Much consideration was given to how it would perform the functions for which it was designed, without diminishing the authority or responsibility of the principal Cabinet members. Its main purpose was to serve as a means by which the President would receive advice coordinated in depth from his Cabinet members having primary responsibility under him for national security.

Care had to be taken to prevent it from becoming a decision-making agency in the foreign field. The President is solely responsible for such decisions under our Constitution.

We studied carefully the set-up and history of a similar organization originally known as the Imperial Defense Council, which was established in Great Britain in 1908, and undertook to benefit from the growing pains experienced by it during its early days.

Principles of National Security Council Operation

I would now like to set forth briefly a number of principles that in my opinion must be observed if the National Security Council is to function most effectively as an advisory mechanism to the President.

First, of the Cabinet officers participating in the National Security Council, the Secretary of State must inescapably be "first among equals" in foreign-policy considerations. It is right and proper that the viewpoints of the Department of Defense and other departments and agencies concerned with the national security should be known through the NSC to the President. Yet the Secretary of State, as the President's principal adviser on foreign policy, must bear the main burden of helping the President to define our political objectives in the world and initiating and developing policies for achieving them.

Second, the military also has an important role to play in the National Security Council. Its responsibility is to make plain the military implications of a desired policy, and to be prepared at all times to carry out commitments arising from political decisions. But it is not the responsibility of the military to determine foreign policy.

Third, the National Security Council, in my opinion, works best when it concentrates on a limited number of primary issues affecting national security. It is necessary at all times to guard against the tendency to burden the Council with lesser problems not properly in its province—operating matters that should be solved through interdepartmental coordinating committees rather than through the NSC.

Fourth, it is necessary to limit the attendance at NSC meetings to those directly and immediately concerned with the problem at hand. I found that when, through laxness, the number of participants was increased—say beyond nine or ten—the benefits to the President were reduced proportionately. Cabinet members, in my experience, were reluctant to express their views frankly and to engage in meaningful debate in the presence of a large audience. The National Security Council was not intended to be, and must not become, a "town meeting."

Fifth, in the NSC it is important to measure the cost of national security policies in terms of necessary manpower, resources, and money, but budgetary considerations should not themselves be the determinants of policy.

Sixth, a strong Policy Planning Staff in the State Department is one prerequisite of an effectively functioning National Security Council. I say this because of my conviction, expressed earlier, that the main burden of initiating imaginative policies in the national security field must fall upon the Department of State. I would add here that the problem of achieving coordinated positions within the departments themselves rivals in difficulty the problem of achieving coordination in the National Security Council.

Seventh, staff assistance cannot be expected to substitute for vigorous personal participation in National Security Council problems by Cabinet members themselves. These officers are charged with the responsibility of advising the President with respect to foreign and military policy. Although these officers are beset by many problems, nothing should prevent them from assuming the primary responsibility of advising the President in their respective fields.

Some of these statements are almost truisms, but they do play a very important part in making the mechanism effective.

The NSC at Work

SENATOR JACKSON. What is your attitude toward the participation by the Bureau of the Budget, or by representatives of the Bureau of the Budget, in the NSC?

ADMIRAL SOUERS. I took a strong position in recommending to

the President that they be represented at the Senior Staff level. I think it is now known as the Planning Board. That was so that budgetary considerations should be considered at that level, but not regularly in the Council itself, except on a case-by-case basis when primarily budgetary or management matters are considered. Budget officials are really not policy-makers. In my opinion, they should not be. They are a staff arm of the President, and the President should determine what national policy, domestic or foreign, should be, and the budget should conform.

SENATOR JACKSON. In other words, your idea is that the President and the NSC should measure the requirements, determine what they are, and then ascertain the resources needed to fulfill these requirements. The Bureau of the Budget comes into the act after a decision has been made as to what really should be done in the area of national security.

ADMIRAL SOUERS. That is correct.

SENATOR JACKSON. I was interested in your reference to the British Imperial Defense Council established in Britain in 1908. Did you find that their experience was helpful in connection with the setting up of the NSC?

ADMIRAL SOUERS. Yes, we did. In 1945, while I was on active duty, I was designated by Mr. Forrestal, Secretary of the Navy, as a member of the Eberstadt Committee for the purpose of covering the intelligence chapter.* We were studying the Imperial Defense Council mechanism at that time. It served a very admirable purpose in England; even though it had many rough times and some British administrations fought it, it was able to survive the Liberals and Conservatives as they came and went. One man, the Executive Secretary, Lord Hankey, started in as a major in the Marines. He stayed there from 1908 until the end of World War II. So he provided the continuity. He was very careful to try to get coordinated advice for the Prime Minister and tried never to take a strong position of his own. In other words, he might tell the Prime Minister, "I can't get this Cabinet Minister to perform," and suggest that he get after him.

He was succeeded after World War II by Lord Ismay. We had quite a visit with him. We explained our mechanism. He thought we had improved on their set-up. They used nothing but *ad hoc*

---

* In 1945, a committee headed by Ferdinand Eberstadt submitted to Secretary Forrestal a report on the unification of the armed services and postwar organization of national security operations. For excerpts from the report, see pp. 291-94.

committees, and we had the stability of a senior staff operating as a permanent working committee. But we set up *ad hoc* committees in certain situations in which technical matters were involved. If we had a subcommittee, we would call upon the head of the two or three departments involved to furnish technical staff to sit with us, to prepare a draft that would coordinate their viewpoints so it could be submitted to the Council for consideration and the President for decision.

They thought that our use of both a permanent working committee and *ad hoc* committees as well as our permanent staff would achieve better results.

SENATOR JACKSON. Do you believe that the NSC papers should normally be prepared by the Department of State?

ADMIRAL SOUERS. The way we functioned before will indicate how I thought it should be done. If the Secretary of Defense wanted guidance on what our policy was in a certain foreign situation, so that he would know how to plan in the Defense Department, he would write a letter to the Secretary of the Council, who would send a copy to the Secretary of State and request him to come up with a draft paper for consideration by the senior staff.

By and large, I found that it was necessary or certainly most desirable to have the State Department initiate the draft, outlining some policy they wished to adopt. They should take the lead. When they would do that, then we would go into the senior staff to get the military implications and, if you please, even the resources implications. We found that we had a far better paper if only one department prepared the first draft than if all three tried to draft it together.

State would get good results by having the head of their planning staff consult one or more from the Defense Department just to help guide him as he was drawing up the paper. It would not be Department of Defense policy, actually, but it would provide the viewpoint of a military man.

SENATOR JACKSON. This is all prior to taking a departmental position?

ADMIRAL SOUERS. All prior to that. They had the right to consultation. So when their paper came over it was not impractical from a military standpoint. Exceptions might be taken to the paper by the Defense Department or by the Army or Navy or Air Force. But at least it would get in what I thought was the important thing— the policy desired by the Secretary of State. Before it was recommended to the President of the United States for action, it had been coordinated to obtain the military and other implications. If they were all agreed, it was simple.

SENATOR JACKSON. I take it in general you rather agree with Mr. Lovett's philosophy, namely, that the Council should be small, that the issues before it should be the critical or key issues, as distinguished from collateral or relatively unimportant issues, and that there should be sharp alternatives presented with debate.

ADMIRAL SOUERS. That is right.

SENATOR JACKSON. I take it that you feel that in the operation of the NSC, in this broad national security area, the Secretary of State should be more or less the orchestra leader in considering the formulation of policy for the President's consideration?

ADMIRAL SOUERS. He must be. After all, the Secretary of State is usually selected by a President because of his past record or experience in foreign-policy matters. The Secretary of Defense is usually a good executive who knows how to run a big business, and it is a different type of selection.

SENATOR JAVITS. There are two things that disturb me. To what extent should we call into the National Security Council not only the technicians but the best brains in the country? When do you call in the best brains in the land—whether it is for a matter of public relations with David Sarnoff, who doesn't work for the government, or somebody else—and when do you not? Has that at any time ever really come up as a problem?

ADMIRAL SOUERS. There have been many discussions of whether we should bring in outside experts, well-informed people of stature, who are not in the government, to give advice, to freshen up the advice that is coming in. There was some talk about having Cabinet members without portfolio to do that because the Secretaries were too occupied with their departments.

I found that the State Department was able to supply some of that by bringing in outside talents, highly qualified people, to assist the Policy Planning Staff in drawing up a desired policy statement.

There were times when we used to bring in the President's advisers on domestic matters, if something would have a repercussion domestically, because I did not profess to be cognizant in that field. But I opposed having advisers to the President apart from the Council, because that could easily cause a conflict between the President's outside adviser and his Secretary of State, if the advice was contrary and he decided with the adviser. But the advisers can be brought into the Council. The staff or planning board is only their work team, as I see it. But even though the outside adviser came directly into the Council itself, there was no reason why they could not also discuss matters at the Planning Board level.

I would make that distinct difference, that they should not stand between the Cabinet members and the President, but they should be advisers to the Council. If the Council members want to use the staff or planning board to help whip the papers into shape or coordinate at that level, I see no objection to that.

SENATOR JAVITS. One other question: Do you think that the National Security Council ought to have any independence as an entity so that, for example, they could, as a council, make some statement or report to the Congress or to the people? Or do you feel that it is strictly a staff agency of the President?

ADMIRAL SOUERS. The way it is set up by statute it is purely advisory to the President. He should make any statements called for to the Congress or the public.

SENATOR MUSKIE. Does the National Security Council in your experience deal strictly with broad goals? Does it deal with strategy or get down to tactics?

ADMIRAL SOUERS. In my opinion, it should confine itself to broad, strategic national planning at the national level. State is expected to be doing its operational planning to carry out the broad program. The Defense Department has planners that adapt its plans to the over-all strategy. But the basic work of the Council should be confined to the broad, national strategic planning.

SENATOR MUSKIE. So it is not an operational agency in any sense of the word?

ADMIRAL SOUERS. It shouldn't be. There should be interdepartmental committees to do the coordinating on operational matters within the framework of the over-all policy.

SENATOR JACKSON. You would say, would you not, that part of the NSC function would be to contemplate what might happen in critical situations, what the remedy might be, and what our position would be—in those situations that have tremendous international impact?

ADMIRAL SOUERS. That is correct.

SENATOR MUSKIE. Would you say that the Secretary of State might very well influence the President to accept a decision as to military priorities that was contrary to the decision of the Defense Department in that same area?

ADMIRAL SOUERS. I should think it would have some effect. It is hard to know what finally influences the President. He could easily be influenced by his Treasury Secretary, if he had great respect for him, after weighing the monetary implications of a course of action. I am sure it would have some effect on him.

SENATOR MUSKIE. In your list of seven principles that ought to apply to the National Security Council, you say that the Secretary of State must inescapably be first among equals.

ADMIRAL SOUERS. In proposing foreign policy.

SENATOR MUSKIE. Not with respect to military policy?

ADMIRAL SOUERS. No. I think he is not expert in that. I would hate to think that the Secretary of State, as the primary adviser, determines military policy. It seems to me that State should be prepared to recommend to the President the policy it thinks is capable of achieving the greatest results in the cold war. The military will show the implications of that course, if adopted, and what it will take to back it up. They will finally say what force it will take, and then it will be a question of pricing it. It will be a question of deciding which weapons will give us the greatest benefit for the least money, I suppose.

Then after all that is brought to play, the President would say, after full consideration of all these discussions, "This is the policy we should adopt." Then the military would proceed with their planning to carry out this basic national policy. It then becomes the President's national policy. By that time it has probably been through the Senate Foreign Relations Committee and so forth. Then it becomes our policy, and the military and the other people carry out their responsibilities in implementing it. It seems to me that that is about as precise as I can be in stating it.

SENATOR MUSKIE. What influence does the National Security Council have on foreign policy? We will put it the other way around.

ADMIRAL SOUERS. The Council itself is purely the mechanism by which all facets of a national security policy are delved into and presented to the President, who makes the decision. But the Secretary of State is still the foreign-policy adviser to the President, and his Department implements it. The military and others are only brought in to be sure the President, who is responsible under our Constitution for making that decision, has all the facts. We tried to give all the facts and viewpoints to him as best we could—not only at the Secretary's level but from further down in the departments, where career officers might be more cognizant. Sometimes it was difficult. The Council is purely an instrument to help the President make these tremendous decisions with a systematic method or organization that will give him all the facts in a consistent manner and to hear any debate if there are differences.

SENATOR MUSKIE. It is more a coordinating agency, then, than a planning agency?

ADMIRAL SOUERS. Well, actually, I look on it more as a coordinating agency to assist the President in weighing all the factors that go into a foreign-policy decision.

This is a very difficult subject, because of the many ideas of how our government runs. In the early days, we had some members of the government who felt that as Executive Secretary of the NSC, I should be the Director, that I should say what the policy should be. But that would be a different form of government. The Congress did not contemplate that, I am sure. They would have called the official a Director instead of an Executive Secretary.

We tried to limit the staff to knowledgeable people. I think it is serving a purpose.

SENATOR MUSKIE. I do not know to what extent I am representative of public reaction to the National Security Council, but it would have been my impression that planning for national security would have a greater part in the Council's function than it apparently does.

ADMIRAL SOUERS. Well, it does have a part. They debate the papers.

The desirable way is to have a deputy to each Cabinet member on the Planning Board, who has enough time to engage in the thinking, exchange of views, and deliberation that is needed for planning. We came near to accomplishing that by having representatives on the senior staff who at all times had access to and the confidence of the members of the Council.

In other words, each Council member would have a representative to assist him to develop policy on the senior staff. Whenever we had that arrangement, where the man really had the confidence of his Secretary, these men debating among themselves could accomplish a great deal without ever surrendering the sovereignty of a department. They developed a broader viewpoint sitting together. Yet they would go back and tie in with their departments.

Wherever we could have the Secretary himself following the planning, with his staff representative, plus his planning staff, we had pretty good results. It would be only if they downgraded the senior staff, and then the member was not really representing his Secretary at all, that we had difficulty.

SENATOR MUNDT. In your experience, did the President preside at NSC meetings or did he get his information through some deputy or assistant or Secretary—perhaps you, who would preside and then relay it to him?

ADMIRAL SOUERS. In the early days, we thought perhaps we would have freer discussion between the Cabinet members if the President did not preside. In other words, we wanted to be sure that the debate would not be cut off by the President saying "I want to do so and so." In that case, the Secretary of State presided by designation from the President. Primarily, we met in the Cabinet Room of the White House, and I would submit the paper, if we agreed or modified it, to the President the next morning. But in all those cases, the President completely controlled the agenda and the individuals who could attend. We kept fighting, always, to hold the number of members down, which is very difficult. Everybody wants to attend.

Starting in 1950, the President presided at practically all the meetings, but he was careful not to state his position. He called on everyone for their individual views.

Before each meeting, when the senior staff had completed a paper, I would send it out to the members of the Council, stating that the senior staff had prepared "NSC so and so, to be considered at the meeting on such-and-such a date." At that time, the very next morning, I would submit a copy to the President, and we would discuss it. I would give him, as best I could, the benefit of the views of the military, the views of State, and their reasons for their views, so that he would have a little background on the paper. He was then just as familiar with it as the other members.

But prior to 1950, we had tried to experiment this other way. We had thought we could have a freer discussion without the President, perhaps, and would submit the paper afterwards. But he was almost ready to pass on the paper by the time it was submitted to him for signature. Even when he sat as chairman, we urged him never to approve a paper until the next day, so that, if anything else arose and he wanted to make comments or modify it in any way, he could.

SENATOR MUNDT. At the Council meetings, did you vote or have a show of hands? How did you arrive at the substance of opinion?

ADMIRAL SOUERS. No, we did not vote. The President simply heard the viewpoints of each. We would have some pretty heated discussions. I always felt it was most productive when we did.

SENATOR MUNDT. In other words, it was the President's decision. He never asked, "How many of you fellows feel this way?"

ADMIRAL SOUERS. The decision was never made by vote. He wanted to know all the facts in the case. My sole job, I felt, was to be sure he got the best that we could get out of the brains he had in his government. If he appointed Secretaries and Assistant Secretaries and they had planning staffs, all I could do was to try to see that he received the best that was in them. It was not my view. I didn't try to prevail.

SENATOR MUNDT. Since this is really the President's decision and he seeks this information, it would seem to me that each President would tailor the NSC to fit his own needs, his mode of operations. Some President may feel he is informed on foreign policy and weak on national defense. Perhaps Mr. Eisenhower feels he is pretty good on national defense—he has spent his life on it—but he might be pretty weak in some other aspect. I suspect they rather tailor the process to be sure that they are shored up in those areas where they may feel a little less certain.

ADMIRAL SOUERS. I expect that is right. It will be used in different ways by different Presidents over the years.

SENATOR MUNDT. Then it probably should be kept as it is in the 1947 statute rather than legislated into any fixed form.

ADMIRAL SOUERS. I think it is well to have a statutory provision for an agency like the NSC, because it should not get lost as you shift and change administrations. But I think the statutory members should be limited to the number you now have. The President can take advice from anybody he pleases, so you cannot stop him from putting others on the Council or asking them to attend. If you told him they could not attend, he could call them in on the side and take their advice instead of the Council's.

SENATOR MUNDT. Were records of minutes kept at that time, or was it informal?

ADMIRAL SOUERS. No, we did not have a stenographer present, because we didn't want a man to feel inhibited in giving his frank viewpoint for fear someone would say, "That fellow was for something unpatriotic," or something else, in the light of later events. We had some of that in the past, when one Cabinet member did keep minutes of Cabinet meetings and he would say how the various members stood on certain subjects. We tried to get away from it. There have never been any minutes of the discussions sent around to anybody, only a record of actions taken.

SENATOR MUNDT. In your experience, were the recommendations usually nearly unanimous? In other words, would they hammer out the idea with concessions to one point of view and another, until there was a pretty general agreement by art of compromise, or would the President ultimately have to decide between two determined points of view, where one Cabinet member took one position and another took a different position—and fairly unyieldingly?

ADMIRAL SOUERS. We did not try to force a compromise. We wanted to be sure, if there were dissents, that they were clearly stated, so that the President would understand the different viewpoints and could reach a sound decision himself. There were several occasions, when we wanted to get ideas across to the President, when we would enumerate different possible courses of action, show where each might lead, and then have a general discussion of the advantages and disadvantages of each.

The National Security Council under President Eisenhower[*]

ROBERT CUTLER

Robert Cutler served as Special Assistant to President Eisenhower for National Security Affairs in 1953-55 and 1957-58. In that capacity, he also was Chairman of the National Security Council's Planning Board and a member of the Operations Coordinating Board. He was U. S. Executive Director on the Board of Executive Directors of the Inter-American Development Bank, 1960-62, and Special Assistant to the Secretary of the Treasury, 1960-62. To these government posts he brought experience in law, banking, and the service of his country in two World Wars. He has been awarded the Distinguished Service Medal, Legion of Merit, and Medal of Freedom.

I voluntarily accepted Senator Jackson's invitation to appear before this Subcommittee, solely in connection with its study directed to matters involving the purposes, composition, organization, and procedures of the National Security Council and its subordinate machinery. My qualifications in this area derive from my service as Special Assistant to the President for National Security Affairs for almost four years—January, 1953, to April, 1955, and January, 1957, to July, 1958. During this period, I was Chairman of the National Security Council Planning Board and a member of the National Security Council Operations Coordinating Board, sat with the Council on Foreign Economic Policy, and served on or dealt with other elements concerned with national security affairs.

[*] Testimony delivered to the Subcommittee on National Policy Machinery in executive session, May 24, 1960.

During my three-year and ten-month tenure as Special Assistant, I presided over 504 meetings of the National Security Council Planning Board and assisted in the conduct of 179 meetings of the National Security Council—48 per cent of all Council meetings held in its 10¾-year existence until that time. The President presided at all but six of these Council meetings.

In this period of service, there was developed a procedural method and a rhythm of Council operation that met with the President's approval; it has been generally continued, I understand, to the present time. The council normally meets about forty-four times a year for two to two and one-half hours, the Cabinet meeting somewhat less frequently. The National Security Council Planning Board normally meets twice a week for three hours or more a meeting, and the National Security Council Operations Coordinating Board meets every week for about three hours.

With the Subcommittee's permission, I should like, first, briefly to describe the operation of the National Security Council machinery, with which I was so familiar; second, to list and comment orally upon what I consider the guiding points of such operation; third, to answer questions.

The Operation of the NSC

First, a brief description of the operation of the National Security Council mechanism. In order to avoid misapprehension of any generalized description, it is necessary to have in mind these criteria:

1. The Council's statutory function is to advise the President on national security policy. It does not serve as a planning or operational mechanism.

2. The Council's statutory function is to integrate all germane views in making national security policy recommendations to the President.

3. The Council also has a statutory duty, subject to the President's direction, to assess and appraise the objectives, risks, and commitments of the United States in relation to our actual and potential military power, in the interest of national security, for the purpose of making recommendations to the President.

4. Thus, the National Security Council mechanism is for the personal use of the President in resolving his will on issues of national security policy. But it is not an exclusive procedure that the President is required to use. In fact, the President may—and does

—use from time to time other procedures and mechanisms for particular national security matters.

5. The Council mechanism's relation to the President is advisory only. It recommends; the President decides.

I thought it advisable to point out that during the early years of President Eisenhower's first term, the Council was concerned with (1) reviewing and recommending revisions of the existing written national security policies of the preceding administration, over fifty in number; (2) preparing recommendations for new national security policies to deal with both gradually changing circumstances and emergency situations. As a result, some seventy policy statements were revised or originated during the first two and one-fourth years I served.

In President Eisenhower's second term, it was possible, in conformity with the President's wishes, to adjust somewhat the Council's primary focus from the necessary considerations and approval of written policy statements more toward oral discussions of national security policy issues. Thus, the annual review in 1957 of over-all national security policy—which usually consumes several months' intensive work each year—was initiated by a series of six Council meetings, at each of which significant issues were discussed on the basis of brief discussion papers, including alternatives, prepared by the NSC Planning Board. Similarly, the 1958 over-all policy review was initiated by similar discussion papers based on the latest national intelligence estimate of the world situation.

Now, may I describe how the National Security Council mechanism would go about preparing a national security policy relative to the mythical state of Ruritania. The procedure would be similar for a wider geographical area, an aspect of the national economy or national defense, or a functional activity of the U. S. Government involving national security, etc.

1. The Ruritania item will be scheduled weeks or perhaps months ahead on the National Security Council Planning Board tentative agenda, in order to give advance notice and enable preparation of material. For this item, the Planning Board will be composed of officials, having the rank of Assistant Secretary or its equivalent, of the departments and agencies that will be represented at the council table when Ruritania is taken up by the National Security Council.

2. At its first of three, four, five or more sessions on this subject, the Planning Board will have before it a national intelligence estimate on Ruritania. It will also have before it a factual and analyti-

cal statement prepared by the responsible department or departments—or sometimes by an interdepartmental committee—on military, economic, political, and other germane factors relative to Ruritania.

Sometimes, this factual data and analyses based thereon are supplied in separate memoranda, sometimes as a consolidated staff study. In the preparation of this factual and analytical material on Ruritania are involved the vast resources of the informed departments and agencies of government, the brains and experience of the operation personnel who work day after day in the particular area of Ruritania and who have learned the hard way the strengths and limitations involved, the very persons who staff the departments and agencies that will be called upon to implement the policy on which they are working when and if such policy receives Presidential approval.

On occasion, though less often on a "country policy," an outside-of-government consultant group may be convened and its views added to the material under study by the Planning Board.

3. The intelligence estimate and the factual and analytical material are explained, discussed, and chewed over by the Planning Board in one or, more often, several meetings. Frequently, a senior representative of a responsible department, a division or bureau chief, or an Assistant Secretary, is asked to attend at the Planning Board table. He will be questioned and cross-questioned about factual subject matter and tentative policy recommendations at one or more meetings. The Board seeks to squeeze out of the material all the juice that it contains.

4. After these proceedings, a draft policy statement is prepared by the responsible department or by an interdepartmental or special committee. This draft will consist of (a) "general considerations" drawn from the intelligence estimate and the factual and analytical material upon which the policy recommendations will be based; (b) proposed "general objectives" of U.S. policy toward Ruritania; (c) detailed proposed "policy guidance" in the different areas of United States–Ruritania relations; and (d) appendixes, covering anticipated financial costs of the proposed policy, and military and economic expenditures and factual data for past and future years. Depending on the size and complexity of the subject, all this material may aggregate from ten to fifty pages, or even more, the annexes being single-spaced.

5. At as many Planning Board meetings as are required, this draft statement is discussed, torn apart, and revised. In the inter-

vals between such meetings, a revised text based on these revisions and on further information is drafted by the Planning Board assistants—the assistants to the Planning Board members—and circulated for consideration at the following Planning Board meeting. In these intervals, the Planning Board members are able to confer with their principals as to the department's or agency's position on developing issues. I used to call this procedure, when I was chairman of 504 meetings in less than four years, an "acid bath."

6. Finally, through this arduous process, there results either agreement on clarity and accuracy of text, correctness of facts, and validity of policy recommendations or, as is often the case, sharp differences of opinion on certain major recommendations or statements. In the latter case, the draft policy paper sets forth clearly and succinctly these opposing views, often in parallel columns.

7. When the draft policy has been thus shaped, reshaped, corrected, revised, and finally stated, it is circulated to the Council members at least ten days before the meeting at which the policy on Ruritania is to be taken up. Thus, sufficient time is provided for the Council members to be briefed on the paper and to familiarize themselves with its contents and for the Joint Chiefs of Staff to express their formal military views on the exact text the Council is to consider, which views are also circulated in writing to Council members before the meeting.

The Joint Chiefs, I might point out, have a representative who sits with the Planning Board, as does the Director of the Central Intelligence Agency. But the Chiefs, you know, are like the College of Cardinals. They are a different body than anything else in the world, and cannot formally give an opinion on a paper until the paper is in final, formal form and has been circulated to the members. We know often very clearly, or we can estimate how the Chiefs will react from their adviser who sits with us, but actually we do not get it in writing until they see the paper that has been sent to the Council members. Thus, the Council has before it in writing the proposed policy or recommendations of the NSC Planning Board and also the written view of the Chiefs on those recommendations.

8. In this standard operating procedure, the views of all having a legitimate interest in the subject are heard, digested, and integrated or, in the case of disagreement, separately stated. In a good number of cases, as I have said, the views of experts or knowledgeable people from outside the government are sought and worked into the fabric at the Planning Board level.

The intelligence estimates, military views, political views, economic views, fiscal views, the psychological impact—all are canvassed and integrated before the President is asked to hear the case argued at the Council table and to come to his decision.

9. At the Council meeting, the Director of Central Intelligence, in his oral intelligence briefing which begins every Council meeting, covers the latest intelligence on Ruritania.

I might add, Mr. Chairman, that this opening of Council meetings with an oral intelligence briefing began in January, 1953. Theretofore, intelligence had been circulated only in writing, and the Director had talked only with the President. It occurred to some of us that it would be a wise move to have every Council meeting opened with fifteen or twenty or twenty-five minutes, and sometimes more, of the latest intelligence from all over the world.

As I pointed out, since Ruritania is to be on our agenda, of course the latest intelligence on Ruritania is included in the Director's weekly briefing.

10. The Council may have three or four, usually not more, items on the agenda. When the agenda item on Ruritania is reached, the Special Assistant explains the reasons for submitting the paper, summarizes the high points in the general considerations, the objectives, the policy guidance, and the annexes. He asks the departments and agencies concerned to express their views on the integrated recommendations.

This is one of the most difficult tasks that we have. You must know your subject better than anyone else, in which you have been helped by getting the paper in shape. You must be able quickly and accurately to turn to the high points and thus give a rounded picture to refresh the Council's mind before it begins its argument.

No matter how qualified people may be, I think that they find it difficult to start off a hard argument unless they have a little intellectual stimulus at the beginning.

11. With respect to the integrated recommendations in the paper, there may be five or six departments which will have responsibilities under the paper; and each of them is asked to make a statement of what he thinks about it. In the event of conflicts of opinion, the proponents are called upon to state their views and are given opportunity to reply. The Joint Chiefs are requested to state their views. Sometimes, these arguments must be carried over to a second or more meetings, especially if there are perhaps five or ten differences of opinion in one paper. It would be unusual to have so many differences in a "country" paper, but in the annual review of

over-all policy it is customary that there will be that many differences, or more, of importance, to be settled.

In my experience, divergencies of views appeared in more than two-thirds of the papers before the NSC. I would like to emphasize this point, for one reads statements made by people who have no real basis of knowledge that conflicts are swept under the rug and there are no differences of opinion. Well, I have helped to run more Council meetings than anyone else, and in the 179 that were under my charge, I would say that more than two-thirds of the papers had differences of opinions in them that were heard and discussed and had to be settled either by the Council coming to agreement after the discussion or, if they didn't agree, then by the President after the discussion.

12. The President is an active participant in the Council discussions. Sometimes, issues that are in conflict are decided by him in the course of the discussion. He has to be very careful not to intervene too early. If you are an affirmative person and you intervene early in the discussion, and you have intelligent Council members, they inevitably tend to feel a wind blowing from one direction or the other. That isn't what the President wants, but sometimes he gets so interested in these discussions that he can't help but jump into the discussion.

Some of these discussions last a very long time. I remember one discussion between the Secretary of State and the Chairman of the Joint Chiefs on a very interesting and difficult subject where they had radically different points of view. Here was a discussion which went on for over an hour between two men of very superior mental ability and very strong beliefs. They spoke with great deference, but with great clarity. This instance was a really fascinating example of the kind of thing that can be done in the Council when it is at its best.

13. Sometimes, the President will decide right in the course of the meeting on one of these doubtful or disputed issues. Sometimes, the President may make his decision a few days later when the draft formal record of action of the meeting is submitted to him for checking, modification, and approval. The record of action, three or four pages long, is a very formal document. It is drafted initially by the Executive Secretary of the Council, working with the Special Assistant, and is circulated in advance of submission to the President to those Council members who were in attendance at the meeting for their comment. It seemed to me only fair to let the Council members have a chance to see what the record was going

to look like, before the staff submitted it to the President in draft form, because they had participated in the meeting it purported to reflect. This helpful innovation gave them a chance to express views again if they wished. Presidential approval of the record of action then determines the national security policy for Ruritania.

14. As the last act, the Executive Secretary's letter, transmitting the Ruritania policy, so approved, goes to the responsible departments and agencies. In the usual case, this letter will advise that the Operations Coordinating Board has been designated by the President to assist the responsible departments and agencies in coordinating their planning to carry out their responsibilities under the policy statement.

So here is a synthesized photograph of how we would proceed to create a policy paper about a particular issue. Like all photographs that are made up this way, no particular case will be like this hypothetical one. And yet it partakes of what exists in all of the cases, really.

Eighteen Guiding Points in NSC Operations

I have selected eighteen points which out of my experience seemed to me to be the most significant. I call them guiding points in the operation of the National Security Council mechanism, as a policy-maker.

1. The NSC mechanism is a personal mechanism for the President to use as one way of making up his mind on issues of national security policy. The mechanism and its operation must be satisfactory to a particular President. The admirable flexibility of the National Security Act permits different Presidents to use the mechanism in different ways.

There are several very significant things that might be said about the concept I have just expressed. When I was fearful that some recommendations might be made that I thought would not be in the best interests of this mechanism, to which I have devoted so much of my strength, I had constantly in mind that the Council is only one way a President makes up his mind. He may make it up in any way that he determines, and Presidents do. He may make up his mind at the Cabinet, and he may make up his mind with some other people, and he may make up his mind when he is alone. He is not compelled to make up his mind in any particular way. I am sure you realize that no law can compel the executive branch to come to a policy decision in a particular way any more than the executive branch could compel the Congress to come to a legislative decision in a certain way.

You have to have a mechanism provided to each President which he finds useful and attractive. That is why I used the word "admirable" in referring to the scope of the National Security Act. I think the National Security Act is a remarkable piece of legislation because it is so sufficiently flexible that two Presidents who are quite different in their makeup have used it in different ways, yet each has found it an instrument responsive to his needs. A third President might use it in still another way. The danger is that the great flexibility of the present statute, which commends it so to Presidents, will in some way, as I once said to Mr. Mansfield, get "embedded in legislative concrete." I am afraid of that.

If the Congress adds people to the Council, a President might say, "I don't want to deal with those people in policy matters." If the Congress excludes certain people from the Council, a President might say, "I want to have these people come. If I can't have my advisers around me, then I will form my own committee and I will use that." In such a case, the Council would become a fifth wheel. This would be a great loss to the United States, in my opinion.

The Council is the President's mechanism. If he likes it, he will use it to the best advantage to himself and as best it can be used. President Eisenhower has put the Council to extraordinary use— about forty-four meetings a year. The first two years I was Special Assistant, we were under great pressure of work. Then, we held fifty-two meetings in each of the first two years, an average of one a week. President Eisenhower likes this Council process, as now developed; he likes the method of presentation; he likes the vigorous arguments in front of him. That is why he finds the mechanism suited to him and uses it so much. Another President might prefer to proceed in another way. From what General Marshall told me, I think Mr. Truman used the Council machinery in a somewhat different way. But that isn't the point I want to make. My point is that it is a good mechanism and has excellent aspects. *Non constat* that everything can be improved.

To give a President a tool he can use and mold to his own use is the reason why the National Security Act seems to me a major triumph of our national legislature.

2. The NSC operates exclusively in the national security field, which is only one part of the President's responsibilities. The Cabinet, which meets about thirty-three to thirty-four times a year, has

vast responsibilities for the President, too. Here we have represented the Post Office; Agriculture; the Attorney General; Civil Service; Interior; Commerce; Health, Education, and Welfare; and Labor. These Departments are great elements in our country's strength: although I am enthusiastic about the sphere and scope of the National Security Council, I must always remember that there are enormous areas of government that are not represented at the Council table.

Somebody said to me a few nights ago, when they heard I was coming to testify: "Why don't you suggest that the Cabinet and the Council be combined?" I replied that I thought this would be a most retrogressive step. The Council was created to carve out of the total government sphere certain areas that should be dealt with by certain of the President's top advisers, leaving in the Cabinet areas that had to be dealt with by all of his top advisers. To put together what had been wisely separated would be a retrogressive step. I feel sure that it would be so deemed in the judgment of you gentlemen, too.

3. The NSC focuses on policy and not on planning or operations.

4. The NSC is advisory only, making recommendations to the President for his decision. This point is very much misunderstood, I suppose because so little is known about the workings of the Council.

I remember reading in a newspaper when we first came down here that the Council was a secret cabal sitting in a back room, that no one knew what they were deciding, and that such a top-secret Star Chamber process was a danger to the liberties of the people. But we must remember that the Council doesn't decide anything, really; except that it decides to recommend certain things to the President. That is my knowledge based on 179 meetings of the Council.

5. The NSC is an established forum for the coordination and integration of the recommendations for national security policy that are made by the principal national security policy advisers of the President.

The idea of integration, if we look at the different walks of life with which we are familiar, is now so well accepted that everybody wonders why one should place emphasis on it. But integration in government, just like integration in the teaching of medicine, is a relatively new concept. In the old days, medical schools used to teach different medical disciplines in separate courses. You learned anatomy in one course, you learned physiology in another course, and so on. But these courses were not married together. In the best of modern medical teaching, the disciplines are integrated more and more.

I understand that integration was so little appreciated by Hitler that in 1940, when he was planning to invade England—a colossal undertaking that had never succeeded since the Romans—he saw his chief admiral, his chief of air, Marshal Goering, and his chief army commander together at an integrated meeting only once in the whole summer. The top leaders were kept separate and did their work separately. Perhaps that is one reason why the planned invasion was abortive. Yet it was as late as 1940 that the largest victorious armed force in the world up to that time had not seized on the concept of integration. The United States found integration necessary when we went into World War II. The Army Service Forces were created to integrate all of the small independent agencies within the Army structure under one over-all chief who could control and direct.

So I bear down on the acceptance of integration and the usefulness that this concept has brought into our government in many ways.

6. The NSC provides an excellent forum for vigorous discussion, with the President participating, at which all interested parties are heard by the President as chairman and by the other members.

May I emphasize this next sentence, because this is what I have found in the Council as it operates at its best? These recurring discussions which come up almost every week, these discussions at frequent intervals, tend to do two things: first, they tend to orient the members toward action as a corporate body rather than as agency protagonists; and, second, they lessen any chance or need for *ex parte* Presidential decisions. I am not saying that you don't still have agency protagonists at the Council table. Of course you do. Department heads are hired to be protagonists for their heavy responsibilities. But, by virtue of these department and agency heads sitting together over a great number of meetings, getting to know each other, getting to know that the President wishes them to advise him as a corporate body and to use their heads the way he has had to use his—the regular, frequent recurrence of this process over a period of time gets the Council members thinking more as a corporate body, more like a good board of directors, than as merely representatives and protagonists of departments and agencies.

My second point is also of tremendous consequence. Nothing is so dangerous to any form of government or of any private enterprise as the *ex parte* decision based on the advice of only one of several sides, privately spoken to the head man.

There are pressures brought on every President to do this or to do that. But a President is always at liberty when he has these recurrent Council meetings every week, to say, "Tell the Special Assistant to put the issue on the Council agenda; then everybody can have a crack at it." In this way, the issue is explored in the light of day, and everybody hears what everybody else has to say about it. This is a great virtue.

7. The formal record of actions of all NSC meetings, together with the approved policy statements, provide a valuable continuity of written policy decisions. I think Mr. Lovett in his testimony referred to this, the value of having a continuous written record of the policy decisions. Until a few years ago, the Cabinet had no regular written record of its decisions. They remained in the memories of the people who were present at the meetings. Since 1954, this has been changed. President Eisenhower initiated the circulation of papers and agenda in advance of Cabinet meetings, with time for them to be read and studied by those to be present so that they would know what they were to talk about, and the formal written record of action taken at the Cabinet to show what had been decided. This may have removed some of the informal charm of the old Cabinet meetings, but it made the Cabinet, I think, a more responsive organization to the President's wishes.

8. The Council should not be so large as to render it infeasible for vigorous, top-secret discussion of cleavages of opinion. Nor should the Council be so small as to miss the views of those who should be heard on the issue to be discussed. There are normally about eleven at the Council table, apart from the Special Assistant, the Executive Secretary, and his deputy—not too large a number, a total of eleven normally participating at the table: the President, the Vice President; the Secretaries of State, Defense, and Treasury; the Directors of the Office of Civil Defense Mobilization and the Budget Bureau; about half of the time the Chairman of the Atomic Energy Commission; the two advisers, the Chairman of the Joint Chiefs and the Director of CIA; and the Director of USIA.

Around the sides of the Council room, away from the table, there are a few Presidential special assistants. These are in irregular attendance. Almost always there is the Special Assistant for Science and Technology, Dr. Kistiakowsky, the Special Assistant for Operations Coordination, Mr. Harr, and the person who now administers mutual security, I think it is the Under Secretary of State. Sometimes Mr. Randall, the Chairman of the Committee on Foreign Economic Policy, is present. There may also be the Assistant to the President and the staff secretary. None of these six or seven persons participates. They attend because the President thinks it is a valuable thing for them to be present.

On rare occasions, as where an important study or report by "inside" or "outside" consultants or committees is to be made, it is convenient to hold a much larger meeting to hear the exposition, but not for discussion.

I do want to say a word about this, because this is a most important feature of the Council, and I know it has been referred to by some of the people who have testified. There is an indefinable line in what changes a profitable meeting into an unprofitable one. The unprofitable meeting is the one that Queen Victoria characterized when she said she didn't like Mr. Gladstone because he talked to her as if he were talking to a town meeting. The profitable meeting is one that has what my law professor, Edward Warren, used to call the pow-wow element. Somewhere between these two extremes, you lose out. It must be small enough to have the pow-wow element. It must not get so big that it turns into a town meeting.

You can divide Council meetings into three kinds. There is the big meeting where you have a Gaither Committee report, a technical-capabilities panel report, or some report on some new thing that is being developed in the Pentagon. Such a meeting is wholly expository in nature. Here you may run up to forty people. This is a Council meeting, but it isn't for the purpose of discussion. It is for the purpose of convenient exposition and information. I have found it much easier to handle this kind of work in one large meeting rather than try to get these top-secret people together at two or three meetings.

The second type of Council meeting is the usual type of which I have been talking, the normal type where there will be eleven or twelve participants at the Council table who are free to talk. The staff people are at the table because they help to run the meeting for the President. Those who sit around the walls say nothing, unless for some reason the President calls on one of them and asks for an opinion on a particular point.

A third type of meeting is one in the agenda of which more people have a proper interest; the attendance must be, therefore, somewhat enlarged. For instance, normally President Eisenhower expects the Chairman of the Joint Chiefs to represent the Chiefs at the Council table, and the Secretary of Defense to represent the service Secretaries. The service Secretaries and the Chiefs are always at liberty to go and see the President in his office whenever they wish. They did so when I was in office. But, sometimes, it is desirable to have them all at the Council meeting for a defense item—three service Secretaries and four Chiefs, seven more to sit at the table. When there are as many as that in attendance, other people think they ought to be there, too. Sometimes such meetings are necessary, whether or not they produce fruitful results. But the important point seems to me to be this. You have to have as many people at a meeting as the President, who is in charge, feels are necessary for the expression of the various points of view that he thinks should be expressed. You should not leave out a small voice with a real interest just because it is small. Civil Defense may not have been the biggest agency, but if it had an interest to speak, it ought to be permitted to come in and speak. It should not be neglected nor should it come in the back door through another participant. That is one criterion.

A second criterion is, of course, to keep down the number of people because there is a tendency for people not to speak as freely if any meeting gets too big. But it is my experience that it is not too big if you have around a dozen participants—plus the three staff people—and also perhaps six or seven trusted advisers to the President sitting around the back of the room. This number has not interfered with free discussion or vigorous debate.

9. Each President must be free to invite to the Council such advisers as he feels are required to represent for him the basic national security concepts of his administration.

In one of your Subcommittee's interim reports, there was some suggestion that perhaps the roles of the Secretary of State and Secretary of Defense should be enhanced in some way. That, I think, is up to each President to decide. I don't think that you could or should put this in a statute. Different Presidents have different concepts of national security, and what is one man's concept may not be another's. If the President is to use the Council as his valued mechanism, which is what we desire, then he must have the people at the table who give him the balanced view which he feels is the correct view of the national security. This is not an overweighting by more voices on one side of the issue than on the other. In fact, balancing the scale is very important.

We are really saying that the Council attendance must be satisfactory to the President.

10. There should be the fullest airing in the Planning Board and at the Council of cleavages of opinion—sharply expressed in papers, carefully explained to the Council with the President present, with opportunity for all sides to be heard and to rebut. I wish that I could count up the hours I have labored to try to make these differences of opinion sharply stand out in a policy statement in parallel columns, so that one could see the difference at a glance even without the accompanying explanation.

11. Policy decisions at the apex of government must be broadly phrased, leaving detailed planning to the responsible agencies aided in coordination by OCB. I have read in some paper or testimony that, in the prior administration, the operative parts of the policy papers were expressed in three or four paragraphs, sometimes in less than a page. In a country as big as the United States, with the manifold things with which we are concerned, policy decisions must be explained in general and not specific language. I don't mean by this that the language should be bland or obscure or poorly expressed. I certainly struggled as hard as I could to try to express clearly what was intended. In 1955, a Hoover Commission task force looked into the operation of the National Security Council. A representative of the task force told me that they had heard from people in the Pentagon that the guidance received in the NSC papers was not sufficiently clear, that we should be more specific. It is my experience that when you give people instructions they do not like, they may say those instructions are not very clear. This is a human thing.

But you can't have detailed policy instructions at the apex of the Government of the United States. They must be broad policy decisions. We should be writing nothing but lengthy papers if we phrased them otherwise than broadly—and clearly.

Numbers 12 and 13 really go together: The fullest, most intelligent use of the vast, valuable resources of the departments and agencies will bring better results than use of a large ivory-tower staff responsible to the President, or of a continuing contract for studies with an enterprise outside of government, or of a continuing, semi-autonomous "political academy." There is no substitute for (a) the intelligence of the day-to-day operator who knows the practical limitations; (b) the hard-pressed operator, who is a better adviser on policy and action than the full-time theoretician.

The NSC policy coordinating staff should be small, highly competent, and well paid, aiding the Special Assistant in his exacting task as Chairman of the Planning Board and Special Assistant to the President and assisting the Executive Secretary.

When I came to the Council in 1953, I had had a little experience in 1951 as the representative on the Planning Board of the new Psychological Strategy Board. In order to study how to make the Council more effective and report recommendations to the President, I took advice from a number of people—Mr. Lovett, General Marshall, Karl Bendetsen, the former Under Secretary of the Army, Professor Elliott—about fifteen of them, as I recall, mostly meeting in small groups for a day of conference. One of the issues then was whether we should have a big staff. Some people thought it should be bigger and some of them did not. I was interested in reading a recent comment of Dean Acheson's: he took a blast at a large staff, which made me feel I must be a wiser man than I am, for that is my view.

I think that you don't want a big staff responsible to the President or responsible to the Special Assistant or through the Special Assistant to the President. You need enough men to help carry the heavy load that the Special Assistant carries—11 or 12 hours a day—to help him do his work. But, for the basic information, the facts, for everything that you need to carry on this enterprise, there are the great resources of our governmental departments and agencies. I was always amazed by the quality of the people that would appear from the departments, if you dug hard enough, on any subject. The amount of information they had was extraordinary, and the quality of expression of this information was high. These are the people you need to get advice from. They will do a lot better than a firm hired by contract on the outside. I will have something to say about employing outsiders in a moment. But here I want to say that the people who can best advise you are the people who have had the hard experience of doing the job and who know what it is to do the job. They will advise you better than the man who has never done the job but who has theories about how it should be done. Perhaps you should have both kinds, to some extent.

After my study in 1953, the President decided to call the subsidiary body the Planning Board rather than the Senior Staff. I suggested that the President himself appoint each member of the Planning Board on the recommendation of the department head and with my approval. We made a ground rule: every member of the Planning Board be an Assistant Secretary or higher. (Usually the Treasury has sent an Under Secretary.) We look over the Assistant Secretaries. The Special Assistant must know the man. When I talked to the Secretary about his choice, I usually knew them—do you think this one or that one is best qualified? We agree on somebody who will be satisfactory to both of us. The Secretary writes a letter to the President and the Special Assistant approves and takes it to the President for discussion and Presidential designation.

This process elevates the Planning Board member. He isn't just appointed by the Secretary of State; he has a letter signed by the President of the United States appointing him.

He must also, of course, be intimately associated with the Secretary. The closer this association, the more useful the person will be as a Planning Board member. When Robert R. Bowie was State's representative at the Planning Board, he lent tremendous impetus and stature to what we were doing. Not only was he interested, able, clear, intellectually aggressive, and strong in his views, but also, because of these abilities and his standing with Secretary Dulles, he was able to get the best people from the State Department to assist when we were talking about a particular subject.

So, it is important to insure that the Planning Board member has the stature and ability which meet the standard required for Assistant Secretary. We were fortunate in having splendid men as Planning Board representatives. They were keen, interested to argue points and interested to get the best, and not willing to give up until the best job possible had been done.

The resources are there in the departments. If you have as a department's representatives a Secretary who is interested in the Council mechanism and a Planning Board member who is competent and interested, you will obtain from that department all of the information you want. That would be my answer to this particular question.

13. The NSC policy coordinating staff should be small, highly competent, and well paid, aiding the Special Assistant to the President in his exacting task as Chairman of the Planning Board and as Special Assistant, and assisting the Executive Secretary.

We have about ten "think" people on this staff. That is a shade on the low side; I think that we could do with two or three more, but not many more than a total of twelve or thirteen or fourteen. It should be a career staff, I think, as Mr. Lovett expressed it in his testimony. It was always the intention that the staff would be built up to a continuing hard core of twelve or fourteen very competent, well-paid people. Their work is fascinating; they will never run into anything in life again as interesting. As long as a man has interesting work and is adequately paid, he is likely to make that work his career. We have been very fortunate in attracting good people to the NSC staff. I would like to have had a few more.

The Special Assistant is a political figure, one who goes in and out with the administration. But the staff, beginning with the Executive Secretary and so on down, should be career personnel. I feel this career quality of the staff is a very important matter.

Number 14 is Robert Cutler's conclusion in regard to a controversial subject that we have argued about for years. "Wise men without departmental responsibilities serving as permanent members of the Council will not produce the most desirable results."

I used to call these wise men "Nestors," but some of my audience didn't know who Nestor was, and so I went back to using the phrase "wise men."

Many people have the idea of putting Nestors without departmental responsibility on the Council. Mr. Baruch is one believer in this concept. Mr. Baruch is a very wise man and a counselor of Presidents. The idea has come to me from all sides: "Don't you think it would be a good idea to have a couple of Nestors without portfolio, sitting as Council members? They would be able to sit all day in their offices and think. They wouldn't have other work to do; just think and bring these thoughts to the Council."

I don't agree with this concept, as a permanent continuing procedure. I will tell you why. If I were the Secretary of Defense, for example, and persons of great ability, like James Bryant Conant or Dr. Vannevar Bush or Mr. Baruch, were sitting at the Council table with the sole responsibility of thinking up and bringing in their thoughts while I was practically running myself ragged carrying on the operations that I was responsible for, I would find it difficult to have these gentlemen telling me of the right policies to guide how I ought to run my department. I would be inclined to say, "Well, if you know so much about this department, why don't you come over and run it, and I can go back home and run my own business."

The "Nestor" concept won't work, I believe. There is a better way to get at the idea embodied in this proposal, which is a very sound idea. I am going to discuss it in a few minutes.

15. Here is a guiding point that lies at the heart of the whole Council operation and of the whole structure of the United States under its Constitution: no arrangement should be proposed or put into action that will tend to cut across the lines of responsibility

which run directly from the President to his department and agency chiefs.

Now, of course, the President can cut any of these lines if he wants to, although I believe it would be unwise. But nobody else can do it. I will give you three reasons why I feel so strongly about this.

In the first place, the orderly conduct of any great department in the government depends on its having a boss who is responsible to the President who appointed him. Whether he is good, bad or indifferent, he is running the department until he gets fired. His responsibility is to the President.

The second reason is this: it is very difficult to get qualified men to head the big departments and agencies. To discourage them by substituting for a direct line of responsibility to the President the intervention of a committee or someone else, is a very dangerous step. It will make it all the harder to get qualified people to run the government's big departments.

In the third place, I believe that every one of these departments has the resources and information to enable these men to run their departments well, assuming they are competent and good men. Therefore, they should be the ones, carrying the load of their department responsibilities, to advise the President. As you read the OCB charter, you will see that this primary law of direct responsibility to the President is carefully preserved. The OCB charter provides that the OCB shall assist the agencies and the departments in carrying out their planning responsibilities under the national security policy. It has no power to intervene, to order, to come between the President and his responsible minister. If one agency says, "I won't do it that way, I don't care what the OCB says," there is no other way to settle the impasse but to take it to the President. The dissenting agency head has the right to do that. His responsibility is to the President and he isn't responsible to any group, even if that group is composed of persons of Under Secretary rank.

Many people believe parliamentary government is better than our form of government. Well, it is a good form of government, but, on the whole, I think that the United States has done pretty well. I believe this direct line of responsibility from an executive department chief to the President who appoints him is basic to our form of government. I want to stand up for it.

16. For the introduction of fresh ideas and points of view other than those generated within the government, the NSC should use

ad hoc consultant groups, carefully selected from outside the government for their specific or all-around capabilities, using them either before, during, or after the formulation of policy recommendations (for the purpose of review). Such individuals or groups may serve from one day to several months, depending on the issues involved. Outside consultant groups may include qualified citizens with prior governmental service. Outside consultants are free from the inhibitions which sometimes tend to affect permanent government staffs.

Since this matter is something that your staff expressed a great interest in, Mr. Chairman, I would like to say a few words about it. During my service as Special Assistant, and because I am a great believer in using consultants on an *ad hoc* rather than permanent basis, I used fifteen separate groups of consultants. The term of service of these groups ran all of the way from five or six months—like the Technical Capabilities Panel under Dr. Killian and the so-called Gaither Committee—down to only two days. A consultant group chaired by former President Dodds of Princeton was able to finish its work in two days.

In these *ad hoc* consultant groups, we can draw on different fields of endeavor, different areas of the country, and different experiences. It is possible to obtain the services of extremely well qualified and intelligent men for a certain amount of time, when they might not be able to come on a permanent basis.

Our first *ad hoc* group, composed of seven consultants, was called in to review a policy that had been decided on. Later on, almost always, we brought consultants in at the beginning or during the course of policy formulation.

It has been said that the views of these consultant groups were not given attention by the Council. Let me answer that from my own experience. In the case of the Technical Capabilities Panel, which Dr. Killian headed in 1954 and 1955, a report was presented to the Council at a four-hour meeting. At fourteen subsequent Council meetings, different parts of this report were taken up and dealt with. For a year and a half, different recommendations of this report were principal items on Council agendas.

I was responsible for requesting the creation of the Security Resources Committee, the so-called Gaither Committee, and I took a great interest in its work and its report of forty pages. (The Killian Committee report was 100 or 115 pages, I think.) Some of the top personnel of the Gaither Committee were received by the President twice, before the report was rendered. Then the full report was presented to the Council at a full, two-hour plus meeting. This was one of the larger Council meetings, convened to hear the report but not for discussion of its contents. I have earlier testified to the convenience of making such sensitive reports at one, rather than several, meetings, at which all interested persons are present.

Later on, the Gaither Committee report was broken down for study into its principal groups of recommendations. It seemed a sensible way to proceed—to break the many recommendations into naturally related groupings and send the groupings to the departments interested in them and require that by a fixed date departmental reports be rendered to the Council so they could be scheduled on the agenda of Council meetings. We held thirteen Council meetings to consider specific groupings of recommendations and departmental reports thereon, and fully discuss them. This procedure went on for the better part of a year.

Out of the some forty separate recommendations, certainly thirty-five were exhaustively considered by the departments and made the basis of written reports. Over a period of seven or eight months, these reports were heard and discussed by the Council. It is quite untrue that the Council paid little or no attention to the Gaither Committee report, as has sometimes been stated. To the contrary, the Council devoted a very great deal of time to its recommendations. That is what we wanted the report for. We appointed all fifteen consultant groups, during my tenure, to report to the Council. As long as I was there, there wasn't a single consultant group that did not have its reports very thoroughly worked over.

Now, when intelligent people cherish ideas, cherish them strongly, and give up a lot of time and effort to propose and forward them, they are naturally disappointed when those ideas are not accepted in exactly the same way in which they were presented. They are apt to feel that their work was for nothing, that attention wasn't paid it, because it wasn't accepted lock, stock, and barrel. Does this mean that the recommendations they made were right? No. But the reason I favored these *ad hoc* consultant groups and valued their work was that they stimulated thinking. They excited people's interest. They had a profound effect. Naturally this is so, if you enlist consultants of highest possible quality. Look at the membership, for example, of the Gaither Committee or the Killian Committee. Here you had some of the greatest scientists in the world at your beck and call. We had Nobel Prize winners talking to the Council, people of that type. To me, it was a fascinating and contributing procedure. You couldn't get this result by hiring a permanent staff. Nor could you get it by hiring some corporation to make these studies. Men of the kind of which I am talking are not purchasable. But you can get them for short stretches of time as a contribution to the national security. They do not refuse the President's invitation on an *ad hoc* basis.

Therefore, I believe, the use of *ad hoc* consultants is the right way. I think a superior way to introduce new and exciting ideas to the Council is to get the best qualified people you can to help on a temporary basis.

17. I think it is a good idea once in a while to use an "outside" private research organization on an *ad hoc* basis.

SENATOR JACKSON. Before you complete that point, could I ask this question: you very rightfully have touched on the problem of human nature and human behavior—the desire of people who have worked hard on an idea, to want it adopted. What impact do you feel there is in trying to get new *ad hoc* committees if so many key recommendations of the previous ones were not accepted? Don't misunderstand me; under our system of government, of course, an *ad hoc* committee is not a substitute for the President or the regular policy advisers to the President.

GENERAL CUTLER. Let me make a slighly roundabout answer, because you have put your finger on the most frequently raised objection to these consultant groups. It is said that they take up too much time of the top people in Washington who are trying to educate them.

Now, even when you have top-flight, qualified people as consultants, they don't know what the current situation is and they have to be educated by up-to-date briefings. Who is going to brief these important citizens? It won't work to have this done by someone way down on the staff. So it means probably that persons at the Secretary level have to do it or have to come for part of the time while other competent people are doing it. But the educational process is time-consuming. Then, secondly, persons who left their university, their business, their bank, their political work, to come to Washington full-time and work as hard as is humanly possible at their appointed job, feel a human and natural irritation with distinguished consultants standing behind them and breathing down their necks while they try to do their jobs. They tend to resent a little being asked by a consultant, "Why didn't you do it this way?"

I have heard this often. And yet it is my over-all experience that the best opinion is that the use of *ad hoc* consultants was a good thing.

Who says that the Council did not accept all of these ideas? How do people know that? It is certainly true that not all of the ideas of a particular report are accepted. But many of the ideas have been accepted, maybe not quite as proposed but in some modified form, perhaps some improved modification dreamed up by a hard-pressed operator. Possibly not all a report's recommendations really were as good as believed. Maybe if the *ad hoc* committee came together in three years, they would agree with this.

One of the things I have learned is that almost as important as a decision itself is the effort that goes into making it, and the stimulation that it provides. It isn't the decision only that is important. It is the tremendous intellectual stimulation that everybody gets in arguing and working over a problem. I have never found that it was hard to get people to come down to Washington to serve as *ad hoc* consultants.

Recently, distinguished people have been used as consultants with the Planning Board as it begins its annual study and review of over-all national security. Men of the caliber of General Gruenther, Dr. Arthur Burns, James W. Webb, to mention a few. They were glad to give up their time and come down to Washington. Why should they not be glad? It is their life at stake just as much as it is anyone's. They never refuse to come.

SENATOR JAVITS. Do any of these people ever actually sit in on the NSC meeting itself, as outside consultants? Do they have a chance to argue their point with the rest of the high-level people?

GENERAL CUTLER. In the early days, this was a practice that was followed. Later, because of the number of people that got involved in these studies, it was more frequent either to pick one person to speak for them all, as was done in the case of Mr. Robert C. Sprague, who came for a long time after a certain report to help follow certain of its recommendations through the Council.

SENATOR JAVITS. The answer is "Yes"?

GENERAL CUTLER. Not as a universal rule. When you have a consultant group with fifty or sixty people on its staff, it is difficult to select who will attend. The President cannot have new people constantly coming into Council meetings. The members would hesitate to talk in front of people they don't know. Perhaps there is a suggestion here we should consider more.

At the beginning, it was customary to have consultants appear. On the other hand, sometimes I can see awkwardness in this procedure. Perhaps we should draw up a list of forty or fifty men, starting with men like Mr. Lovett and that type, who would be qualified to be called on for consultation and who would agree in advance to give brief periods of service from time to time. They could be brought up to date every couple of months for a couple of days.

This is a thought which might help, along the lines you have just been asking about. It would establish a set of consultants.

The last point (18) is this: the quality and caliber of the operators, far more than the quality or quantity of the mechanism, count the most—whether you are talking about the Council, or a league, or a law school, or business management or research. What one needs in government, as in all human enterprise, is what a friend of mine calls "the pursuit of excellence." This is a wonderful phrase. Leadership lies in the pursuit of excellence. This is so in all walks of life. You don't get results by money, and you don't get results by high office, you get results by the services of the best men you can obtain for the job. We can help mechanically. We can always improve mechanisms, but—above all things—let us seek to improve the caliber and the quality and the devotion of the operators.

Procedures of the NSC

SENATOR JACKSON. Because the NSC is at the summit in the executive branch, next to the President, and one of the "tools" that is available to him to advise him, there is a certain temptation to try to pump a lot of things into the NSC. Shouldn't this temptation be avoided, so that the big issues can be dealt with effectively and in time?

GENERAL CUTLER. Mr. Chairman, aren't we getting on dangerous ground here? On the one hand, it has been said in some circles that the President does not mind the store, that he delegates too much. Now you are asking if the NSC should not winnow all of this harvest and bring up to the President only the "big" issues. It seems to me there is an antithesis between these points of view. You must have a series of written policies—geographical, functional, and administrative. The government is so big that it has to be run on the basis of something that is written out. But as you get it written out, and as you shake yourself loose from having done this, the act of current review doesn't take nearly as long as it did in the early stages. The Planning Board can review one of the policies it has previously worked on in perhaps two and one-half meetings and the Council can deal with maybe two or three such reviews in one meeting. In the early days of an administration, this work will take much longer.

However, I agree that, as the Presidential cycle permits, more time can be spent focusing attention and discussion on fewer significant subjects. I didn't say on significant subjects, but on fewer significant subjects.

SENATOR JACKSON. I realize that the problem is to have matters presented to the President so that he can, in consultation with the NSC, identify the areas that the Planning Board, for example, should prosecute with great diligence. There would be other areas of lesser priority. It occurred to me that the NSC itself could be more effective if the agenda is such that it can concentrate on things that are identified as predicative of great trouble ahead unless something is done to prepare for them.

GENERAL CUTLER. Sir, the waves of scientific discovery have beset us with all kinds of policy issues that neither you nor I dreamed about fifteen years ago. The advance of science has increased the Council's workload. Sometimes we have been criticized because we did not tackle these matters soon enough. Things that looked at first about the size of a man's hand now look as big as a whale.

SENATOR JACKSON. You do have in the NSC the Secretary of State and the Secretary of Defense, who can help to identify the issues and assist the Council and the President in bringing them up. My thought was that this should come up through the departments, naturally, and that the President's top Cabinet advisers in the national security field, being present in the NSC, could assist in this process, too. I was not saying that just the Assistant to the President for National Security Affairs should take unto himself the selection of the significant issues.

GENERAL CUTLER. There is one more red light, to put in the path. When we first came to Washington our responsibility was quite novel, from the President on down. Therefore, we proceeded a little slowly. Not all areas of national security were originally deemed by the President to be suitable for this Council mechanism we were trying to develop. It was my effort constantly to get the President to put more and more areas into the Council rather than to decide them outside of the Council.

Parkinson's law is involved: If matters that belong within the Council's spectrum are decided outside it, there is a tendency for another department to feel that if one such matter wasn't before the Council, why does another such matter of that department have to come before the Council. Gradually, this way, a great many matters may slide out. So I have been driving the sheep into the pen until they are pretty well all included now. I feel that the President likes the way the Council now operates, and he uses it a great deal, and he always comes and takes a lively interest in it. Naturally enough, I don't want to take a step now to open the gate and let a lot of those sheep slip out so that they are attended to outside the Council.

Yet I do feel a great sympathy for the point of view we were just talking about—in the proper time of the Presidential cycle, trying to focus on fewer of the significant issues.

There is a cycle in the term of a President, particularly if he has two terms, which is very noticeable. Thus, the first two years of President Eisenhower's first term were extremely active Council years, because we were reviewing the old policies, revising them, and making new policies. When the second term began, the situation had begun to be different. We had already had our own policies approved in the first term, and we did not have to make the same kind of review of them. We review all policies every year or so, but it is different, because you are reviewing that with which you are familiar and not that which was entirely new to you. Therefore, in this second term, the President was able to do what he had long wished. He directed the Council's focus to be more on oral discussions of significant topics.

Now, this is a cycle that every President is going to face. Eventually, in each cycle, there comes time to be less busy with the formulation of written policy and more busy with discussion of a smaller number of significant issues.

MR. PENDLETON. When the final decision is made, is that by a vote? Does it occur at the same time, or the following day? Just what occurs?

GENERAL CUTLER. It may occur in one of two ways. As the argument goes around the Council table, this member has talked twice, this one has talked three times, and other members have talked once; the disputed subject has really been hashed over. Someone has to bring about the decision. More often than not, this precipitating function is usually left to the Special Assistant. When he thinks that a consensus has been arrived at, or that most of the people think one way, while he has been busily trying to make an appropriate pencil note as to what has been decided, he elevates his voice above the argument to say, "Mr. President, on this point I would understand that the consensus is about as follows."

Then, if there is no objection, in as small a time as possible to see whether anyone is going to talk any more, the Special Assistant moves on to the next point. There is a great deal of business to be done and no time to waste. If the President does not object, that means that this is all right with him. Sometimes he says, "No, that isn't what he said," and then you have to carry on the debate further. Some points he will leave for decision until the Special Assistant brings the draft record of action to him. The Council meets usually on Thursdays. I used to take the draft record of action to him on Saturday morning and go over it with him; it would be as I drafted it, and also with the Council members' comments.

The President frequently would get out his pencil and rewrite the decision the way he wanted it, instead of my way or someone else's way. The President took that kind of an interest in the formal record of action. Of course, there were more or less routine actions that were generally agreed upon. But he would go through the record of action and put his initials on it. When he did, that was it. No paper was ever sent out until he had OK'd it. He didn't always actually put "DDE" on each record of action. Sometimes I would write "DDE by RC" under his authority. These records of action, as approved, will be found in the records of the Council.

MR. PENDLETON. On the budget-making process, how has that been brought into the policy-making process of the NSC level?

GENERAL CUTLER. Well, it has been brought in a great deal more than when we started in 1953. One of my aspirations has been to bring the budgetary process more closely into the Council's mechanism. I think it was Mr. Lovett who commented on the difficulty of doing this, for the Federal budget is wonderfully and fearfully made. The Government is working on three budgets all at the same time. That is a very hard task to get into proper focus. Yet if I ever had to do this job again, one of the principal things I would try to do would be to bring into still closer relationship the budgetary operations. Especially, I think, this could be done in the early part of each budgetary cycle. The fiscal year 1962 budgetary cycle is starting now, the budget that will be presented to Congress in January. The hen is sitting on the nest now and the egg will be gradually coming out during the next seven months.

Now, we want to get into the issues in the early part of the cycle. I don't mean we should or can deal with all of these figures, for that would be inconceivable for a body like the Council. But we could identify the big questions and have them brought up before the Council. I think this would be a very wholesome thing.

I tried to get such a thing put into operation just before I left. We tried to work out an arrangement on how it could be done. I don't think it has worked as well as we hoped. That does not mean that it should not be tried.

The Council is much more in the budget-making process now than it was when we first came to Washington. But I don't think it would be realistic to say that the Council sits down with paper and pencil and works out the figures. But it is familiarized with the process as it goes on, and it knows what is going on. The vast defense budget is exposed to the Council before any decision is taken on it, usually two or three times. This is an innovation, which some people did not care for because it wasn't done that way before.

I agree with what I think the chairman is suggesting, and what your question indicates, that a still closer relation would be helpful if it could be effected. The closer the relation, the better off we would be, I think.

SENATOR MUSKIE. We would be interested in the manner and speed with which newly announced or revised policies are implemented at the operating levels of government.

GENERAL CUTLER. It is sometimes said that the Council is not designed for rapid action. I think it is hard for a body like the Council to act with rapidity. And yet, during my experience, I can remember three instances where (with a very short time to prepare material), because of intervening events, the Council acted very quickly. The Planning Board had to work under great pressure, in some of these cases day and night, in order to produce some very much shorter papers than I would have ever preferred the Council to act on. I have seen the Council take action within two or three days in matters of extreme emergency. It can be done if it is the President's wish to carry an urgent matter through the mechanism and not decide it in another way. It is difficult to get enough information, put it together, have it presented and studied, and come to a decision, but it can be done. To say that the Council is so slow and ponderous that it can't act quickly goes too far. I think perhaps it would be fairer to say that it isn't the most apt mechanism for quick action, but if quick action is required, I have seen it act in three or four days. Where it acted with great rapidity, its policies were implemented very, very quickly.

SENATOR MUSKIE. If, in the implementation of a major policy

by an operating agency, the result in a specific instance is an incident that has an important impact upon our world position in the eyes of the other nations, is the machinery of the National Security Council so set up as to permit it to take action with respect to (1) the handling of the immediate reaction of the U. S. Government to this incident, and (2) revision of national policy or of the national policy that resulted in the incident?

GENERAL CUTLER. If the President of the United States were to decide that he wished to convene the Council to advise him on any matter that affected the national security, he could do it. The Council could be assembled and it could consider the matter, and it could advise the President and he could take or not take its advice, as he saw fit.

SENATOR MUSKIE. Is the relationship between the President and the National Security Council such that it would be one of his first inclinations to initiate such a consultation?

GENERAL CUTLER. Well, the President has used the Council a great deal. He likes this mechanism. But he may choose other mechanisms or he may choose to decide it himself or in concert with some of his trusted advisers. It really is what the President decides he wants to do, I think. When I was Special Assistant, I suppose that I saw the President four times a week, and we were in constant communication with each other.

The relationship between the President and the Council through his Special Assistant is very close. It has to be so. It meets every week, sometimes twice a week. (I don't think that I ever knew of it meeting more frequently than twice a week.) But it is a very convenient form of obtaining advice on matters of national security. People are accustomed to it and they have been doing it for seven years now, meeting together and discussing things. The Council is no longer a lot of strangers meeting. I think the President considers the National Security Council a very useful mechanism. Yes; I do. If he does not, I certainly wasted a lot of my life in serving him in connection with it.

The Secretary of State[*]

CHRISTIAN A. HERTER

Christian A. Herter, Secretary of State from 1959 to 1961, came to his position after two years in the post of Under Secretary. During World War I, he served abroad and in the State Department. He has had a long career in elective office: member of the Massachusetts State House of Representatives, 1931-43; Representative in the U. S. Congress, 78th-82nd Congresses; and Governor of Massachusetts, 1953-57. Since 1962, he has been the President's Special Representative for Trade Negotiations.

I welcome the opportunity to offer this committee my views on those aspects of the national policy machinery with which I am most familiar. My comments are based on reflections arising from my service as Under Secretary and Secretary of State, and of course as a member of the Committee on Foreign Affairs of the House of Representatives.

Fundamental Considerations

It seems to me that several fundamental considerations underlie the questions concerning the Department of State you have asked me to discuss today. While these are generally well understood, they might bear restating, to be sure we are on common ground.

First of all, under the Constitution and the historical development of our government, executive responsibility for the conduct of foreign relations and the enunciation of foreign policy resides squarely with the President. As this committee knows so well, the course of events of the past two decades has given to these responsibilities dimensions that are awesome, to say the least.

[*] Testimony delivered to the Subcommittee on National Policy Machinery, June 10, 1960.

Second, it follows that the fundamental mission of the Secretary of State is to assist and support the President in the discharge of his responsibilities for foreign affairs. Unlike, I believe, any other major department, the basic authority of the Department of State is left completely to the discretion of the President. The basic statute of the Department of State provides that the Secretary of State "shall perform and execute such duties as shall, from time to time, be enjoined on or entrusted to him by the President of the United States, agreeable to the Constitution."

Third, as became evident after the conclusion of the last war and becomes more apparent with each passing year, international affairs no longer have an existence separate from domestic affairs, and they can no longer be treated except in the context of the entire range of governmental activities. Practically every government department and agency has, to a varying degree, a proper concern and, in some instances, responsibility for one facet or another of international affairs. Conversely, the Department of State is properly concerned with facets of domestic affairs that have major impact upon our foreign relations.

Before proceeding further, I should like to make several observations on the considerations I have just enumerated.

The burden of the President's responsibilities for international affairs is almost indescribably heavy. I think all of us must be sympathetic and helpful in doing what we can to provide him with the highest possible caliber of assistance, both with respect to his immediate staff and in each of the various departments of government concerned.

The relationship between the President and the Secretary of State is, of necessity, a very personal one. Over the years, it has varied with circumstances and personalities and will undoubtedly continue to do so. The relationship can never be considered fixed beyond the tenure of either incumbent, and any effort to make it so would hamper rather than enhance effective performance.

Every President, in his own way, has defined the role he wishes his Secretary of State to carry out. President Eisenhower set forth quite clearly on repeated occasions his concept of the function of the Secretary of State. Typically, he stated on June 1, 1953, that—

> I personally wish to emphasize that I shall regard the Secretary of State as the Cabinet officer responsible for advising and assisting me in the formulation and control of foreign policy. It will be my practice to employ the Secretary of State as my channel of authority

within the executive branch on foreign policy. Other officials of the executive branch will work with and through the Secretary of State on matters of foreign policy.

These principles have been adhered to in succeeding years. I would doubt that any more explicit or enlarged statement is necessary.

I do not wish to leave the impression, by my emphasis on the discretion that must be available to the President, that there are not enduring guideposts within which we can approach the questions we are considering today. In my opinion, the Secretary of State should, under the President, have in his relations with other departments a clear primacy in foreign relations and in all matters with a substantial effect on foreign relations. This is not to say that he should be charged with operating all the programs carried on abroad in support of our national security goals, but that he should have clear primacy as to policy on these programs. Nor is it to say that he should normally have the power of decision upon matters crossing departmental jurisdiction simply because they involve foreign affairs. Rather, the Secretary of State should be looked to for the formulation of recommendations to the President, when appropriate through the National Security Council, which take into account the considerations and views set forth by other departments. Assistance of this nature enables the President to focus effectively on foreign-affairs problems of transcendent importance. In following these principles, it is hard to state general rules that will be self-enforcing. It is more a matter of recognizing that the activities and programs are for a foreign-affairs purpose and should therefore be guided by the official responsible for foreign affairs.

In my opinion, good organization alone will not suffice for the solution of foreign-affairs problems of the magnitude and complexity that confront us today. While I am well aware of the value of good organization and soundly conceived relationships, I find that I subscribe to the sentiments of those who place even greater value on the human element—on the devotion, ability, and experience of the personnel of the State Department and the other principal departments of government. This is why I have been such a strong advocate of the moves made in recent years to strengthen the Foreign Service—and, indeed, the entire Department of State. While I have been pleased with the progress made in matters such as training and integration of the foreign and domestic officer corps, I recognize that there is much that remains to be done. This is a long-range program, and I very much hope that it will continue to have the support of my successors and of the future Congresses of the United States.

The Department of State

The ability of any Secretary of State to serve the President depends not only on his own capacities but also on the support available to him from the Department of State. The responsibilities customarily assigned to the Secretary of State for providing leadership to the government as a whole in the international field require the participation of many parts of the department. Its capacity to provide leadership at all levels is dependent, in the final analysis, not upon fiat but upon the competence, judgment, energy, and comprehension of the many officers who are involved.

I should now like to speak to the questions relating to the Department of State that were posed in the Interim Report of this Subcommittee.

First are those concerned with whether the Secretary of State should have a more dominant role in the formulation of over-all national security policy: "Are the responsibilities of the State and Defense departments in national security policy-making now correctly defined and divided? If not, what changes are needed?" In my judgment, they are correctly defined and the division is working well. I do not believe that any major improvement in the relationships between the departments of State and Defense would result from further efforts to define their respective responsibilities. A more immediate and profitable target is for the State Department to improve its capacity to provide timely political guidance to the Defense Department and, reciprocally, for the latter to improve its capacity to provide timely military advice. I should emphasize that this is being done not only at the senior levels but at all levels in the two departments. The advice worked into problems at the lower levels is frequently the most helpful.

The functional and organizational aspects of State-Defense relations are, of course, important. More important, however, is the continuing development of personnel in both departments who share understanding and perspective in the gray area where foreign policy and military policy come in contact or overlap. In this regard, the common experience shared by personnel of the two departments who attend the war colleges and the Foreign Service Institute is very helpful. In addition, I think it would be worth while to have a greater exchange of personnel between the two departments. The men loaned would function as an integral part of the host agency, contributing their own special knowledge, and would return to their parent agency at the end of the tour with the broadened perspective acquired through shoulder-to-shoulder work. We might, with such a program, over a period of years, develop a nucleus of highly trained senior officers within the two departments, each having a profound and comprehensive understanding of the subject matter and viewpoint of the other department. If this understanding were regularly and consistently brought to bear on the solution of problems of mutual concern, much more good would be accomplished than could result from efforts to adjust and refine the respective responsibilities of the two departments. I should add that the broadening of personal contacts among senior officers resulting from such an interchange would be a major asset in insuring the continuity of a productive relationship between the departments of State and Defense.

"Should the Secretary of State be formally charged with more responsibility in connection with our defense posture and the defense budget?" No. First of all, I regard somewhat skeptically the word "formally" as contravening the basic concepts that the Secretary of State is the agent of the President and that it is unwise to prescribe how the President may utilize him. More to the point, however, is my belief that participation by the Secretary of State in the NSC, in the Cabinet, and in confidential discussions with the President affords ample opportunity to advise the President on the defense posture and defense budget. In addition, I feel free to advise and consult with the Secretary of Defense on these topics, and I do so.

"Should the Secretary of State be asked to testify in the Congress concerning foreign-policy implications of the defense budget?" The Congress is entitled to obtain whatever advice it deems necessary to insure the enactment of wise legislation. In recent years, a number of steps have been taken in the executive branch to insure consideration of foreign-policy implications in determining the defense budget. It must be recognized, I think, that should the Secretary of State testify on the defense budget, he would undoubtedly be supporting decisions in which he had already participated. These budget decisions, as I have seen them, are not made in a vacuum, and the departments are fully aware of each others' interests.

"Would it be desirable to create a "super Secretary of State" who would be responsible for the over-all direction of foreign affairs, and who might have under him additional Secretaries of Cabinet rank for such areas as diplomacy, information, and foreign economic matters?" Although I can fully understand and sympathize with the general objectives desired by those who advocate a so-called super Secretary of State with Cabinet-level agencies reporting to him, I do not believe that such a proposal would be desirable. There are a number of factors that cause me to question it. Among them is the assumption of equivalence for areas such as diplomacy, information, and foreign economic matters. I do not believe the areas are, in fact, equivalent. If these three principal areas are to be equated, it will then become necessary to establish what I fear would be an excessively large coordinating mechanism at the level of the super Secretary of State. Instead of being relieved of burdens, he might find his load increased.

This is not to say that I disagree with the concept that our foreign economic and information activities ought to be under the control of the Secretary of State. It may be desirable at some time for the overseas information activities to be brought into the department in a semi-autonomous status somewhat similar to that successfully followed with the ICA.

The Interim Report next poses questions concerned with lightening the burdens of the Secretary of State: "Would it be desirable to create a Minister of Foreign Affairs of Cabinet rank responsible to the Secretary of State who would represent the United States at Foreign Ministers' meetings? Would any other arrangement help, such as appointment of ambassadors at large?" The underlying question here is whether it is possible to lighten the negotiating burdens of the Secretary of State in order to give him more time to discharge his responsibilities at home. I do not consider feasible the proposal to create a Minister of Foreign Affairs. When Foreign Ministers meet, they are meeting as their governments' chief advisers on foreign affairs. Since the Secretary of State would continue in this country to be that chief adviser, another representative, no matter what his rank and title, would create problems for the other Foreign Minister.

I am coming to the conclusion that it would be desirable for the Foreign Ministers to curtail the occasions upon which they themselves attend meetings. To do this would require greater delegation to principal subordinates and greater reliance on the normal mechanisms of diplomacy. Additionally, when there are some eighty-five nations who must deal with each other, we may have to dispense with some of the ways of protocol that we no longer have the time to afford.

Relations with the Defense Department

"What is the proper relationship between State and the Joint Chiefs of Staff (and/or the Joint Staff of the JCS)? Should a representative of the Secretary of State participate in discussions of the JCS when appropriate?" The Secretary of State, the Secretary of Defense, and the Joint Chiefs of Staff form, and should continue to form, a well-coordinated and smoothly working team in both the planning and execution of national security policy.

The two departments naturally have very extensive relationships on a multitude of subjects, which enable the State Department to inject foreign-policy considerations into military affairs at all stages. Secretary Gates and I confer frequently and we also participate in larger meetings, such as the NSC and the Cabinet. An Under Secretary of State confers regularly with the JCS, and the Assistant Secretary of State for Policy Planning meets regularly with the Joint Staff of the JCS and officers of the Department of Defense. State, Defense, and military officials work directly together across the board and without any formalities and especially so when there is a premium on speed of action. In addition to our broad and fruitful policy relationships with Defense through the Office of International Security Affairs, we have direct relationships with the three services on a variety of subjects.

I believe it would be a mistake to have a State Department officer sit with the JCS as a representative of the Department, but I would not rule out the long-term possibility that a senior officer might be assigned to the JCS in an advisory capacity. While such an official might not participate in the deliberations of the JCS as an official spokesman for the State Department, he might have a role comparable to that of a political adviser to a unified military command.

Next are the questions directed toward improvement of planning in the departments of State and Defense: "Should officials with more diverse backgrounds and experience be brought into the Policy Planning Staffs of State and Defense? Is there a need for a joint State-Defense-JCS Planning Staff? Can greater use be made of *ad hoc* interdepartmental task forces on special issues of national security policy?" We have long recognized the need for officers of diverse backgrounds on our Policy Planning Staff. I think that we have succeeded fairly well in meeting this need. Naturally, we shall continue to select with great care the members of this staff, so as to insure a balance of knowledge and background.

A Joint State-Defense-JCS Planning Staff would have the merit of bringing together diverse backgrounds but might have the drawback of being apart from the operating departments and out of the mainstream. The firm connection with reality that proximity to operations gives is certainly a requisite of useful planning. This is one of the reasons why the Planning Board of the NSC has been so useful: its members are active participants in the operations of their own departments as well as members of a joint planning staff. Additionally, we have utilized interdepartmental task forces for planning on special issues, and we have found it to be an excellent means of bringing to bear upon a problem the best knowledge of several agencies.

Lastly, there is the question about a joint career service embracing senior officers selected from State, Defense, and related national security agencies: is it practical and worthwhile? The joint career service proposal strikes me as being a rather drastic and administratively cumbersome approach to the very desirable objective of developing policy-makers with nonparochial viewpoints and wide experience. As I suggested earlier, I believe the interchange of selected personnel between the Departments of State and Defense and the use of joint task forces on planning might go a long way toward meeting this objective and should be tried before we resort to the more drastic proposal for a joint career service.

In conclusion, I wish to thank the committee for this opportunity to meet with it.

More Help for the Secretary of State?

SENATOR JACKSON. I think we are all conscious, and certainly the public is, of the enormous burden the Secretary of State must carry. I think it is second only to that of the President. Are there some changes that might be made in the organizational structure of the Department that would somewhat lighten that burden and make it possible for the Secretary to spend more time on the critical issues? We are aware of the requirement that he travel to many, many places but while the Secretary is going from place to place, we have critical issues that must be decided at home.

SECRETARY HERTER. This is a very real problem. I don't pretend to have the answer to it, but I would like to sketch out just what the problem is. I am drawing now on my own experience as Secretary of State.

I have been in office as Secretary of State for 414 days. I have been out of the country during that time for 156 days, or 38 per cent of the time. This obviously poses very real problems from the point of view of the internal administrative operation of the State Department and the constant contacts and necessary service it must provide the President.

This growing tendency to be required—and I use that word advisedly—to go overseas is a part of the technological development of the time, in one respect, because travel is so much quicker than it ever was before. But it has become a virtual necessity as a result of the treaty structures and alliances we have built up over the years. As you know, we are a member of the Organization of American States. We are a member of NATO. We are a member of SEATO. We are a member of the principal committees of CENTO. In addition to that, the United Nations General Assembly opening is now attended by foreign ministers. This last year, I think there were more than sixty foreign ministers in attendance at New York. The contacts with them there and the presence of the principal officer of the State Department have become practically a requirement.

If it were possible to find some alternate in the Department, regardless of what the title was, who could take some of that burden from the Secretary of State—that is, the necessity of attending these alliance conferences, on which our allies count very heavily for consultation and for periodic meetings—if it were possible to find someone, that would be excellent. But, particularly because of the sensitivity of many countries that they are being downgraded or that those in one alliance are being considered as less important than those in another alliance, they are never satisfied except with the top individual. They feel that, if anybody else is assigned to the task of representing the United States, it means that for some reason we are now paying less attention to, let us say, South America, or Asia, than Europe or the Middle East. This makes it very, very difficult for the principal foreign officer to avoid that particular type of meeting.

I feel that the day is coming, and coming pretty soon, when there will have to be another conference equivalent to the Congress of Vienna to discuss this type of problem. As you know, the question of visits of high-ranking officials to other countries has increased by leaps and bounds, again with the facility of travel. The protocols that have been established in years gone by require a degree of attention to those visits that is extremely time-consuming. Just the mere physical operation of going to airports, seeing people off at airports, accompanying them on visits, having to give so many dinners and return dinners—all of which are set by these protocol arrangements that have gone on over years and years—is a very time-consuming process, and a very difficult process.

But, again, there is no substitute for the individual who happens to be holding the position I am holding now. I think the time has come when internationally we ought to revise, if we can, the whole question of the exchange of visits, and how we handle them. The question of the recognition of Under Secretaries with special capacities for attending international conferences, and things of that kind, should be looked into. Until we can reach international agreement on that, however, we have this very serious problem of not being able to find a substitute without seriously offending a good many nations to whom this means a great deal.

As you know, in the last two years, we have created a new Under Secretary of State to assist in the over-all problem. We now have a Secretary of State; two Under Secretaries who, by the power of delegation that Congress has given, can be alternated in the special responsibilities of economic or political affairs; two Deputy Under Secretaries of State, in addition to the eleven Assistant Secretaries who are largely specialists in their geographic and functional bureaus.

The question that keeps going through my mind is whether, if we create another new high-level position with a new title, it will take the load off the Secretary or whether there will still be the demand for him and a feeling of being downgraded if they don't get him. I have not been able to answer that question in my own mind.

SENATOR JACKSON. I sympathize with your problem. It does seem to me that unless we come to some kind of resolution of this problem it will not be possible for the Secretary of State, with his broadened responsibilities, with new elements that relate to power and therefore to diplomacy, to do the job. He may be abroad and dealing with an urgent matter when we at home have a critical decision to make. If he has to do both, I just don't see how we can compete effectively with our adversaries. We are bound to make mistakes.

SECRETARY HERTER. I might add just one thing that is also quite time-consuming, and that is a good many committees of the Congress are not satisfied with an Under Secretary of State as a witness and insist on the Secretary.

SENATOR JACKSON. Having served on the Hill, I think you understand that problem, too. I wondered if you had any comment with reference to the appointment of ambassadors at large—a device that has sometimes been used to lighten some of the burden.

SECRETARY HERTER. I have always felt that it is a desirable thing to have a limited number of ambassadors at large. There are so many unexpected things that come up where it is very difficult to take anyone at a high level away from his operational responsibilities and assign him to specific tasks. I think that if it were possible to assign two or three ambassadors at large to the Department for what you really might call trouble-shooting duties, without designation to a given country, it would be a very useful thing.

SENATOR JACKSON. Especially, I would think, if the ambassadors at large are men of experience, of substantial international reputation, this would help to add to the importance of the position.

SECRETARY HERTER. It would.

The National Security Council *

SENATOR JACKSON. In your judgment, what is the most useful and proper role of the NSC in assisting the President? Can it best serve the President as a large body with elaborate supporting structure that prepares formal papers, or as a small group of the President's principal advisers who would discuss, usually without a formal paper, current matters of importance and major policy changes?

SECRETARY HERTER. My impression is that on the whole it is working pretty well. The question of size is a relative thing. As you know, the law prescribes the members of the National Security Council but also gives the President permission to bring in as participants such government officials as he sees fit. Insofar as the Planning Board is concerned, and the papers that are brought in, I think that in a way facilitates the work. I think that unless you have some guidance for the discussion and the issues to be discussed are pretty well pinpointed, you may wander all over the place, even if it is a small group. I think a certain amount of paperwork is absolutely essential.

SENATOR JACKSON. Would you not say that there can be a danger

* Testimony delivered to the Subcommittee on National Policy Machinery in executive session, June 10, 1960.

in the NSC that an effort is made to cover too many problems? Do you not feel its use as an advisory body to the President is at its best when they try to limit the areas of discussion and debate to the really critical issues, and then try to take some concrete action on them? In other words, would it be better to try to keep out a lot of collateral issues?

SECRETARY HERTER. In general, I think it is true. On the other hand, it is quite an extraordinary thing that you often start with a comparatively small issue that maybe relates to one country or one particular problem, and it will bring out a very large issue in the course of the discussion. So again, it is pretty hard to generalize as to just where you should draw the line and who should have the authority in drawing the line as to what comes before the National Security Council. The Planning Board, of course, does a good deal of screening in that respect.

SENATOR JACKSON. General Cutler has indicated that during the time he served as Special Assistant to the President for National Security Affairs—and he was there quite some time, on two different tours—the emphasis in the NSC gradually shifted, that is, in the sense that less time was spent in the preparation of formal policy recommendations and more time on prearranged informal discussions and debate of important issues based on the so-called discussion papers. Based on your experience, do you think this is a useful shift in emphasis?

SECRETARY HERTER. Yes, I do. I think this has been an evolutionary process.

SENATOR JACKSON. It has been a healthy change?

SECRETARY HERTER. I think it is a very good change.

SENATOR MUSKIE. It seems to me we ought to insure, to the extent that it is possible, that strongly held differences of opinion, which are vital and important, should rise to the National Security Council level. I am not sure there is an organizational answer to this.

SECRETARY HERTER. I have sat on it now for three years, and I can assure you that there are very lively discussions there and very lively differences of opinion that are held absolutely freely before the final decisions are made.

SENATOR MUSKIE. Are these differences of opinion between departments or differences of opinion within a given department that rise to the National Security Council?

SECRETARY HERTER. Usually between departments. On the other hand, the Joint Chiefs very frequently have a different view from the Defense Department that they want to express and always have a right to express.

SENATOR MUSKIE. Are differences only on the level of the Joint Chiefs or the Secretary of Defense brought to the National Security Council or differences at lower levels?

SECRETARY HERTER. If we went to the colonels and the captains, we would never be able to resolve anything.

SENATOR MUSKIE. I am going to read two comments on the NSC and ask your reaction to them. These were made by William Kintner. He suggests three standards for the national security policy process:

> Any national security policy mechanism equal to the challenge facing us must, therefore, be such that its personnel have: first, sufficient *perspective* to be able to see our national security problems in their entirety and utilize every available means, public and private and in flexible combination, in their solution; second, sufficient *objectivity* to devise coordinated plans and policies, and impartial review and analysis of operations so that essential goals are achieved by the operating agencies without debilitating compromise or without their working at cross-purposes or independently of one another; and, third, sufficient *time* to devise broad, imaginative and coordinated action programs, long-term in their scope and inclusive of aspects of our social, economic, and political life likely to be overlooked by the department or agency head in his inevitable preoccupation with daily operations. . . .
>
> One reason why the U. S. Government has not as yet evolved a more rational staff system for the top levels of its national security organization is the confusion that exists in many minds between the planning function at the national level and the operational duties of the executive departments. The various governmental departments have always been afraid that a staff at the President's level would assume some of their prerogatives and functions. They are perfectly willing to have the general planning function done by interdepartmental representatives, because they feel they can practically dictate the result of such planning.*

SECRETARY HERTER. This is something I tried to touch on in my prepared statement. It is really the concept of the ivory-tower planning staff versus a planning staff of people who are in constant touch with operational problems. I think you get more real-

---

* William R. Kintner, formerly in the Office of the Secretary of Defense, now Professor of Political Science, University of Pennsylvania, "Organizing for Conflict: A Proposal," *Orbis* (Summer, 1958).

istic planning from those in constant touch with the operational problems than from those who are completely divorced, as we would have them here, from any operational relationships—an outside staff made up, presumably, of individuals who did not represent departments.

In planning work we try to get as many diverse points of view as we can. This may mean that in the process of consultation and shaking down, you get to a common denominator that sometimes is not a desirable thing. But from a practical point of view, there is never a piece of paper that comes up to the National Security Council, that does not have split views on it. In other words, in the Planning Board they just don't reconcile their views. This has to be done at the level of the National Security Council itself, with the President making the final decision but with the various department heads having a chance to express themselves on split views.

If I read Mr. Kintner correctly, what he has in mind is that the Planning Board would tell every department how to run its show.

SENATOR JACKSON. If I may turn to the OCB for a minute, which has the responsibility of coordinating the plans that the departments and agencies must carry out in connection with policies adopted by the NSC, do you feel this is an area warranting further study to see if improvements could be made?

SECRETARY HERTER. I would never say there was any area in which improvements could not be made. I was Chairman of OCB for two years. The feeling of utility varied an awful lot. At times you felt that you were being very useful. At other times, you felt you were fanning the air or spending a lot of time reviewing minutiae. There are two phases of it. The members of the OCB eat lunch together every Wednesday. In those discussions, where there is very little staff, anything can be brought up, and those discussions are extraordinarily useful. Again, it is a little like a staff meeting. When you get into the formal sessions, you again apply yourself to paper-work. Sometimes you get yourself so bogged down in the editing of a word or sentence that you say, "My God, why am I spending so much time on this?" Other times, pretty important decisions are made and made very quickly.

If there were not the OCB, you would have to have something similar. That is always the answer you come up with. There has to be one coordinating body somewhere where you can air out differences in the operational end of things, and often you find that something may have been decided upon but runs into operational difficulties that require a complete reassessment. From that point of view, it is very valuable.

SENATOR JACKSON. Could it be improved upon if they could concentrate on fewer matters?

SECRETARY HERTER. That is a question mark in my mind. We have some eighty-five nations to deal with today. Most of the OCB's operations are in the international field. That is where the coordinating process is required. Sometimes we get into a domestic matter where the individual officer concerned comes in. But the mere fact of our geographic divisions in connection with the individual countries and the problems in those countries makes a good interdepartmental review of what is going on in the country a healthy process. It means a lot of work. You often get kicks: why do I have to come up with a new evaluation of how the operational process in connection with some NSC decision is working? I think it is a healthy process to take a good look at yourself at regular intervals. While sometimes taking a good look at yourself and completely reviewing an existing situation does not produce any particular change, or only very minor things come up in connection with it, the mere fact that it has been made comparatively recently gives you some assurance that you are not letting a situation drag because it is not being reviewed. That means that a lot of matters do come in, inevitably. More and more, as you know, our problems have shifted from areas where you consider a whole group of countries together; we now have these independent countries which have separate problems. More and more, you have to subdivide, because there is too much in an area that you just can't cover.

MR. PENDLETON. Mr. Secretary, do you believe at the present time that the NSC covers too many issues?

SECRETARY HERTER. No.

The Secretary of Defense*

THOMAS S. GATES, JR.

Thomas S. Gates served continuously in the Department of Defense from 1953 to January, 1961, as Under Secretary of the Navy, as Secretary of the Navy, as Deputy Secretary of Defense, and then as Secretary of Defense. He was a commander in the U. S. Naval Reserve in World War II. He is Chairman and Chief Executive Officer of the Morgan Guaranty Trust Co.

In common with a great many others, I have followed with interest the hearings you have been conducting to explore the organizational machinery now employed within the government to reach policy decisions and to plan for the future. An objective review of policy-making machinery is most useful and constructive, and I am pleased to have an opportunity to discuss the subject with you.

The Defense Department

In the letter inviting me to appear before this committee, Mr. Chairman, you directed my attention specifically at two questions:

The first question is: "Is the Department of Defense now properly organized to discharge its responsibilities adequately today and in the years lying ahead? If not, what changes are desired?"

In my judgment, the Department of Defense has at present a sound basis of organization on which it can discharge its responsibilities. An organization as large and complex as the Defense Department is always subject to administrative improvement. In the future, the emergence of new problems, new concepts causing a shifting of emphasis in procurement and research, and the ideas contributed by successive administrators—all could indicate that changes in both structures and operation are desirable. Since weap-

* Testimony delivered to the Subcommittee on National Policy Machinery, June 13, 1960.

ons technology and military strategy are undergoing a continuous and increasingly rapid evolution, there probably can never be an ideal or permanent solution. A primary need will always be flexibility, therefore, to be used as necessary to meet changing requirements.

Certain major changes were made with the adoption of the Reorganization Act of 1958. It is too soon to evaluate these completely or to determine whether others are needed. One of them, the creation of the position of Director of Defense Research and Engineering, has already proved to be of great benefit and has made a major imprint on our operations. The centralizing of authority in one office empowered to make certain that maximum use is being made of our resources for research in all military services—people, facilities, and dollars—was a forward step of significant importance. The streamlining of the line of command from the Commander in Chief to the unified and specified commands, eliminating the extra step that formerly involved the military departments as executive agents, has proved highly satisfactory and could be of critical importance in a time of emergency. Other improvements contained in the 1958 act have been beneficial.

I would suggest no further statutory changes until we have more thoroughly digested this 1958 reorganization and learned, by living with it, whether any further changes in the law might be indicated.

Meanwhile, administrative measures to improve our operations can be taken within the framework of the 1958 reorganization act. I trust it is in order to note certain recent actions of this nature.

Much attention has been focused on the workings of the Joint Chiefs of Staff. Some people have expressed concern that on some important matters the Chiefs do not reach unanimous agreement and thus, it is suggested, do not give the Secretary of Defense clear, firm recommendations. Various solutions have been offered by those experienced and those inexperienced in the ways of the military. We are dealing with matters of judgment. We are considering subjects of great complexity. Senior military men of integrity do not compromise their views when they think our national security is at stake. They will have differences of opinion, and it is both natural and helpful to have them.

A procedure was instituted whereby the Secretary of Defense and the Deputy Secretary of Defense sit with the Joint Chiefs weekly, usually on Monday afternoon and more frequently if desirable, to discuss major issues. This has produced several important results:

1. We are exposed to the various views as they develop.

2. We have an opportunity to make certain by questioning that there is a basis for evaluating these different views.

3. A better basis is created for a sound decision between two or more possible courses of action.

4. The time required to make decisions is shortened.

To illustrate this procedure, I can give you this summary of results. Since January 21, there have been six specific issues on which decisions had to be made, in addition to a number of other matters for discussion. These issues involved command arrangements, military planning and doctrine, and matters pertaining to the military assistance program. Five of the six decisions were made before the meeting ended, and the other was made within a week. There are others pending, of considerable importance, but this is the kind of improvement that can be made through administrative changes in internal procedure.

Another major change we have made recently is to establish the Defense Communications Agency. This centralizes control of all our long-haul communications under a single officer, who reports through the Joint Chiefs of Staff to the Secretary of Defense. This should result in improved efficiency of our communications. It is an organizational concept we shall watch with interest.

The Secretary of Defense and the NSC

The second question specifically asked in your letter, Mr. Chairman, was, "How can the Secretary of Defense best contribute to making the National Security Council an effective advisory mechanism for the President?"

Mr. Chairman, I should like to emphasize that, in my judgment, the National Security Council is functioning effectively and efficiently as an advisory mechanism to President Eisenhower. It has functioned in that manner through all the time I have been exposed to its operations. Since the National Security Council is an advisory group, I am sure each President will use it according to his own way of doing business. I can assure this committee that President Eisenhower participates actively in all Council meetings; the pros and cons of any issue are thoroughly and ably debated at the meetings; and the President himself makes the decisions. All this, in my judgment, is exactly as it should be.

Recently, I have read some public comment suggesting that the

Council may be too large, suggesting that the meetings are conducted in a so-called mass atmosphere, that too much of the essential debate may be taking place at lower staff levels, that top-level discussions have become smothered in papers, and that the Council is somehow insulating the President from so-called hard facts and hard decisions. Frankly, I am at a loss to know the basis for such observations, because as far as I am concerned—and I am a member of the National Security Council—not one of these suggested criticisms can properly be applied to the current practices of the National Security Council. The size and character of the meetings vary with the agenda. For example, it has been the practice to have experts present when they can be helpful to a discussion in their particular fields. Vitally interested agencies may be represented when they should be informed in detail because their responsibilities are heavily involved. I cannot tell this committee what habits and practices may have prevailed at other times or will prevail in the future, but I do know, of my own knowledge, that these faults have not existed during my activity with the Council under President Eisenhower.

In my opinion, one can never fully separate the statutory composition of any agency from the personalities of the individuals involved. This applies to the National Security Council, and it applies also to the daily relations of government officials at all levels. All members of the Security Council, along with the responsible officers and employees in their departments, function together smoothly as a team. To illustrate this, I have known Secretary of State Herter and Under Secretary Dillon for years. I enjoy working with them. The members of the Office of International Security Affairs, that part of the Defense Department most concerned with military matters involving foreign policy, work closely and smoothly with the Department of State. In an average day, there will be several hundred separate contacts between individuals in the two organizations—by meeting, phone call, or exchange of correspondence. Similar contacts are made daily between the State Department and the military services and the Joint Chiefs of Staff.

There is, I think, a common recognition on both sides of the Potomac that most foreign-policy issues have major defense connotations, and conversely that even routine military activity may have major foreign-policy implications. In addition to the lessons of experience, professional training programs at the National War College, service war colleges, and the Military Assistance Institute stress the relations between political, economic, and military factors in our security policies. State Department personnel are attending military schools.

Thus, at the highest political levels, at Washington staff levels, and at the "Country Team" level, planning and implementation of national security policies by Defense personnel reflect increasing integration of political, economic, and military considerations. We have long realized that the defense program cannot be prepared in isolation.

Working relationships between the State and Defense departments are excellent; I am told they have never been better.

Defense Department Organization and the Budget

SENATOR JACKSON. I take it that, insofar as authority given to you by the Congress is concerned, you have ample authority to deal with problems of organization and reorganization within the Department of Defense. I mean, you are satisfied with your statutory authority?

SECRETARY GATES. I am at the present, yes, sir.

SENATOR JACKSON. Do you have any general ideas as to the trend, looking ahead a year or two, where the needs for further reorganization will occur?

SECRETARY GATES. I have certain preliminary thoughts, largely in the fields of management and of planning and policy. I think that we could or should continue to review our administrative procedures and try perhaps to perfect them. I would be interested in exploring these two areas to see whether we could perhaps make further improvements. Until we tried this administratively, I do not believe we would want to propose legislation. If we did, it would involve a fundamental change in the statutory appointees.

SENATOR JACKSON. You feel you should exhaust the remedies that Congress has already given you before coming in and asking for more?

SECRETARY GATES. Yes, but not rest on our laurels, but continue to try to think how we can improve and perhaps make future recommendations for change.

SENATOR JACKSON. The onerous job of preparing a budget is well known to you: you have been wrestling with it now for eight years. Each service has a comptroller; the Defense Department has a comptroller; and guidelines are issued. I wonder if you have any thoughts about improvements that could be made in this area.

SECRETARY GATES. It is a procedure that many persons work on for many months. You start with military requirements at a service level. You go through the service's priority review under their comptroller and senior military people. You go through various interested Assistant Secretaries of Defense, particularly with Research and Development now with authority in this field. You come up through the Defense comptroller into decisions that we all participate in. It is a long, almost a year-round, process. We have already started to work on the 1962 budget and we do not yet have the fiscal year 1961 budget approved by the Congress.

So it is a laborious and difficult process. It has one collateral advantage, and that is you learn an awful lot about the programs and business when you go through it. People become very well informed.

Senator, the only improvements I can think of we are already making. Last year, Mr. McElroy brought the JCS into the budget discussions in a specific manner for the first time. I intend to do this, too.

The other one is that we are going to try to have an earlier and greater participation in the budget procedure on the part of the Assistant Secretary for International Security Affairs, which will put the foreign-policy implications into the budget earlier in the Pentagon's planning than it has been heretofore.

We have made a great deal of progress in apportionment in the years I have been here. It used to be almost unbelievably difficult to get apportionment procedures through rapidly. I think now the apportionments come through reasonably promptly.

The Secretary of Defense in Partisan Politics

SENATOR JACKSON. Suppose that both political parties agreed in their platforms or otherwise, *first*, that in the selection of people in the national security field, partisan politics would not be considered—at least not as the fundamental criterion in the selection of people for the job and, *second*, that once they were selected, they would stay out of partisan political activity.

SECRETARY GATES. I would be happy to say what I think.

Over the years that I have been familiar with the problem—and by that I mean starting before World War II and earlier—there have been many instances when people of opposition parties have held office in the Department of Defense, or in the service departments before the Department of Defense was created. There are people today in this position. I think this has been fine.

As far as I am concerned, I would be in accord with any resolution or guidance that the Senate would give a new President to the effect that partisan politics should not be paramount or be decisive in terms of an appointee in the Department of Defense.

SENATOR JACKSON. I am pleased to hear you make that statement. I would hope that both political parties, during the coming conventions, would lay down some general policy rules on this. As far as I am concerned, this would not be construed as reflecting on any one administration, because, as a matter of history, it does not. These things have occurred in all administrations.

SECRETARY GATES. The other part of your question has always been difficult for me. I would prefer personally, and most of my associates would prefer, to be disassociated from any political activity while holding office in the Department of Defense. As a matter of fact, I have made a few speeches to Republican audiences— one or two for money-raising when I was in the Navy Department —but I believe direct political activity is unwise.

SENATOR JACKSON. It is not good politics sometimes.

SECRETARY GATES. Except—this is the balance that I do not know quite how to appraise—that the administration, whichever administration it may be, has to depend on its statutory appointees to defend its programs, particularly when they are under attack.

SENATOR JACKSON. I agree that the administration, through its Secretaries, should defend its position with all its vigor. My question refers to direct political activities.

SECRETARY GATES. In my judgment, we have too big a procurement program, too big a cross-section of American industry, too big a responsibility to nonpartisan committees of the Congress—bipartisan and nonpartisan—to engage in direct political activity. I hope we do not.

Officer Exchange between State and Defense

SENATOR JACKSON. Secretary Herter suggested to this Subcommittee that it would be worth while to have a greater exchange of personnel between the departments of State and Defense. He suggested that "the men loaned would function as an integral part of the host agency, contributing their own special knowledge, and would return to their parent agency at the end of the tour with the broadened perspective acquired through shoulder-to-shoulder work." What are your comments on that?

SECRETARY GATES. I have been discussing this with him: we

agree completely. This is an objective we both have and hope to put into effect, at least in a preliminary pilot plant manner, to see how it will develop. I think only good can come from it.

I would be opposed to putting a man in a ten-year position in the State Department. I think he ought to go in for a normal tour of duty and then go back to his service. On that basis, I think there would be very few sensible arguments against the interchange. There might be some feeling about it because people like to stay in their own competitive world.

We should be careful not to create a special kind of military corps, a State Department–Military Corps of some character or another, or an elite group of officers that would be sort of different. But I think we should put in the career promotional system for good officers the opportunity for some of them to become better informed on political-military matters.

An Above-the-Department Staff Agency?

SENATOR MUSKIE. There is a point made by W. W. Rostow in the *Harvard Alumni Bulletin* of May 25, 1957, which I think is worthy of comment. He says: "High level policy tends to emerge in one of two forms: either as general statements so broad that operators can go on doing what they are doing, interpreting policy statements as they will; or as tough, practical compromises, allocating money or other scarce resources, in which the pattern of policy is much less important to the outcome than the bargaining weight of the negotiators. First-class ideas cannot emerge from a committee of hard-pressed bureaucrats any more than a first-class book can be written by a committee of professors."

SECRETARY GATES. This is something one has to think about. He is talking about the whole philosophy of doing business in Washington. Certainly there are sometimes compromises that are tough and practical, and certainly there are sometimes statements that are too broad. We try and battle out policy statements so that they are definitive. But when you cover a very complex and comprehensive field, you sometimes have to leave them broad.

I would say this statement is neither true nor false. It perhaps carries a connotation that is a little more critical than I would be, and I would not agree that some of the things exist. I think there have been some first-class ideas produced by coordination at top level. I do not know of any committee that has written any books.

I think this is a generalized statement that would be better if it had made a more specific analysis.

SENATOR MUSKIE. Mr. Rostow has made his case so badly, in your judgment, that I hesitate to call your attention to his conclusion. He says; "What shall we conclude? Instinctively—as good Americans—we think first of institutional change; and indeed, the NSC would be vastly improved if it had an independent staff of first-rate men, freed of ties to particular bureaucracies, paid to think in terms of the totality of our policy problem, empowered to lay proposals on the table."

SECRETARY GATES. This is an ivory-tower staff created out of first-rate men freed, apparently, of all experience and association with the problems. I do not believe it should be organized that way.

The National Security Council *

SENATOR JACKSON. From your knowledge of the NSC, how does it work best as an advisory mechanism to the President—when there are fewer people in attendance dealing with a few big issues, or when they cover many issues with many people?

SECRETARY GATES. I would not draw much of a distinction based on the numbers of people present, Mr. Chairman. Sometimes it is smaller than at other times—for example, when important military matters are involved, the service Secretaries and service Chiefs are there; that immediately adds seven people, including the Commandant of the Marine Corps. When we have special briefings for the NSC, we may have experts who have worked on these briefings there to make the presentation. (They do not participate in the policy discussion and usually leave after the briefings are finished.) I would not feel that there was a distinction to be made between the number of people present and the work of the NSC.

SENATOR JACKSON. Let us put it this way. Do you feel that the membership at least should be held down? You don't want it to be a big body if it is going to be advisory to the President?

SECRETARY GATES. No.

SENATOR JACKSON. At times there have been meetings when you could hardly find the statutory members in the crowd. The tendency to bring in a lot of other people is always great in a body like that.

* Testimony delivered to the Subcommittee on National Policy Machinery in executive session, June 13, 1960.

SECRETARY GATES. There have been large meetings of the NSC for special briefings, where a number of responsible people were present and it was important to have them informed of the briefings. But the freedom of discussion has been usually confined to a very modest group.

SENATOR JACKSON. Would you say that the best use of the NSC would be to concentrate on a smaller number of extremely important issues rather than trying to cover many issues?

SECRETARY GATES. I feel that the system we have been using is sound and that items that come before the NSC are of importance. I don't think that I can recall an occasion when we could have disposed of the item in as sensible a manner without bringing it there. Of course, certain items are more important than others. I feel, from my experience, that in principle the NSC has been working well.

SENATOR JACKSON. What about the work of the Operations Coordinating Board? Do you feel it has been functioning well?

SECRETARY GATES. Yes. My personal experience with the OCB was limited to a very short period. That was during the time I was Deputy Secretary of Defense from last June until December. I was one of the group of Under Secretaries who attended the OCB Wednesday lunch meetings. I felt the meetings I participated in were most helpful for coordinating the actions and implementation of NSC policies. Those were always attended, in those days, by Bob Murphy from State and the AEC man and the ICA representative and the Under Secretary of the Treasury. I thought they were helpful and useful; out of them came a good method of follow-through. I think the OCB mechanism or something like it is vital to assist in coordinating the implementation of NSC policies.

SENATOR MUSKIE. Do disagreements within the Defense Department on important matters rise to the level of the National Security Council as freely as they should?

SECRETARY GATES. Of course, the National Security Council is not the only time that the Joint Chiefs and myself meet with the President. We meet on many other occasions. If there is any strong disagreement that affects important military policy, I would say that a Chief should present his case to the President directly, and he does. Frequently, they have expressed strong opinions in the NSC, when they are present for the military discussions. Also, the Chairman of the Joint Chiefs of Staff is a regular attendant at the NSC meetings, and he feels it part of his responsibility, if it is solely a military discussion, to recognize the position of a given service as being different from his own, and to state it. So the service's strong conviction on an important subject is available.

SENATOR MUSKIE. Is there a major impact, or an important impact, made by the National Security Council on the actual defense program?

SECRETARY GATES. From the standpoint of the policy of the defense program, there is a most major contribution made. The major defense policy is approved by the National Security Council and the President. This is the policy within which the defense programs are developed. If a unified commander has a strong point of view about something he wants to do unilaterally, we don't take this to the National Security Council. We try to handle this within our own responsibilities. If it is so strong that it worries us, that we feel we need broader review, then we seek the broader review. We would not take a speech or something of that character beyond the Department of Defense if we felt that we had confidence in our own collective thinking that we should not do so.

When any person with grave responsibility can bring an additional light on an important subject where I myself have a doubt as to my own wisdom or the wisdom of the majority or minority of my advisers, I think the only sensible thing to do is to get that advice and throw all the light you can on the subject. I would not know how to operate any other way.

SENATOR MUSKIE. On the implementation of policy, the Council tends to accept your judgment and that of the Joint Chiefs of Staff?

SECRETARY GATES. And the President. If someone wants to contest that in an important matter, then it could be reopened. It does not stay static.

We have a responsibility to carry out policy actions. There is a check-and-balance follow-through. Major policy decisions are reviewed annually. I think that policies are reviewed by the OCB on a six-month basis. I have a responsibility to see that NSC policy actions are carried out. If they require coordination by the OCB as determined by the guidance of the NSC, that is done.

SENATOR MUSKIE. A question on the general value of the NSC: as an important department head and an experienced one, do you feel that NSC gives you thinking time that you would not otherwise utilize as effectively or even have at all?

SECRETARY GATES. The mechanism is this: The International Security Affairs charter, which includes more than just international security affairs, established two offices composed of nine professional people, full time, on NSC responsibilities. The first review is held in those offices. The subject is then farmed out to the services, which have their own departments and their own people on NSC matters, in the politico-military division of the military staff under the Chief. The service Secretary himself has a large amount of responsibility. Then the services' positions are reassembled by ISA and reviewed in close consultation with the Joint Staff. This position is taken up at a Planning Board session (twice a week) at which the Assistant Secretary of Defense is the Defense representative. It is brought to the Under Secretary or to myself, usually to both of us, and we review it with the people who have worked on it. This meeting, which may last any amount of time, depending on the item, then prepares me to represent the Department at the NSC meeting.

From there, through the record of action, it goes back to the Secretary of Defense, to the services, and to the OCB working groups, which may develop plans and may even come back to me for further action at a later date.

So this is the mechanism we use. It is considered of major personal importance to a service Chief and to a service Secretary and to myself, that we participate thoroughly in the position that the Department of Defense will take.

SENATOR MUSKIE. Through this process, is there a tendency to emphasize compromise and accommodation at the expense of maintaining sharp alternatives?

SECRETARY GATES. I think there is usually a fairly strong position involved if we want to take it forward for action, and we take it forward in articulate and strong form. If there is a matter that is not quite that important, one that perhaps could be done one way as well as another way, then we say so when we bring it up. But if it is a strong position, it is then the Department of Defense position—representing the military departments, the Joint Chiefs of Staff, and the civilians who participated in it.

The Executive Office of the President*

NELSON A. ROCKEFELLER

*Nelson A. Rockefeller, Governor of New York,
served as Chairman of President Eisenhower's Advisory Committee on Government Organization
from 1953 to the end of 1958. In 1958, he was appointed consultant to the McElroy Committee on
the Organization of the Defense Department. His
government service in Washington under three Presidents includes his service as Assistant Secretary of
State for American Republic Affairs under President
Roosevelt, Chairman of the International Development Advisory Board under President Truman, and
Under Secretary of Health, Education, and Welfare
and Special Assistant to President Eisenhower for
Foreign Affairs.*

I deeply appreciate this opportunity to appear before you. This
Subcommittee is performing an outstanding service to the nation.

The nation's problems, the world's problems, press upon the
policy-makers in Washington with ever-increasing urgency and in
ever-growing complexity. In seeking solutions to these problems,
there can be no substitute for able men in government—men of
vision, of capacity, of courage. But not even the best of men can
perform to the fullness of their abilities, nor will men of ability be
attracted to government or encouraged to stay in government, if
inadequate organization frustrates accomplishment. In its extensive
exploration into the question of improving the organization of
government, this Subcommittee is addressing itself—importantly,
constructively, and with nonpartisan objectivity—to a fundamental
need of this government in dealing with a world of danger, of op-

* Testimony delivered to the Subcommittee on National Policy Machinery,
July 1, 1960.

portunity, and of fantastically rapid change. That need is to provide the framework within which able men can perform the great deeds demanded by the challenges of our times.

I know from personal experience that no man is more deeply concerned with this question than President Eisenhower. During the six years of my chairmanship of the President's Advisory Committee on Government Organization, fourteen reorganization plans presented by the President were adopted by the Congress. The President's vision, breadth of concept, and creativity made possible the substantial advances in government organization achieved in recent years. In addition, they profoundly influenced the thought behind specific proposals I shall make to this Subcommittee, although, naturally, I alone assume responsibility in recommending these proposals for your consideration.

With recommendations from the President, the Congress at its next session, as a first order of business, should set about adapting the government's machinery to the needs, the urgencies, the demands for decisive action that the times require. I am confident that the work of this Subcommittee will be of great value in accomplishing this.

As a fundamental step to be taken either at this Congress or at the next, I recommend the extension of the Reorganization Act of 1949, which expired last year. This legislation provided the basis for the reorganization plans adopted in the last decade and, in my opinion, should be renewed.

Governmental reorganization is necessarily a matter of cooperation between the legislative and executive branches. Understandably, it is a matter in which many toes will get stepped on, many vested interests within the government feel imperiled. The blunt truth is that—despite all past progress—the present structure of the federal government is still not geared to support the President in developing and executing integrated policy, thoughtfully and purposefully, either in the complex areas of national security and foreign policy or in the equally complex area of domestic affairs.

Few realize the tremendous load the President carries in his multiple responsibilities as Chief of State, Chief Executive, Commander in Chief of the Armed Forces, the man constitutionally responsible for the conduct of our foreign policy, and leader of his political party. More than fifty departments and agencies of the government report directly to him. Their number imposes upon him an almost impossible burden—to resolve conflicting approaches and divergent advice, and, from such sources, select and set a determined course of action.

In fact, international affairs involve, one way or another, the activity and responsibility of every department of our government. There are also some eighteen independent agencies, as well as sundry boards and commissions, involved in aspects of international affairs. The field of foreign economic aid alone involves four government agencies and six international financial organizations.

In an effort to bring order to this array of agencies, a host of interdepartmental and interagency committees has been set up. These have come to number approximately 160 in the field of international affairs alone.

This overelaborate pattern of interdepartmental committees has been designed over the years in an earnest effort to meet the legion of complex problems in both foreign and domestic affairs. The simple fact is this: the committees of a democratic government cannot hope to meet or master these problems by simply trying to outnumber them. The critical need is for a revamped structure of government. The structure of our government today too often moves slowly, even sluggishly, to meet this world of swift-moving change. It tends to be stiff and static—when it should be quick, alert, and creative. There is, therefore, a growing public awareness and concern about the structure of government and the efficiency of its decision-making process. And one great proof of this public concern and interest is the existence and the work of this Subcommittee.

With all this in mind, I deeply believe that the time has come when we can look forward to achieving important reforms at the next session of the Congress. I have no illusions about the complexity of these tasks. In the light of my own experience in federal government, and having undertaken, as Governor of New York, that state government's first reorganization in thirty years, I am well aware of the toughness of the problems. Yet, I believe very strongly that both the clear need of the nation and the quickened concern of the people make this a necessary, and a realistic, time for action.

Let us proceed, then, to the major specific areas of action, both foreign and domestic. In both these areas, the structure of government demands reorganization to assist the President in wisely formulating and effectively executing national policy. As early as 1955, former President Herbert Hoover recognized this sweeping need by suggesting the creation of two appointed Vice Presidents with specific responsibilities respectively for foreign and domestic affairs. This problem was given active and detailed study by the President's Advisory Committee on Government Organization, while I was chairman of that committee.

I welcome this opportunity to make the following recommendations in these two important fields:

1. Foreign affairs and national security: (*a*) creation of the post of First Secretary of Government to assist the President in the exercise of his authority in this whole area; (*b*) further reorganization of the Defense Department to achieve unified doctrine, planning, and command.

2. Domestic affairs: (*a*) creation of the post of Executive Assistant to the President, to be head of a newly created Office of Executive Management; (*b*) consolidation, in certain areas, at the departmental and agency level, of functions now scattered among various Government agencies, particularly in such important fields as transportation and water resources.

FOREIGN AFFAIRS AND NATIONAL SECURITY

Let us examine how further—and more forceful—support may be given to the President in his constitutional responsibility for the formulation, coordination, and conduct of foreign affairs.

The Problem

The problem is too complex to be soluble simply by adding more authority or more power or more functions to the Department of State. Foreign operations involve the Department of Defense and other major departments and agencies—each with its own special concern with, and attitude toward, international problems.

The crux of the problem is to help to develop a coordinated Presidential policy and program which can then be administered, on a day-to-day basis, by the existing agencies of government. The proliferation of agencies and committees has tended to increase and complicate—rather than ease and clarify—the burden upon the President to define and direct policy. The reason is obvious. The more numerous and varied the sources of divergent advice and advocacy—from departments, agencies, committees and individuals —the less chance or time is left to the President for reflective, overall, long-range defining of purpose and planning of policy.

The proper role of the committee, in our government, is a subtle and delicate one. The system of committees works well, of course, in the Congress; it is basic to the legislative process, providing machinery for concession and consensus as well as means for mustering votes for final legislative decision. And committees also have a proper and important place in the executive branch—either by sharing counsel among those empowered to act or by conducting *ad hoc* studies on specific problems.

But excessive government by committee can be anything but constructive. In the field of executive action, it can reduce the level of government action to the least bold or imaginative—to the lowest common denominator among many varying positions. In such circumstances, policy may be determined not for the sake of its rightness but for the sake of agreement. And then the bold and imaginative action most needed, in these critical times, becomes least probable or possible.

The Objectives

The essential objectives are three.

First, in support and furtherance of our national purpose, we must integrate fully, at the Presidential level, the international political, diplomatic, economic and social, military, informational, cultural and psychological aspects of foreign affairs.

Second, we also must relate and integrate these matters—from the perspective of the responsibility of the Presidency—with all of our compelling domestic concerns—economic or social, financial or regulatory—as all these affect our national conduct in the world.

Third, we must provide the governmental structure that can effectively assist the President in developing objectives and policies, in all the area of foreign policy and national security, so clear and so thoughtful that they will give unified and purposeful direction to America's unique role in serving—and enhancing—the future of freedom.

The Recommendations

To achieve these objectives—equally vital to our national security and our world role—I recommend two broad courses of action.

1. I recommend creation of the post of First Secretary of the Government to assist the President in exercise of his constitu-

tional responsibility and authority in all the area of national security and international affairs.

(*a*) The First Secretary should be appointed by the President, subject to the confirmation of the Senate.

(*b*) He should have statutory designation as Executive Chairman of the National Security Council.

(*c*) He should exercise authority as delegated to him by the President, and be subject to withdrawal of such authority by, and at the will of, the President.

(*d*) He should be empowered, at the discretion of the President, to act for the President in international matters at the prime ministerial level, with the Secretary of State operating on the level of the ministers of foreign affairs.

(*e*) He should have a staff of his own and be empowered to use and reorganize all of the interdepartmental planning machinery of the government in the area of national security and foreign affairs.

While the First Secretary, deriving his authority from the President and acting on his behalf, would have a status above that of the Cabinet, the operating responsibilities of Cabinet officers would not be changed. Thus, the Secretary of State would continue to be in charge of the day-to-day conduct of diplomacy. So, too, the Secretary of Defense would continue to be in the direct line of Presidential command of the armed forces.

As Executive Chairman of the National Security Council, the First Secretary could be delegated the authority, by executive order or by legislation, to appoint the Chairmen of such supporting groups as the Operations Coordinating Board, the Council on Foreign Economic Policy, and the National Advisory Council on International Monetary and Financial Problems.

2. I recommend the reorganization of defense planning and command to achieve, under the President, unified doctrine and unified direction of forces.

(*a*) The Chairman of the Joint Chiefs of Staff should be designated principal military adviser to the Secretary of Defense and the President, and be responsible for development of over-all strategic doctrine.

(*b*) The staff of the Joint Chiefs should be organized on a unified basis under direct authority of the Chairman.

(*c*) All officers above the rank of brigadier general or the equivalent should be designated officers of the Armed Forces of the United States—not the individual service of their earlier careers—and their promotion should be placed in the control of the Department of Defense.

(d) Full authority should be given to the Secretary of Defense over all military research, development, and procurement, so that he may assure the most productive utilization of research and development funds.

(e) The budget process of the Defense Department should be revised so that Congress appropriates all funds to the Secretary, thereby fixing in him a focus of fiscal responsibility similar to that held by other departments.

DOMESTIC AFFAIRS

The urgencies are as clear and great in the area of domestic affairs as in the areas of foreign affairs and national security. Here, too, the President needs the service and support of a structure of government assisting him more effectively to define national purpose and execute national policy, in meeting the swiftness and the complexity of the problems and challenges of our time.

The Problems

Such is the nature of this period of history that the problems confronting the government have seemed to multiply even faster than the agencies created to cope with them. To be specific:

There is the sheer number of departments and agencies reporting to the President—in essentially domestic affairs, no less than eight departments and some forty agencies.

There is the ever-widening scope of problems confronted within the Executive Office of the President itself. This Office includes such diverse duties as those of the Bureau of the Budget, the President's Assistant for Personnel Management, other specialized officials within the White House Office, the Office of Civil and Defense Mobilization, and the Council of Economic Advisers.

There is the constant and ever more difficult task of resolving conflicts between program objectives and budgetary limitations.

There is the ever-increasing volume of legislation pending in the Congress each year, including legislation proposed by the President—all reflecting new problems, freshly and forcefully challenging all departments of government.

And there is the need for thoughtful long-range planning and development of policy—made ever more difficult, and ever more necessary, by problems ever more complex.

The Objective

The President alone simply cannot undertake to meet the volume of problems and functions today demanding his attention, study, and action. To ignore this would be to strain the structure of our government at its apex—to allow it to be weak where it must be strong. The essential objective, then, is to give to the President a strong supporting structure within his own Office for policy formulation and concrete decision.

A second objective is to assure that, at the level of the departments and agencies themselves, there is an organizational structure adapted to meeting the key domestic problems of today.

The Recommendations

1. I recommend the creation of the post of Executive Assistant to the President and Director of the Office of Executive Management, to assist in planning and management in domestic affairs.

There should be created immediately under the President a new Office of Executive Management. Five key functions should be transferred to the new Office of Executive Management, to be carried out by five bureaus created within the new office. Each bureau should be under the direction of a noncareer official appointed by the President. The Director of the new Office would report directly to the President.

(a) Bureau of the Budget: functions—budget formulation and administration.

(b) Bureau of Legislative Clearance and Coordination: functions—review, clear, coordinate, and develop legislation proposed by the executive branch and the administration's position with respect to other legislation pending in Congress.

(c) Bureau of Program and Planning: functions—to develop and coordinate recommendations concerning executive branch programs, including participation in long-range studies and planning.

(d) Bureau of Organization and Management: functions—coordination and improvement of the organization and management functions of the executive branch, including accounting and statistical programs.

(e) Bureau of Personnel Management: functions—assistance to the President in exercising his leadership in personnel management throughout the executive branch.

The Office of Executive Management, if created along these lines, would serve the President more effectively than the present structures of government in the general management of administrative matters—budgetary, personnel, planning, and organizational activities. The Office would assume the functions of various units within the Executive Office of the President and would remove over a period of time, the need for numerous temporary staff arrangements established to meet special problems.

Even with an ideal organizational structure at the White House level, the President's responsibilities with respect to domestic affairs cannot, any more than in the field of national defense, be effectively performed without sound organization at the departmental and agency level. All too often, the location of a particular function within a department or agency is more a matter of history than of logic. Thus, in a number of areas, improved governmental machinery is essential to sound policy development in meeting the critical and emerging problems of today and tomorrow. In these areas:

2. I recommend the consolidation of functions that are now scattered among various government departments and agencies, particularly in such important fields as transportation and water resources.

The field of transportation is a good example because of its critical importance to the growth of our economy in time of peace and to the defense of our nation in time of war. In spite of general recognition of the importance of transportation, we still do not have today a single focal point within the Federal Government for the formulation of over-all national transportation policy, accompanied by broad powers to develop such policy and coordinate the activities of other agencies.

To remedy this, I recommend the creation of a new Department of Transportation, to which would be transferred all governmental transportation functions now located both inside and outside the Commerce Department. These transferred functions would include all the responsibilities of the Federal Aviation Agency, as well as the present promotional and administrative functions of the regulatory agencies: the Interstate Commerce Commission, the Civil Aeronautics Board, and the Federal Maritime Board.

Another example—equally clear—is the area of water resources policy, where a dispersion of responsibilities has made the development of a coordinated and coherent government policy very difficult.

CONCLUSION

I have outlined—briefly—a program of some specific measures to assist the President and the executive branch of the Federal Government in meeting the clear responsibilities and compelling challenges before it. I believe such measures will enable the executive branch, in all areas of national policy, to give direction more firm and unified, and decision more swift and thoughtful.

No citizens are more keenly aware than you, gentlemen, of what is ultimately at stake here. The matters discussed seem technical and mechanical. They rise, in ultimate meaning, far above this level. They are tests—practical tests—of whether free government can work, and can work well. They are tests that come at a time when the processes of freedom—the workings of democracy—stand under fire and under challenge in the world at large. They are tests that we, as a people and as a nation, can and must meet.

Effectiveness of the Policy Process

SENATOR MUSKIE. In your judgment, is our government now producing decisions adequate to our needs?

GOVERNOR ROCKEFELLER. I think the mechanism is such that some decisions that should be made never come to the point where they can be made. In other words, the President is the only one who can make certain decisions; the process is such the issues do not come up to him; they are compromised in committees, where I think in many cases compromise is not the right answer. A decision should be taken by somebody with authority to make it.

In many cases, we are not making decisions on issues that nobody knows about because they are never up for decision. In other cases, decisions are made where all the pertinent information is not brought to bear. This is a very difficult problem because these things are so completely interrelated, domestic and foreign and all aspects of foreign. I think the mechanism I suggested would give an extension to the President's arm and authority, which would be sufficiently organized to accomplish on a more effective basis what the President tries to accomplish now but which the present mechanism makes very difficult.

SENATOR MUSKIE. What you are saying, then, is that our government is not now producing decisions adequate to our needs, but that the fault lies in the machinery. Would you say that it lies wholly in the machinery?

GOVERNOR ROCKEFELLER. Obviously, human weakness all along the line is bound to slow down the decision-making process. If somebody makes a recommendation that is not the most penetrating or wisest, then the final decision obviously is not going to be as good as it should be. I think, considering human weaknesses and considering the machinery, the best job under the circumstances is being done. I think the changes I suggest are urgent, though, if we are going effectively to understand the implications of actions abroad and actions in our own country.

SENATOR MUSKIE. Would you agree, and I think you do, from your statement, that the constitutional powers of the President in foreign policy and defense are such that the Congress can and should do nothing to dilute those powers?

GOVERNOR ROCKEFELLER. I certainly agree with that.

SENATOR MUSKIE. Thus, we cannot and should not undertake to create machinery that the President would not want to use.

GOVERNOR ROCKEFELLER. I agree with that.

SENATOR MUSKIE. As a matter of fact, he can't be forced to use it if he does not wish to use it.

GOVERNOR ROCKEFELLER. That is right.

The Role of the First Secretary

SENATOR JAVITS. Your suggestion for a First Secretary interests me enormously. I think it is a very original and provocative idea. I would like to point to the fact that you say the First Secretary should have a staff of his own and be empowered to use and reorganize all of the departmental planning machinery of the government in the area of national security and foreign affairs. Is it your idea that he shall be confined to the area of national security and foreign affairs or that he should also cover domestic affairs?

GOVERNOR ROCKEFELLER. I don't mean him to cover domestic affairs except to be responsible for the reconciliation of differences between our domestic interests and our foreign or international interests. This is one of the areas of conflict that gets compromised in government and that needs, in my opinion, to be dealt with more decisively and more rapidly than the committee system allows. The longer a problem or conflict is left, the more difficulty develops from it; the faster decisions are made that are sound and that reflect the best over-all interests of the country, the better off we would be.

SENATOR JAVITS. So, unlike the French system, where you do have a strong President with a Prime Minister, you would have the First Secretary confine himself to the coordination of national security and foreign affairs with domestic affairs.

GOVERNOR ROCKEFELLER. I think the executive assistant to the President in charge of the Office of Executive Management would be very helpful in working with him. Our domestic activities enter much more immediately into the economic, political, and social life of our people. I don't think you could superimpose over the departmental decisions in the domestic field the same kind of delegation by the President that you can in the international field.

SENATOR KEATING. I am very much interested in your suggestion about a First Secretary. Your concept, am I correct, is sort of an Assistant President to make decisions in some cases and in certain areas final decisions, unless they are overturned by the President?

GOVERNOR ROCKEFELLER. I think it would be safer to refer to him as an assistant to the President rather than Assistant President. I think we have to be very careful that there is no differentiation or subtraction of the President's powers.

SENATOR KEATING. I agree with that. The First Secretary concept is certainly preferable in my mind to the one suggested by former President Hoover for a Vice President in charge of domestic affairs and a Vice President in charge of foreign affairs. I do like the title "First Secretary." It is his functions that I am interested in. Your idea is that he would have the power to resolve a conflict between the heads of various government departments.

GOVERNOR ROCKEFELLER. Yes. I would not limit the First Secretary to being simply an arbitrator between departments. I think there is a very important need for the encouragement of centralized thinking, planning, and strategy that involves all the factors. There is no spot for that today in a staff that can be used and led by someone who has this kind of delegated authority. I think he could play a very important role on the positive side as well as being an arbitrator and decision-maker in the event of disputes.

SENATOR KEATING. One objective or result of it would be, in your thinking, that the President himself would have more time to think?

GOVERNOR ROCKEFELLER. That is correct. He would have more basic information that was not compromised and watered down to use in connection with his thinking.

SENATOR JACKSON. I have been interested in what you had to say about the First Secretary. I believe Mr. Eisenhower has spoken, too, of the importance at least of seriously considering this. Do you have the impression that he feels that it might be helpful?

GOVERNOR ROCKEFELLER. Beyond saying "Yes, I do," I would not want to elaborate. I do think he does.

SENATOR JACKSON. You had an opportunity while serving as an Assistant to the President to acquire knowledge of the problems that are inherent in the Office of the President under present conditions.

GOVERNOR ROCKEFELLER. And, as Chairman of President Eisenhower's Committee on Government Organization, I worked with him on this problem.

The Role of the Vice President

SENATOR CLARK. Do you not think we ought to make a better utilization in our organizational structure of the office of Vice President, an elected public official, who I don't think should be relegated to merely presiding over the Senate? I wonder if you have given any thought in your reorganizational suggestions as to what could be done with the Vice President.

GOVERNOR ROCKEFELLER. We studied this question at great length, as to how the Vice President could play an active role in the executive branch. But all of the experts in the field interpret the Constitution as barring anybody with a position in the legislative branch of government—which he does, as presiding officer of the Senate—from holding any office (policy, administrative, or operational) in the executive branch of the government. So you have a constitutional problem. If you want to sponsor a constitutional amendment, then maybe we could get a change in that structure.

SENATOR CLARK. Don't you think, though, that the President could constitutionally delegate a number of important functions to the Vice President temporarily, just as he could delegate them to an appointed officer in the executive branch?

GOVERNOR ROCKEFELLER. That was not the conclusion we came to in studying this question. It was impossible. Some of the functions we have been talking about for the First Secretary Mr.

Hoover suggested be handled by an appointed Vice President. We studied very carefully if they could be handled by an elected Vice President, and the consensus was not only that it could not be constitutionally, but that it would raise all kinds of questions administratively within the executive branch of the government. It is not like a state, where, when the Governor goes out of the state, the Lieutenant Governor is Acting Governor. When the President goes out of the country, the Vice President is not Acting President. He has no more authority than before.

SENATOR JACKSON. The Vice President is an important member of the National Security Council, under the National Security Act of 1947. What other duties might be acceptable for him? He can participate in an advisory capacity. He does have by statute a responsibility that far transcends his constitutional duty. As a matter of fact, these other duties take up 90 to 95 per cent of his time under certain conditions.

GOVERNOR ROCKEFELLER. What we have been talking about here is not an advisory function. We are talking about authority delegated from the President to make policy and operating decisions in the government.

SENATOR CLARK. I was thinking that the President could delegate to the Vice President a great deal of the quasi-ceremonial duty that takes the President all around the world in the interest of goodwill. He could delegate to him certain diplomatic negotiations if he saw fit and generally utilize him as an arm of the executive to a much greater extent than presently. I think this has been done during the last seven and a half years quite substantially, would you not agree?

GOVERNOR ROCKEFELLER. Yes, I do. You will find if you study the inner workings of the executive branch that it is one thing to undertake ceremonial functions, but it is another thing to undertake diplomatic negotiations where there are others who have responsibility for those negotiations. It does lead to trouble and difficulties and confusion.

The National Security Council*

SENATOR JACKSON. Some witnesses have indicated to us that the NSC has tried to do too much, in the sense of involving itself with too many policy questions, some of not great importance. They

* Testimony delivered to the Subcommittee on National Policy Machinery in executive session, July 1, 1960.

would like the NSC to concentrate on a smaller number of important policy questions. What is your general idea on that?

Would you preface your answer by stating for the record your association with the NSC and its subordinate agencies?

GOVERNOR ROCKEFELLER. I attended all the NSC meetings for a year, in 1955, when I was working for the President as Special Assistant. I attended many of the Planning Board meetings and had a representative from my office who sat in on those. I was Vice Chairman of the Operations Coordinating Board. Then I was chairman of a planning coordination group which was established when I came to the White House to develop a more imaginative, creative approach to the carrying out of NSC policy.

Prior to my arrival, and I think it was the Director of the Bureau of the Budget who happened to be a sponsor of this, they felt that there was a need for a more imaginative pursuit of objectives stated in NSC papers than was developed by the departments, particularly from the psychological point of view. Therefore, this planning coordination group was set up with representation from State, Defense, and CIA. It had certain secret assignments but it also had this broad assignment. However, this was bitterly resented by the State Department, which felt it was an invasion of its authority and responsibility. The result was that the lack of cooperation from that area made effective functioning impossible after about six or eight months. You can go against a wall of opposition so far, and then it is useless. So I recommended the abandonment of the operation. But it was evident that there was a feeling that more creative and imaginative thinking was needed. I think this is the kind of thing the First Secretary could put into this.

I made some recommendations about the Operations Coordinating Board that were subsequently carried out—namely, that the President's representative be chairman and not the Under Secretary of State; that it have a staff of its own and not a borrowed staff from the departments; and that it be given other than advisory authority. (It is advisory now. That was *not* carried out.)

Going back to your question, I would say it has two phases. Structurally, the Planning Board is so constituted that it is like these other committees we were discussing. A major question is presented to the Planning Board, and the various interested parties—namely, the departments, each with its own role in relation to the area under discussion—work carefully with highly skilled representatives to get language into the position paper that, while it does not violate the objective, protects their own position and their own special responsibility—I don't say interest—in this field. You get a watered-down version before it comes to the NSC, and language that permits considerably more freedom than would appear on a superficial reading of the document.

SENATOR JACKSON. There is a tendency to compromise?

GOVERNOR ROCKEFELLER. To compromise and also to get permissive language that is not too obvious in the phraseology. This is quite an art, this business.

SENATOR JACKSON. You feel, I take it, that what should occur is that these matters should be presented to the NSC from the Planning Board with sharp alternatives, so that you can encourage debate and discussion.

GOVERNOR ROCKEFELLER. Yes. If you have a man who has stature, and the staff to support him of the kind that I was suggesting, and who has the responsibility for this mechanism and these other mechanisms, he can prevent the watering-down of a paper by simply taking more of a responsibility in its development, or, as you suggest, by presenting alternatives. If he rather than a department presents those alternatives, they are going to carry more weight. When the President comes into the meeting, and this paper is there, he will have been briefed by the First Secretary and will know the background. Also, the alternatives and the strength of the paper, in my opinion, will be increased very importantly, because the First Secretary could make decisions in the process of developing this material that today nobody has the authority to make.

SENATOR JACKSON. What you are saying, as I interpret it, is that where there are critical problems, the various points of view should be presented so that the President can exercise his constitutional responsibility and make the decision. I gather you feel that there is a tendency sometimes in the departmental process to save the President work—which certainly is helpful where problems are not highly important and where they really should not be passed on to him—but that there is a vital area relating to national security that is a constitutional responsibility of the President, and that problems in this area should be presented to him in such a way that he can see the clear-cut alternatives and then make the decision.

GOVERNOR ROCKEFELLER. I feel very strongly that way. I think the public does not recognize the degree to which the Planning Board really does 95 per cent of the work. It is not very often that a paper is changed by the National Security Council. The real work is done in the Planning Board, on these position papers; very few items are taken up without a paper, and very few papers are substantially changed.

SENATOR JACKSON. Did you get the general impression that the tendency was to agree and compromise in the Planning Board so that all the departmental interests would be taken care of, rather than to develop papers with sharp alternatives so there would be an encouragement of debate and discussion?

GOVERNOR ROCKEFELLER. I think that almost is the necessity under the structure and system they have.

SENATOR JACKSON. You feel that in part, at least, the way the Planning Board is set up generates this result?

GOVERNOR ROCKEFELLER. Yes, because there is nobody with authority to make a decision when there are differences of opinion. Therefore, the paper can only get done by compromise. I think there needs to be a strong Presidential leadership at that level, the Planning Board level.

SENATOR JACKSON. We have had testimony suggesting that the Secretary of State should be in a position of primacy in this area—the orchestra leader dealing with all of the elements that go into national security. What do you think of that suggestion as an alternative to your concept of the First Secretary?

GOVERNOR ROCKEFELLER. If you could go back to the original concept of Secretary of State, when he had the national seal and so forth, he was in a sense in this position. However, if you now elevate him to a position of super-Cabinet responsibility—which this involves, because he has to be able to make decisions between departments—you then have a Cabinet officer with a constitutional responsibility delegated by the Congress in his function, arbitrating in a dispute between himself and another department. So he is sitting over himself making decisions. It is pretty tough to have the party in a discussion finally say, "All right, I decide I am right," rather than a third party who is not responsible for these immediate operations, exercising that authority on behalf of the President.

Another reason is that if the Secretary of State is elevated to the concept we are talking about here, it would put such an additional load on him that he would not be able to negotiate with his counterparts, the ministers of foreign affairs, and would be largely precluded from going to conferences. Then you would have to have somebody else, a Deputy Secretary of State—and I think the ministers of foreign affairs of other countries would feel they were being slighted if the Secretary of State himself did not come. So you run into a very serious time factor on this.

We had thought of setting up a Department of Foreign Affairs in the Department of State. You could organize the State Department with a Department of Foreign Affairs, a Department of Economic Affairs, and a Department of Informational Affairs. But it would be very hard to establish the authority and prestige of that Department internationally, because the Secretary of State is the man they want to see and talk to.

We felt it was easier in the long run to create a new office which in a sense goes back to some of the original concepts this nation had in establishing the Secretary of State instead of a Secretary of Foreign Affairs.

SENATOR JACKSON. I gather that what runs through your mind is that if national security is to be properly coordinated, the one who is doing it must in fact be above other Cabinet officials because he will be calling on them and in a sense directing them to do certain things that are essential and necessary to bring about this over-all policy on national security, involving as it does military, economic, political, and psychological factors.

One thing that troubles me about your proposal is whether you would be able to get a good, strong Secretary of State and Secretary of Defense if you have this singular super-Secretary right in the White House.

GOVERNOR ROCKEFELLER. In my opinion, it would facilitate the function of both the other posts. I have been Assistant Secretary of State and had a great deal of contact with the military department through OCB and through the reorganizations and so forth. As a matter of fact, at one time I agreed to become Deputy Secretary of Defense. So I am pretty familiar with their problems. I think a First Secretary would be someone with whom they could discuss their problems and with whom they could sit down, who is more available than the President is, so that they could get these things straightened out at the Presidential level without having to go to the President, which is impossible from the point of view of the limitation on his time. I don't think it would downgrade them. They might think so at first, but their functions and responsibilities are so tremendous they don't need additional prestige. What they need is decisions and time and authority to carry them out. This man could give it to them.

I know this is also true in the domestic field. For instance, when

I was Under Secretary of Health, Education, and Welfare, and Mrs. Hobby was Secretary, we would come on such questions of policy as federal aid to education. We wanted to sit down and talk with somebody in the White House as to what national policy was on this. There was not anybody there who was responsible for that except in the Bureau of the Budget. Of course, their enthusiasm is less than complete for any program that is going to involve more money.

There is very important need for Cabinet officers and their deputies to have somebody in the White House to whom they can go to get policy guidance and who will participate with them in the planning and thinking for the future in other than money terms.

SENATOR MUSKIE. Really this is a super-Cabinet that you are thinking about.

GOVERNOR ROCKEFELLER. President Hoover was perfectly right in the two suggestions he made, except they raise so many taboos because of the Vice President being an elected official.

SENATOR JACKSON. You get into constitutional problems.

GOVERNOR ROCKEFELLER. Yes. I don't think you can put somebody in the domestic scene who has authority over a Cabinet officer because these things are too hot in terms of domestic political life—I don't mean partisan political life—whether water or economics or so forth. A man could serve the President in this area far more effectively than he is now serviced, even though he has I don't know how many dozen special assistants in different fields.

SENATOR JACKSON. To get back to the question I asked, I had the impression in World War II that Mr. Hopkins' role caused some friction with Hull.

GOVERNOR ROCKEFELLER. No question.

SENATOR JACKSON. During the latter years of Mr. Hull's tenure as Secretary of State, I had the impression that he was quite unhappy about Mr. Hopkins' role. This leads me to the question whether an Acheson or a Dulles would accept a First Secretary over them.

GOVERNOR ROCKEFELLER. I talked about this position to Secretary Dulles on various occasions. In fact, I worked with him on the development of this concept. He was completely for this. He visualized himself in that position.

SENATOR JACKSON. You made the answer very easy.

GOVERNOR ROCKEFELLER. That is right. I don't think you have to worry as long as the position is there before people take the other posts. The only difficulty would be to superimpose the First

Secretary over existing personalities. I think it is so needed and so recognized by all that there would not be real difficulty. This will facilitate everybody's work.

SENATOR JACKSON. I want to go back a moment to the Planning Board and the process of developing papers. Unless the principals discuss the paper and alternative courses of action in the NSC, will they really understand what the policy is?

In other words, where you have hard alternatives, and you have debate and discussion, don't you really come up with a final Presidential decision where everyone fully understands the policy? When you attempt to compromise and meld it in with everything, it has something of everything and no one knows what it really means. They each interpret it from their own parochial point of view.

GOVERNOR ROCKEFELLER. I think that is a very fair statement. But in order to have a really intelligent discussion on the kind of question which comes before the National Security Council, in my opinion there has got to be some additional material available. I feel the need for what I call a position room. When you discuss problems in Africa, I would like to see these National Security Council meetings held in a position room. On the walls you would have the pertinent economic factors, a map showing which countries are being discussed, which country has come from colonial status to independence when, what the economic problems are, what the political structures are. I think you have to have certain background information for many of the members of the Council who are not familiar with these questions. They need to have a factual briefing so that they can bring that to bear on the discussion of the paper.

SENATOR JACKSON. As a matter of fact, the way it works out practically, the statutory participants in the NSC are heavily burdened with their own operating responsibilities.

GOVERNOR ROCKEFELLER. That is right. They don't have time to brief themselves. General Marshall used this system a great deal. I thought he did a superb job of understanding the collateral factors relating to the decision in question and in having factual information available and interpreted before the decision was made. Visual presentations are very useful, I think.

SENATOR MUSKIE. With respect to the Planning Board, did you find that there was a tendency for disagreements within a department to be smothered?

GOVERNOR ROCKEFELLER. Yes, before they got to the Planning Board. There is no question. That is natural. Again, if the First

Secretary and his staff are functioning properly, and he controls the mechanism of the interdepartmental agencies related to the National Security Council, he would be aware of that kind of situation and would see that it got the opportunity of reflection.

SENATOR MUSKIE. It strikes me that OCB ought to perform three functions: one, that of liaison in the process of implementing policy; second, to review the effectiveness of the implementation; third, to judge the effectiveness of the implementation. The OCB should therefore have the power or authority to bring to the attention of the NSC and the President the failure to implement adequately. Would you agree with that?

GOVERNOR ROCKEFELLER. I agree completely. I saw that at first hand for a period of a year. There is no question about the wisdom of it. There are thirty-six OCB working groups, and these groups review the programs and appraise them. They are almost exclusively chaired by State Department personnel. It is very hard for someone, no matter how honest and empirical he tries to be, to review the work of his own department and say that it has been a partial failure or an utter failure, and then to call it to the attention of the National Security Council. I think this is one of the weaknesses. I don't blame State for wanting to have their own people as chairmen of these committees, but it does make it difficult—I am not criticizing individuals, it is natural. I worked very hard trying to get independent reviews back to the NSC. But in so doing, I ran into the feeling on the part of the State Department that here I was interfering, and they would go to the President and complain, "That man is causing trouble. He is raising havoc with an orderly, effective procedure."

I think you've put your finger right on it. We have to get fast appraisals, honest appraisals, and have the courage to admit something is not working, a policy is not right, a program is not right, and revise it.

This goes back to your first question, concerning the amount of material that comes before the Security Council. I think myself that too much time is spent on position papers that go for a year; everything is frozen for a year. There needs to be much more flexibility with planning in depth—not just on a calendar basis— that leads to a constant review; and there needs to be somebody who can bring up a question that is not on the calender when things look as though they were going to get hot. The calendar is frozen months ahead.

SENATOR JACKSON. Some of the people we have talked to said

that the NSC process should be tied in more closely with the budgetary process. Do you have any comments on bringing the two more closely together?

GOVERNOR ROCKEFELLER. This is where I think the Office of Executive Management is terribly important. You will have a man there who is over the budget and in a position with the planning group and various other groups under him to sit down and talk with the First Secretary and see that these things are done, so you don't get a purely monetary domination thwarting the execution of agreed-upon policy.

SENATOR JACKSON. If an NSC decision, as approved by the President, is to have meaning and be effective, it requires a budgetary implementation. You feel that the Office of Executive Management might be in a position to provide that?

GOVERNOR ROCKEFELLER. Yes. The head of that office should be able to work with the First Secretary in seeing to it that these things flow. In other words, he is the operating man who sees that these programs don't get bogged down or blocked. He has the responsibility that is one step higher than the Director of the Bureau of the Budget.

MR. PENDLETON. Governor, two conflicting allegations about the operation of the NSC structure have appeared from time to time in the press. One has been discussed here: the compromise of issues before they reach the final level. The other is the overcrowded agenda. Obviously both can't be true.

GOVERNOR ROCKEFELLER. I think both are true. I think there has been too much compromise on the items, and I think there are too many items coming before the group. The agenda—at least when I was there; I can't speak with authority today—was too long. You had to wait in line to get on: the plans were a compromise that in some cases—I won't try to make an estimate of the percentage—did not reflect the best interest of our nation.

MR. PENDLETON. Taking first the question of the overcrowded agenda, could you solve that by bringing fewer problems to the NSC?

GOVERNOR ROCKEFELLER. Yes, I think you can. If there is a person who has the President's authority, delegated by the President to make decisions, I think it would be unnecessary to bring some of these matters before the NSC. I think they could be settled the way you would in any operation. There is a conflict or difference of opinion; a hearing is held; points of view are discussed; and the decision is made. I don't think they need to come before the National Security Council. Some of them are much too complicated to be intelligently decided on by people who are not familiar with the background in a half-hour discussion. These things need to have staff work by the person who has the authority—leading up to his making a decision.

MR. PENDLETON. But the way the NSC operates now, as I understand it, it is consultative to the President. It puts before him decisions to make.

GOVERNOR ROCKEFELLER. That is the concept. In actual practice, the Planning Board makes the decision, in the paper, and it is very seldom that the paper is substantially modified.

MR. PENDLETON. On the question of compromise at the Planning Board level, Mr. Cutler said this: "In my experience, divergencies of views appeared in more than two-thirds of the papers before the NSC." Mr. Gray said, "In fact, more than half the policy statements that are sent to the Council from the Planning Board contain split views, largely on important issues on which one or more of the NSC agencies have indicated a strong divergence of opinion." (This is from an article prepared for delivery at the 1959 annual meeting of the American Political Science Association.) I take it you disagree with their opinions?

GOVERNOR ROCKEFELLER. No, I don't disagree that there were split views in papers that came before us. I would not know the percentage. Bobby Cutler was responsible for the operation; he was Special Assistant for Security Affairs when I was there. But the fact that there is a split on one or two questions does not mean that there were not widely divergent views on a dozen other questions that were not reflected. You just could not bring these things up in the number of differences that exist. I personally would rather see those decided by someone with authority, who is informed, who is close to the President, and who has his confidence, rather than see them compromised by representatives from ten or a half-dozen departments who, by the very act of compromise, have got to reach a lower common denominator.

This gets down to the question of whether you give authority to individuals to make decisions or whether you let groups compromise. I don't think myself that we can substantially improve the system without some form of higher authority who can really speak for the President, with his responsibility.

MR. PENDLETON. You don't think under an approach like that that you would hear the charge that the President is being shielded from major issues?

GOVERNOR ROCKEFELLER. No, because if you have an executive assistant who is working with you and he has your confidence, he can give you the point very quickly—when you are working together, as they would be, intimately.

In New York State matters, I see this—a man whom I trust, for instance, the secretary to the Governor, works on policy and operating problems; the department heads see him; and he will come to me. I can get from him in five or ten minutes the essence of the problem. I know him. I trust his judgment. I know his background. We have worked together for years. When he says something, I get the feel of the thing and I can make that decision very fast, if he feels that he should ask me about it. Or he will inform me of decisions he has made. I just have not the time to hear these people. If a department feels very strongly that they have been short-changed on a decision and that it was wrong, they will come to me and I will listen to them. But he is a fairminded man and they have confidence in him. That, I think, is the kind of relationship that is true in any big operation. There needs to be a delegation of responsibility.

SENATOR JACKSON. What it really gets down to is that the NSC, being an advisory body, should concentrate on the highly critical issues, so that the President can be exposed to them and make the decisions. These other matters of lesser importance, involving differences and so on, should not get into the machinery so as to reach the Presidential level. I gathered from the analogy you used that his First Secretary would give him a daily briefing or as need arose. This gets down to the people you have confidence and trust in.

GOVERNOR ROCKEFELLER. Exactly. You can't get around that. The President would then have more time to put into creative thinking, planning ahead, visualizing these emerging forces and how we are going to develop policy and programs to deal with them and shape them. Then we are taking the initiative not only at home but in the world scene. I think it is of tremendous importance that we not be dealing with other people's man-made crises but that we be shaping our own forces.

The Budget and the Policy Process[*]

MAURICE H. STANS

Maurice H. Stans, investment banker, was Director of the Bureau of the Budget in the Eisenhower Administration, 1958-61. He came to that post from service as Deputy Postmaster General, 1953-55, and Deputy Director of the Bureau of the Budget, 1957-58. President of Western Bancorporation, Los Angeles, 1961-62, he is now senior partner in William R. Staats and Co.

Mr. Chairman and members of the committee, I very much appreciate the invitation to meet with you today and to discuss some of the problems related to organizing our Government for national security. Certainly this subject is vital to our future as a nation, and the committee is to be commended for the serious attention it has focused on it.

The committee's careful and judicious consideration of the points of view offered in these hearings can lead to valuable conclusions that will strengthen the national capacity for survival. This will be true even if the committee concludes that, in many areas, past and present procedures are not susceptible to significant improvement, since the endorsements of the committee, where appropriate, will strengthen the confidence of our citizens in the management of our affairs in these times of stress and tension.

Although the responsibilities of a Director of the Budget are manifold, it seems to me that there are two areas of particular interest to this committee: (1) the assistance given to the President in respect to the Federal budget; and (2) the aid provided to the President in regard to the organization and management of the Federal Government. Within this compass I thought it might be

[*] Testimony delivered to the Subcommittee on National Policy Machinery, July 31, 1961.

helpful if I were to devote some time in these initial remarks to two separate areas in which in one way or another I carried responsibilities—the budgetary process and the organization of the Executive Office of the President. These two subjects relate, of course, to the efficiency of the staff assistance available to the President.

The Budget Process

For perspective, I would like to touch first on a few elementary facts about the budget process:

1. The Bureau of the Budget is a statutory arm of the President. In budgetary matters it does not operate in a vacuum. It undertakes to carry out the express or implied policies of the President. It acts as it believes the President would act if time permitted him to deal with each particular situation in the light of all the known facts.

2. The annual budget is the President's budget. The decisions it reflects are his, not only as to programs and activities but as to fiscal policy. In other words, the major budgetary function of the Bureau is to evaluate priorities and issues for the President and to advise him of their relation to his policies. All of the Bureau's activities in the budget process are directed to the end of preparing a document that represents the President's concept of national needs and priorities. From this, the Congress exercises its judgment in making appropriations.

One even more elementary fact; budgeting is choosing among spending alternatives. If there is enough money to meet all demands and no choices are necessary, then the plans are no longer a budget but a spending list. Actually, there is never enough to go around, which means that it is necessary to fix the priority of claims on resources. Priority may be recognized by inclusion of a request in whole or in part, or by rejection.

It is natural, then, that there may be dissatisfaction with this process by those dedicated, determined people in the government agencies who seek more funds than they receive. They sometimes fail to see that their own budget requests are based on subjective, provincial points of view. Only the President sees the over-all measures of the nation's needs and can keep them in proportion. (If I may be permitted a less serious note, I think the matter is summed up in a phrase that I used some time ago and that has since been publicly referred to as "Stans' Law": "Effective budgeting is the uniform distribution of dissatisfaction.")

Thus, it is also natural in budgeting for an organization as large as the Government of the United States that there be misunderstandings. These misunderstandings result in various accusations, some of which have crept into these hearings: The Bureau of the Budget is "arbitrary and capricious"; it "fixes ceilings"; it is "preoccupied with balancing"; it "controls our defense policies"; and so on.

My first and perhaps major point here today is a defense of the budget process and of the Bureau of the Budget as essential to the nation's organization of its activities. If there were not a budget process basically similar to ours, there would be fiscal chaos. If there were not a Bureau of the Budget, there would have to be another agency under another name performing the same functions.

With all this as background, I come now to the matter of how the process works and how it can be improved to the advantage of the President, of Congress, of the national security, and of the taxpaying public. It has seemed to me that perhaps it would be most useful if I were to discuss seriatim some of the principal questions raised about the budget process during the past year—both before this committee and elsewhere.

The question that appears to have been raised most frequently is whether our national security processes and our budget processes have been closely enough related. During my term of service as Director of the Budget, I was quite convinced that they were.

This is not intended to mean that there are no opportunities for betterment in the mechanics of budget analysis and presentation. Some notable improvements were made in the last few years, other changes are now being planned, and, as times goes on, there will surely be found many ways of making the significance of budget proposals more clear. But I do mean that there has been every reasonable opportunity, I believe, for the exposure, communication, advocacy and evaluation of program ideas advanced by all agencies, including the Defense Department, and that the President formulated his budgets under these conditions.

Perhaps the second most frequently raised question has been whether the budget process, over the past few years, has permitted the Budget Director to impose ceilings on the Department of Defense.

More than two years ago, I testified under oath on this question before the Preparedness Investigating Subcommittee of the Committee on Armed Services of the Senate. For your own records I should like to repeat again what I said at that time in response to the question, "Have you fixed a ceiling or formulated a target for the 1961 budget?" My reply was—

> Well, I want to answer that carefuly, because the choice of words is very important. I have not fixed a ceiling this year and did not fix one last year. I do think that it is important, in considering a budget of this size, to take a look at it at various levels. By that, I mean I think the Department of Defense should determine what kind of defense it can provide for $40 billion.
>
> If this is done and everything is given its proper ranking in priority, then it can be determined whether or not it provides an adequate program, which items are next in rank of priority that should be considered, and which items are marginal or least essential. This does not mean I think that the defense of the country can unquestionably be satisfied for $40 billion. It means that as a matter of method, I think the Department should start with a figure of that general magnitude and see what kind of a budget it can prepare at that level, and what, if anything, is then left out that is still sufficiently important that it has to be added.
>
> That, in my opinion, is not a ceiling at all and it is not a target either. It is a method of procedure that I think is a desirable one to follow. I think all agencies of the Government should use a similar approach.

In the context of today's hearing, with the committee looking for constructive ways of improving the budget process, I would like not only to reiterate this view but to express a related thought. There is a tendency at budget time for both defense and other agencies and subordinate units to look at a budget for one year as a "floor" for the next year, with new programs and other growth entirely additive. To accept this would be to ignore the responsibility to require the older items to compete properly with the new in priorities. Every item in a budget request should be severely tested, and this cannot be done unless some flotation process is found to bring to the top the lesser or marginal items of the previous budget. This is why I believe so strongly that a budget base for one year should start at a point significantly less in total than the previous year, and that items proposed for addition to that base should be evaluated in relative importance and need, whether old or new. Only by this means will less important programs ever be retired or reduced.

This leads to the question raised in one of this committee's early reports whether there might be advance preparation of alternate budgets for major national security programs. The report noted: "Some wish to see one proposed budget at x dollars, another at perhaps 10 per cent below this level, and still another at perhaps 10 per cent above. Such a procedure, they hold, will permit policy-makers to see more clearly, and sooner, what is sacrificed and what is gained at various expenditure levels. Can and should this be done?"

In actuality, in the development of the Defense budget the past several years, this is substantially what was done. Since we had to take some common starting point, we selected the total expenditure figure for the current year and asked the Department of Defense what the adequacy would be for the next year of a budget that provided either the same amount of money, or 10 per cent less, or 10 per cent more. The Secretary of Defense used this formula, but with other percentages.

Pursuing the matter a step further, however, it has also been suggested that the budget document itself might well reproduce these alternative possibilities. I have considerable doubt whether this would be feasible. The budget must necessarily reflect decision rather than indecision, and in any event the budget message itself can and should provide in regard to certain major programs some explanation of why a particular course of action was selected. It is the responsibility of the President to recommend, and it is not conceivable to me that any purpose would be served by parading anywhere in the budget some or all of the items that he does not recommend.

Five-Year Budgets

Another question that frequently arises is whether or not we would profit from budgeting for longer periods of time—say for five years. Here I believe we should distinguish carefully between planning and budgeting. There is no question but that *planning* for years ahead is desirable. However, *budgeting*, in the sense of seeking appropriations for such periods of time, could create several types of serious problems.

The net effect of a multi-year budget for any period for any program is to give that program an absolute priority over all other programs that do not enjoy such an automatic availability of funds. In other words, in the preparation of each year's budget, it would be necessary to allocate to such a program whatever amount had previously been appropriated in advance, regardless of the requirements of other programs. Assuming that funds are not unlimited, and since the controllable portion of the annual budget is relatively small, this could effectively destroy budgetary management. And, depending on the year in which it was approved, a five-year program budget could deny to one or even two succeeding Congresses any control over that program through the appropriations process.

One of the most serious objections to any five-year budget lies in the fact that it is almost impossible to project requirements so far ahead, even if one pays no attention to the priorities of competing programs or the projected availability of funds. The five-year projection may turn out to represent more than is actually required, so that adherence to the plan would represent a waste of funds. If the projection turns out to represent less than is required the result is to place completely undesirable restraints on the program.

A fair question is whether what is really intended in discussions of multi-year budgets is the provision of some minimum amount for a three- or five-year period, with these amounts augmented each year to meet presumably new and pressing requirements. In such case, of course, it is no longer a three- or five-year budget.

None of these objections applies to long-range planning, and that is certainly to be encouraged. As you know, it is relatively easy for the Government to start an activity with a small amount of money, with clear knowledge that subsequent expenditures will be much greater. Unless the full implications of present programs are projected well into the future, the aggregate significance of enacted commitments may not be recognized, and this can have a disastrous effect on future fiscal management of the Government.

For some years, the Bureau of the Budget has required most of the agencies to develop three-year estimates of requirements, and these have entered to some extent into the President's consideration of new proposals. Without doubt, this procedure can be improved and extended, but I would express the caution that any public use of future projections should be clearly labeled as tentative and for planning purposes only, so as not to imply any commitment of future resources.

The committee will undoubtedly be interested in knowing that in January of this year I delivered to the President a ten-year projection of future government spending. Although this is a public document, it does not seem to have received the attention it deserves. As a guide to future planning, it provides a projection of amounts of spending by 1970 at three levels: one somewhat austere, one that carries on the trend (and commitments) of the last decade or so, and one in between these extremes. Further study and work along this line should be encouraged.

Organization

Perhaps the most important question which can be raised with respect to organization for national security is to ask what process can best assure that the total intellectual resources of the government are made available to assist the President in making crucial policy decisions.

Several points are critical here. First, in making such policy decisions, the President must have available the advice of all those counselors whose responsibilities bear on the matter at hand; there is no substitute in the making of policy for the participation of those who will be charged with carrying out that policy. Secondly, and equally important, is the matter of confrontation—of assuring that proponents of alternative courses of action or of modifications to proposals—debate each other before the President; no other procedure will as rapidly expose the totality of facts bearing on the problem. Thirdly, and also very important, communication of policy factors and decisions must be precise; this means that oral reports of considerations and policy conclusions will not do, because they are too often incomplete and inaccurate or become so, as they pass through agency networks. Carefully written and debated policy statements, approved by the President, are essential to avoid confusion and worse.

Just how a President assures that these goals are achieved is, of course, a matter for his own determination. Personally, however, I thought the national security policy process as it has evolved over the last decade and as I participated in it met these requirements well.

A second question that might properly be raised is how the Executive Office of the President might be better organized to meet the President's requirements. In that connection, I would like very much to recall to you certain points that President Eisenhower made in his last budget message:

The duties placed on the President by the Constitution and the statutes demand the most careful attention to the staffing and organization of the President's office. While the present organization of the Executive Office of the President reflects many constructive steps taken over a period of years, much remains to be done to improve the facilities available to the President. The first requirement for improvement is for the Congress to give the President greater flexibility in organizing his own office to meet his great responsibilities.

Specifically, the Congress should enact legislation authorizing the President to reorganize the Executive Office of the President, including the authority to redistribute statutory functions among the units of the Office; to change the names of units and titles of officers within the Office; to make changes in the membership of the statutory bodies in the Office; and, within the limits of existing laws and available appropriations, to establish new units in the Executive Office and fix the compensation of officers. Such action would insure that future Presidents will possess the latitude to design the working structure of the Presidential Office as they deem necessary for the effective conduct of their duties under the Constitution and the laws. Enactment of such legislation would be a major step forward in strengthening the Office of the President for the critical tests that will surely continue to face our Nation in the years to come. These matters are obviously devoid of partisan considerations.

My experience leads me to suggest the establishment of an Office of Executive Management in the Executive Office of the President in which would be grouped the staff functions necessary to assist the President in the discharge of his managerial responsibilties. In an enterprise as large and as diversified as the executive branch of the Government, there is an imperative need for effective and imaginative central management to strengthen program planning and evaluation, promote efficiency, identify and eliminate waste and duplication, and coordinate numerous interagency operations within approved policy and statutory objectives. The establishment of an Office of Executive Management is highly desirable to help the President achieve the high standards of effective management that the Congress and the people rightfully expect.

I have given much personal study to the assistance the President needs in meeting the multitude of demands placed upon him in conducting and correlating all aspects of foreign political, economic, social, and military affairs. I have reached the conclusion that serious attention should be given to providing in the President's Office an official ranking higher than Cabinet members, possibly with the title of First Secretary of the Government, to assist the President in consulting with the departments on the formulation of national security objectives, in coordinating international programs, and in representing the President at meetings with foreign officials above the rank of Foreign Minister and below the rank of head of state.

I would urge that this legacy of thought by an outgoing President, after eight years of experience with the burdens of office, be seriously considered by this committee.

Conclusion

Now, in conclusion, I would like to recall one other paragraph from President Eisenhower's fiscal-year 1962 budget message, in which he said:

> The budget process is a means of establishing Government policies, improving the management of Government operations, and planning and conducting the Government's fiscal role in the life of the Nation. Whether that role is increasing, decreasing, or remaining unchanged, the budget process is perhaps our most significant device for planning, controlling, and coordinating our programs and policies as well as our finances. Thus the President and the Congress will always need to give attention to the improvement and full utilization of the budget system.

As to ways and means for improving the over-all budget process, I would have two suggestions:

First, although the President presents one budget for the entire government to the Congress each year, the Congress considers the budget in a multitude of pieces rather than as a whole. Financing methods outside the regular appropriation process (so-called backdoor spending) are one phase of the problem. The complete separation of the handling of tax legislation from the consideration of appropriations and expenditures adds to the total difficulty. There would be marked gains if the Congress could find a mechanism by which total receipts, total appropriations, and total expenditures could be considered in relation to each other.

Secondly, I believe that future Presidents ought to have the authority to veto items of appropriation measures without the necessity of disapproving an entire appropriation bill. Many Presidents have recommended that this authority be given our Chief Executive and more than 80 per cent of the states have given it to their Governors. It is a necessary procedure for strengthening fiscal responsibility and a proper way by which, in effect, the President can ask the Congress to reconsider an item. As in the case of other vetoes, the Congress would have the authority to override an item veto.

I would not be wholly in character if I did not end with one plea. The protection of the nation's security requires that we be economically strong as well as militarily strong. We could lose the cold war as easily by the pursuit of unsound fiscal policies that resulted in impairment of our money and our economic strength as we could by neglect of our military resources. In times of tension such as the present, the budgetary flexibility we need to meet emergencies can be provided only if all Americans exercise restraint in their demands for more nonmilitary domestic spending programs. I hope the committee, in whatever conclusions it reaches, will emphasize this point.

Long-Range Economic Projections

MR. TUFTS. I am glad you referred to your ten-year projection. What was the purpose of this projection, and does it indicate that in your judgment such projections may be useful as a part of the budgetary process?

MR. STANS. The purpose of the projection was to carry out the belief that it was very important for the general public, for the Congress, and for the President to look ahead for a somewhat longer period of time than one year and see what the consequences of existing legislation and existing activities of the government agencies would be in terms of dollars. This would be a good guide to planning ahead, to measuring relations between revenues and expenditures in each of the years, and it would be a good indication of the extent to which new programs and new activities might be undertaken by the government without straining our fiscal resources.

I think this exercise was the first that has ever been done along this line, and, of course, it has many of the inadequacies that a first effort, has, but it does project for 1965 and again for 1970 what the expenditures of the government might be according to three different basic premises. One premise is that we would carry on on a relatively austere basis, taking care of the real needs of the country but not going into a great many of the other demands that are made for Federal Government activity. The other extreme would, in effect, project the trends of recent years which, as you know, have been very strongly upward, and assume that all along through this period there would be new and additional programs urged upon the Federal Government and adopted by it.

The third course that was laid out was one of some compromise between the two points of view. Under the austere program, we could have for fiscal year 1970 a budget in the magnitude of $84 billion. Under the more generous type of projection which carried on the trends of recent years our budget would be in excess of $122 billion. In medium terms, it would be about $97 billion. If you assume that the normal growth of our economy would produce a gross national product of about $750 billion by 1970, which I think is the generally accepted assumption at this time, and the tax rates were unchanged, we would have an annual revenue of about $120 billion in 1970. Under the high spending projection we would run a deficit in 1970, and we would have deficits in most of the intervening years. Under the low projection, we could, I believe, take care of the basic needs of the country and we could have substantial amounts available for debt reduction and for tax reduction in the intervening period. The general purpose of exposing these figures is to encourage discussion of which of these courses of action we really want our government to take.

MR. TUFTS. Which of the three levels do you think is the most realistic projection?

MR. STANS. I would find that a little hard to answer without expressing a political view and I would rather not. My personal conviction is that the lower projection would be the best for the country, as it would allow more of our national income to be spent in the area of private choice.

MR. TUFTS. We always have to keep the revenues and the expenditures in mind. Your study projected, chiefly, expenditures except for a few comments on revenues. I wondered whether a projection of expenditures alone might not result in a somewhat misleading impression of the government's over-all position in the future.

MR. STANS. I would hope that it is not a misleading impression. I would concede that it is an incomplete one. Our difficulty was that in the time we had to complete this analysis, before January 20, we could not explore all the elements in our revenue picture. One of the things that gave us trouble was the question of how, in projecting revenues, we could recognize the impact of business cycles along the way or of changes in economic conditions. Only because of the complex of items to be considered and the limited amount of time did we fail to include in this projection a revenue assumption. We felt that the projections of the expenditures themselves were the real meat, however, of the question of trend in

Government programs. This was a significant start on some type of long-range planning, some kind of long-range thinking about the kind of government we wanted to have by 1970.

MR. TUFTS. Do you think the time has come when projections of this sort would be helpful to the Congress in its consideration of national policies, and that such projections should be made available to the Congress perhaps as part of the budget message or in some other way?

MR. STANS. I would hope this would be recognized as a very valuable tool in Congress, in the consideration of appropriations and tax policies, and that stimulation of discussion generally around the country would cause people to think about what course of events they wanted the government to enter into in the future.

The National Security Council*

MR. STANS. I would like to comment on one other area: the activities and procedures of the National Security Council. As I said in my statement: "The question that appears to have been raised most frequently is whether our national security processes and our budget processes have been closely enough related. During my term of service as Director of the Budget, I was quite convinced that they were."

Let me now add to this: as you know, President Eisenhower determined that the National Security Council should be the channel through which recommendations for national security policy should reach him for decision. At the beginning of his first term in office, President Eisenhower added the Director of the Budget to the list of officials participating in all NSC meetings. He further directed, for the first time, that all policy papers considered in the NSC be accompanied by financial appendixes in order to assure that the current and future financial implications of all policies under consideration were fully appreciated. Not only did these procedures assure that the NSC and budgetary processes were related throughout the year as activities were reviewed, but the budget requests of the major national security programs were the subject of explicit NSC consideration each year prior to finalization of the President's budget.

In view of the composition and frequency of NSC meetings, the thorough and extended discussions of program issues elsewhere

* Testimony delivered to the Subcommittee on National Policy Machinery in executive session, July 31, 1961.

at budget time, the many special meetings with the President on such matters, and the fact that important budgetary questions were the subject of frequent discussions between the Budget Director and the heads of agencies—and at the staff level—throughout the year, I do not feel that there were any significant gaps in the relations of national security processes and the budget process, under the procedures in effect during this period.

SENATOR JACKSON. Referring to your statement that the purpose of the financial appendixes was to assure that the current and future financial implications of all policies under consideration by the NSC were fully appreciated, will you tell us something about the success of the financial appendixes? Did this device accomplish what you say was its intended purpose?

MR. STANS. I would say that it accomplished basically the main purpose, which was to give an order of magnitude to the substance of the particular discussion and the particular paper. It was not in any sense a budgetary commitment for the future, and the President always reserved the right to apply other considerations and adopt other figures in the preparation of the budget. But it did successfully indicate the general magnitude of the problem under consideration.

SENATOR JACKSON. In what form were these programs submitted to the NSC for its consideration? I think you have emphasized the importance of precision in such discussions, if the decisions are to be meaningful. Were the programs presented in such a way as to meet this requirement?

MR. STANS. Most of the programs presented were in the form of papers of one kind or another supplemented in many cases by slides, charts, graphs, and oral explanation. The policy papers generally were the subject of debate wherever differences of opinion existed, and when the matter was decided by the President, the policy paper became in substance an expression of his policy in the particular area involved.

SENATOR JACKSON. At what point in the budgetary process did the NSC give explicit consideration to our national security programs?

MR. STANS. I would say continuously during the year. There were many subjects that came up in the National Security Council, particularly in defense, but sometimes in atomic energy and sometimes in connection with mutual security, that carried budgetary implications. There were many cases in which the Director of the Budget participated in the discussions, either questioning or calling attention to facets of the proposals that the President then took under consideration.

The major consideration of the budget as a whole took place late in the calendar year and shortly before the budget was completed.

SENATOR JACKSON. Was this all in connection with discussion of what our strategy should be, both short-range and long-range? Was there plenty of discussion involving all the factors going into a strategy?

MR. STANS. Yes. I will not say there was any process by which every aspect of the defense program was allocated a time and a place on the agenda, but as issues came to focus—in continental defense, in strategic striking forces, in civil defense, and in other areas—these were debated and discussed in the National Security Council. Where it was possible to do so, the financial implications were part of the discussion. Conclusions and decisions were reached by the President in the course of the action.

SENATOR JACKSON. Did you run into disputes with the services over the price tags, as set forth in financial appendixes? Generally, would there be an agreement as to what a given course of action would cost in terms of dollars?

MR. STANS. Generally, there would be agreement, and only infrequently would there be disagreement as to the price tag. I would say the principal reason for this was that most of the matters that came before the National Security Council had their preview in the Planning Board. The processes of the Planning Board brought together the various considerations and viewpoints on the figures as well as on the other aspects of the policies.

SENATOR JACKSON. When did the last administration start indicating the price tags in financial appendixes?

MR. STANS. In 1953.

SENATOR MUNDT. Were records kept of these National Security meetings—minutes or transcripts?

MR. STANS. There were not actually minutes in the sense of recording all of the discussion, but there were action papers reporting the Presidential conclusions and directives. In other words, there was a written record of the President's action with respect to each subject that came before the Security Council and it not only indicated his decision on each matter but who had responsibility for carrying it out.

SENATOR MUNDT. Was the Budget Bureau represented adequately

at the meetings? Would you be there alone, or would you have your specialists in the particular field that was being discussed?

MR. STANS. The Budget Bureau had dual representation, in the sense that a regular member on the Planning Board participated in all the discussions and the Director appeared in the National Security Council. I can think of only one or two occasions on which anyone else accompanied me to a discussion at the National Security Council, and that may have been an occasion when some special knowledge was required.

SENATOR MUNDT. But the procedure provided that if you needed technical help, you could have it at your elbow.

MR. STANS. That is right, provided it was cleared in advance.

The Budget and the Policy Process*

DAVID E. BELL

David E. Bell served as Director of the Bureau of the Budget in the Kennedy Administration from 1961 to 1962, when he became Administrator of the Agency for International Development (AID). Joining the Budget Bureau staff in 1942, he worked in key posts in the Bureau and in the White House. He was administrative assistant to President Truman, 1951-53.

Mr. Chairman and members of the Subcommittee, I am very glad to appear before you today. The series of impressive reports that came from the hearings conducted by this Subcommittee last year has been of considerable interest to those of us concerned with establishing the pattern of management and operation of the new administration. We look forward with interest to any report that may come from your present hearings.

You have asked me to discuss with you the role of the budgetary process in national security policy-making and execution, particularly as it appears from the viewpoint of the Bureau of the Budget. I should like to place before you three or four ideas that seem relevant to your inquiry.

The Federal Budget System

First, let me remind you very briefly of the basic origin and meaning of the federal budget system. Speaking broadly, the federal budget as we know it today is the product of a statute enacted by the Congress forty years ago, at the crest of a movement to reform obsolete fiscal procedures. The Budget and Accounting Act of 1921 included two major reforms that remain the basic founda-

* Testimony delivered to the Subcommittee on National Policy Machinery, August 1, 1961.

tions of the system today: one was the requirement that only the President (not his Cabinet officers or agency heads) may transmit a request for funds to the Congress; the other was the requirement that the President must transmit annually to the Congress a complete budget showing all his proposals for spending and for raising the funds to support that spending.

These two reforms were of great significance. They gave to the President—and they give him today—a major means for unifying and setting forth an over-all executive-branch program, and they give him a major responsibility for evolving a federal budget that reflects his judgment of the relative priority of different federal activities. Thus, the President's budget necessarily reflects his policy judgments; the Congress, in acting on the President's budget, necessarily reviews those policy judgments as to the relative importance of alternative uses of national resources.

Thus, the essential idea of the budget process is to permit a systematic consideration of our government's program requirements in the light of available resources; to identify marginal choices and the judgment factors that bear upon them; to balance competing requirements against each other; and, finally, to enable the President to decide upon priorities and present them to the Congress in the form of a coherent work program and financial plan. The budget operates as an extremely effective element of discipline on the President and the executive branch, because it requires that each proposed use of resources—for defense, science, natural resources, or whatever—be tested against others and against the total size of the budget.

In passing, I might add that it seems to me that the Congress, because it considers budgetary matters for the most part in fragmented form, does not face quite the same necessity to consider the effect of separate budgetary actions in relation to each other and to the entire budget. The Congress might well seek methods that would assist it in giving a more sharply focused consideration to such matters.

The Budget and National Security

My second preliminary observation is that budgeting for national security is a most complex matter, because the national security itself involves so many factors. Our security plainly depends in large part on our own military strength, and planning and budgeting for military strength is difficult in a time of rapid changes in weapons technology. But in addition to our own military strength, our national security depends in part on the military capability of our allies, which requires combined international planning and, where military assistance is involved, our budgeting process must consider the relative importance of direct military outlays and indirect outlays through military aid.

Over and above military outlays, budgeting for national security requires us to consider the addition to our security that may be made by contributing to the economic and social development of other countries through foreign economic aid. And, finally, budgeting for national security requires us to consider the underlying strength of our national economy—the requirements of economic stability and growth, and of the skill, education, and morale of our people.

It is plain that considering the national security in this broad sense requires the President—and the Congress—to make a difficult series of choices for which we do not have a satisfactory set of criteria. How do we weigh the value, for example, in terms of our national security, of a marginal outlay for military force as against a marginal outlay for basic scientific research or for strengthening higher education? Difficult as such questions may be, they are real choices; they affect our national security in a true sense; and we have to make them as best we can.

Lines of Improvement

Against this background, I should like to suggest three lines of improvement in our budgeting for national security.

The first is to make sure that budgeting and planning are in step. Logically, budgeting and planning are two sides of the same coin, two aspects of the same process. A budget is the financial expression of a plan. On some occasions in the past, however, it has been possible for budgets and plans to be established on different bases—that is, there might be an "approved plan" to have certain forces in being, and simultaneously a budget providing for a different level of forces.

We intend in this administration to make sure that we plan to do only what we are willing to budget for—and to budget fully for what we plan. To accomplish this requires an appropriate interlocking between budgeting and planning at each step. This begins in the departments—in Secretary McNamara's mind, budgeting and planning are regarded, as they should be, as two aspects of the same process.

A similar objective guides the work of the Bureau of the Budget and the other units of the Executive Office of the President and the White House Office. All of us endeavor to tie budgeting and planning tightly together in the work that precedes Presidential decisions. We in the Bureau have established close working relationships with the Special Counsel to the President, the Special Assistant to the President for National Security Affairs, the Special Assistant to the President for Science and Technology, and others who advise the President in reaching decisions on national security policy. We have also strengthened our working relation with the Secretary of the Treasury and the Council of Economic Advisers, in an attempt to make sure that our economic and budget policies are fully consistent and that our budget and fiscal policies will contribute to the strength and vitality of our economy, both in the long run and in the short run.

A second avenue of improvement in the process of budgeting for national security is to extend our time horizon further into the future. As far as the Department of Defense is concerned, it is Secretary McNamara's intention to prepare and keep up to date at all times a fully worked out plan and budget for defense programs extending five years into the future. I am not sure we can reach very soon the same goal with respect to other aspects of national security activities, but this is clearly the direction in which to move. In national security budgeting, and indeed in budgeting for all purposes, we must work with longer periods than the single year that used to be our standard. I am pleased here to acknowledge the very useful groundwork laid by my predecessor, Mr. Stans, in the closing period of the Eisenhower administration. Among other steps in the direction of longer-range budgeting, Mr. Stans, last fall, directed the Bureau staff in preparing a ten-year projection of the federal budget for the period 1960-1970, which was most informative.

The fact that we want to move toward longer-range budgeting does not, however, mean that we can do so easily. While some Federal agencies—such as the Federal Aviation Agency—are accustomed to thinking several years ahead, others are not, and it will take some time before we can obtain fully useful long-range projections from all agencies. However, even our initial steps in recent months to extend the budgetary time horizon have paid dividends, in my opinion, in permitting us to understand better the issues that will determine the size and nature of the budget in future years.

Our purpose here is to improve our lead-time for recognizing important developments in public policies and for organizing to find solutions. Whether these issues relate to outer space, housing, education, transportation, urban affairs, science, defense, or whatever, we hope to be able to detect them sooner and meet them more adequately and with a better sense of priorities.

In closing, I should like to point to a third avenue of improvement in budgeting for national security—an avenue on which we have, I think, still far to go. Our budget for national security must reflect and can only be as good as our strategy for national security. I think everyone would agree that the United States has much to do to develop a fully satisfactory strategy for our security. What is the proper mix of military and nonmilitary measures? How can we guide the inevitable processes of change in Asia, Africa, and Latin America to produce free institutions and not Communism? How can we step up the rate of economic growth? On these and many other issues affecting our national security, our budgeting can only be as good as our underlying strategy. Much of what is needed is quite beyond budgetary consideration, and improvement must come from analysis of our situation in the world, and imaginative thinking about the courses of action that are open to us.

In at least two respects, however, we can, I think, point to progress through the budget-planning route. One of these is the development of the so-called program packages in Defense Department budgeting. This process of functional budgeting, under which the expenditures for strategic warfare are grouped together, as are those for conventional war, and so forth, permits more accurate comparative analysis of alternative possibilities and a more realistic understanding of what is proposed. As far as military planning and budgeting are concerned, we believe that this will represent a considerable step forward over the older method of grouping expenditures by service—Army, Navy, Air Force—or expenditure category —personnel, procurement, research and development, etc.

A second step forward is the decision that underlies the administration's approach to the foreign-aid program, namely, to build our economic and military aid efforts around "country programs." This permits us to consider in proper relation to each other the various alternative military and economic measures we can take to assist a given country and, moreover, to relate our aid appropriately to the country's own efforts, to our political objectives in the country, to our diplomatic and information efforts, and so on.

Thus, I believe the use of "program packages" in defense budgeting, and "country programs" in foreign-aid budgeting represent major advances toward sensible planning and budgeting for national security.

I do not wish to minimize the basic difficulty of the problem, however. When we face the hard questions of how much of the nation's resources we should devote to national security and what is the optimum combination of activities to which to devote them, we cannot avoid a considerable degree of uncertainty and considerable room for differences of judgment. We have much to do to improve our understanding of these matters and the analytical framework of ideas which assists us in dealing with them. Any light your subcommittee can shed on these complex and difficult problems will be most helpful.

An Office of Executive Management?

SENATOR JACKSON. Governor Rockefeller testified at some length on the need for reorganization of the Executive Office of the President. Among other things, he proposed the creation of an Office of Executive Management, of which the Budget Bureau would be a part. President Eisenhower strongly supported this proposal in his last budget message. Mr. Stans has also warmly endorsed the proposal.

Are you familiar with the proposal and, if so, do you have any comments as to whether, in your judgment, it would be useful to the President?

MR. BELL. Mr. Chairman, this is not a matter that I have investigated fully or at any length. As I understand it, there were two ideas involved: one was simply to change the name of the Bureau of the Budget to recognize that it is an institution that has several functions in addition to the budgeting function. This is correct; it does have other functions, as you gentlemen know. It is the President's principal adviser on organization and management matters. It helps him to coordinate his legislative program. It has a special function in reviewing and coordinating the statistical forms used by different federal agencies to make sure that they don't overlap and that the inquiries made of private parties are as simple and inexpensive as possible.

Thus, the Budget Bureau has a series of functions in addition to that of helping the President prepare his budget. Consequently, some people have suggested that its name is obsolete and that it should be termed something else. I don't think, myself, there is much to it. Perhaps I am a bit of a traditionalist, but it seems to me it is a fine name and we ought to keep it.

There is another element, however, if I understand the proposition correctly, in the notion of establishing an Office of Executive Management. This is the notion that the President should have, in effect, an administrative Vice President. This idea I am a little doubtful about, frankly. I am not sure that it fits the conception of our federal government.

I think the set of functions now combined in the Budget Bureau make a useful package of great assistance to any President. I believe each President over the last twenty or thirty years, and each Budget Director, would agree.

To attempt somehow to upgrade this position, or perhaps to replace it with a superior position, which would have a broader reach and which would somehow be more of a business manager for the government as a whole—I doubt very much that that is the direction which would really represent progress.

By and large, the federal government is organized so that each head of an agency is fully responsible for its operations—for the policy, for the substance of the activities that are carried on, for the funds that are spent, and for the organization and administration of that agency.

To have the responsibility thus combined and focused on the individual head of each agency is, in my opinion, the correct way to get the best sense of responsibility and the most effective management.

The Bureau of the Budget does provide advice to the President on the over-all management and organization of the executive branch and that is very useful. Furthermore, the Budget Bureau does perform important functions to stimulate the adoption of new and better management methods. To illustrate: we have a small staff of three or four people constantly at work in the field of automatic data processing. These are very good men, experts in their field. They are attempting to advise different federal agencies as to when it will be effective, economical, and useful to adopt automatic data processing in one form or another, and also when it would not be effective, economical, and useful. They try to teach federal officials to resist overzealous salesmen of electronic computers and so on, as well as to advise them when such computers would, in fact, be very helpful to the government's operations. Therefore, the Budget Bureau does perform, in a sense, an advisory role that assists the various federal agencies. I hope that we can do more of this as time goes by.

But this is a different thing from proposing in some manner or other to establish on the President's staff an official who would somehow control the administration of the different federal agencies. That concept is very doubtful, it seems to me. Insofar as that is what is involved in the notion of an Office of Executive Management, I am a little skeptical of it.

I would like to repeat, however, that I have not fully explored this notion. It has not come up in the present administration in a form that required me to go through it to the bottom. It may be that I am arguing here with a concept that the proponents of an Office of Executive Management would not, in fact, put forward. It seems to me sensible, appropriate, and efficient that the head of an agency be the top manager of that agency, as well as its policy-making executive. I would think it a step backward to split policy-making and managerial responsibility. We have them joined now in the head of each agency; I think that is the way it should be.

Congress and the Budget

SENATOR HUMPHREY. You have commented on the importance of the integration of long-range planning with the budget procedure and then you said, "In passing, I might add that it seems to me the Congress, because it considers budgetary matters for the most part in fragmented form, does not face quite the same necessity to consider the effect of separate budgetary actions in relation to each other and to the entire budget. The Congress might well seek methods that would assist it in giving a more sharply focused consideration of such matters." I believe that one of the great weaknesses in the budget process is on the legislative front. I imagine you are going to be hesitant to comment about this. You are a prudent man.

MR. BELL. Senator, I do try to be prudent in these matters. One thing occurs to me, however. I think possibly the right way to approach this matter, to analyze it and try to reach a solution, is to think in terms of the needs of the Senators and their organized methods of doing work, and of House Members on the other side. The problem is to get enough information and understanding in your mind and those of the other Senators. The problem is how to organize the procedures and available information, the judgment of your staff members and people in the Executive Branch you can draw on, so that you can master very complex problems.

It seems to me this is the right point from which to start out, these are the right questions to be asking as you face this issue. In the fundamental philosophy of the legislative process, each Senator and each House Member is supposed to know enough and to have enough judgment to participate in decision-making on nearly everything that comes before him. He obviously can't be expected to know all the details about everything, but he has to master a very wide range of issues.

How he can do that—with the problems changing all the time, with the agencies as they exist or as they can be altered in case alteration would help to meet these problems, with the kind of staff assistance, the kind of information techniques that are available—this is the problem.

One step that might help would be an extension of a system the House Appropriations Committee has begun to use, which I think is undoubtedly very useful. In recent years, the Director of the Budget and the Secretary of the Treasury have appeared before the House Appropriations Committee for two or three days to go over the whole budget, to talk about it as an integrated whole, before the Appropriations Committee broke up into its various subcommittees to take up the different agency budgets.

It is a small step but, it seems to me, a significant one and illustrative of the kind of thing you are talking about—getting groups of Senators together for briefings of various kinds on broader subjects than they normally meet to consider.

Anyway, the only comment I am really trying to make is that I think the right way to take hold of this problem is to think of it as a problem of getting information and facts and ideas into the minds of the members of the legislature.

The Problem of Pay

SENATOR JACKSON. I wonder if you have any comments as to what we might do to get better people in government. I am sure you agree that one of the real deficiencies that we face in many areas is our inability to obtain and keep the type of talent we need.

MR. BELL. I think the most effective means of getting good people is to have good leadership, to look for people who are competent, and to give them responsibility. President Kennedy has had good luck in getting able people into the administration because there is clearly a job for them to do. He wants to put them in positions of responsibility. He gives them challenges, and a challenge is, I am sure, the Number One consideration in getting first-class people to come into government.

However, I see no reason why they should have to come in at great financial sacrifice, and many of them have had to do that. I think the matter of executive pay is very serious. There is no doubt that it needs to be considered. Whether the Congress will be willing to consider it in the near future or not, I cannot say. It seems unfortunate that we pay our Cabinet officers a good deal less than the vice presidents of second-level corporations. This does not seem to reflect an adequate recognition of the relative importance of the activities involved. Yet, at the same time, I should think it is quite clear that government salaries at the upper levels will never be fully competitive with those in private life in many lines.

So it is not a matter simply to decide on the appropriate scales. There is no doubt that at the present time the government is having the greatest hiring difficulty in the ranges just below the top executives.

As I have indicated, Cabinet officers may well come into government because of the challenge of the job. Good men who have either worked up from below or come into government from the outside, at the second, third, or fourth level in the departments, may be willing to hold those jobs for a while. But these are typically men with family responsibilities, and they cannot stay at those levels indefinitely. As you well know, this is one reason why there has been such a proliferation of nonprofit corporations that do scientific or other technical jobs for the government: they can pay higher salaries than those of the Classification Act of the Federal Government. We are having great difficulty in getting and holding top-flight scientists. We find this true of not only scientists, engineers, and technicians, but also lawyers. The Department of Justice is asking the Congress to take all of its lawyers out of the Classification Act.

The Congress has been making numerous exceptions in recent years. There are hundreds of jobs now that are deliberately exempted from the Classification Act because the Congress has recognized that its pay scale is too low. To get the kind of people the Federal Government needs to carry out its work requires permission to pay higher salaries.

The National Security Council*

SENATOR JACKSON. Mr. Bell, could you explain in broad terms the basic philosophy of the new administration in its use of the NSC and other interdepartmental coordinating mechanisms?

MR. BELL. I think there are probably two major points that could usefully be made.

First, the President is using the National Security Council as I believe it was intended to be used under the statute—namely, as an advisory body for him as he confronts the major questions of national security. He meets with it frequently, and the discussions have included those major matters which are the President's principal concern in the field of foreign and military policy at the present time.

The second point, which represents a considerable change from recent years, as I understand it, is that the President is deemphasizing the interdepartmental committee.

Instead, President Kennedy is using a system under which he places responsibility on a Cabinet officer, or a top subordinate in a Cabinet department, for preparing an analysis or coming up with recommendations on a given issue or subject. This Cabinet officer or top subordinate is expected, himself, to arrange for whatever coordination is needed in order to obtain the views of other departments concerned and to make sure that the matter, which is to come before the President and the National Security Council, has been considered by others in the government who ought to consider it.

The person on whom the President has placed responsibility—most frequently, a Cabinet officer—is not, however, supposed to come forward with a combined report that is finished and all the President has to do is stamp it "yes." Quite the contrary, he is expected to bring before the President his own conclusions, his own analysis, his own recommendations for action. It may well be that other departments differ strongly. The President expects that this will be the case and expects the issues to be argued before him and with him. He participates very vigorously in such discussions in Security Council meetings, or in such other meetings as may be convenient to him, at Hyannis Port or wherever it may be. This, I

* Testimony delivered to the Subcommittee on National Policy Machinery in executive session, August 1, 1961.

think, is a striking attribute of the present system. I understand that it is somewhat different from what happened in recent years, although, of course, I am not personally familiar with that period.

SENATOR JACKSON. This administration has abolished the Operations Coordinating Board. Insofar as you are concerned, do you feel a satisfactory substitute for policy follow-through has been created?

MR. BELL. First of all, I am not at all sure that the Operations Coordinating Board was a satisfactory method for following through on decisions. If you ask the question in a little different form, if you ask whether I am satisfied that this administration has a satisfactory system for following through on Presidential decisions, I would say we have a basic understanding of how it is supposed to be done. I certainly would not claim that in every case it is being done as effectively as it should be.

The essential pattern for execution, again, rests on a system of direct responsibility on the Cabinet members; in some cases, the responsibility is given to an Assistant Secretary, particularly the geographical Assistant Secretaries of the State Department. Those officers and the staffs that work with them are expected to be in a real sense the significant centers both for policy-making and for following through on Presidential action, for making sure that the different parts of a Presidental decision affecting a given area or country are appropriately pursued, that the things that are supposed to happen in fact do happen, and that they happen in correct relationship to each other.

The office of the Assistant Secretary of State for a geographic area has really been upgraded very substantially in this administration. These Assistant Secretaries are frequently the key people on whom responsibility is placed for pushing ahead with a given set of decisions. If there is any one place that the functions that were supposed to be carried out by the Operations Coordinating Board have come to rest, it is with these Assistant Secretaries.

However, there are, of course, many decisions with which those officers are not particularly concerned. For example, in the case of decisions that affect primarily the U. S. Information Agency, or the Department of Defense, the essential responsibility goes to Secretary McNamara or Mr. Murrow.

The staff of the Special Assistant to the President for National Security Affairs, Mr. Bundy, performs a secretariat function in that it keeps up with actions taken under the President's decisions.

They are not responsible for seeing that the action takes place. They are responsible for knowing whether it has taken place and for reporting it to the President. They keep a score sheet, but they are not the responsible action organization.

SENATOR JACKSON. In other words, in lieu of the Operations Coordinating Board, you are relying on the traditional departments or agencies?

MR. BELL. That is right. I want to emphasize, though, that none of us would claim that we are achieving perfection in these matters.

SENATOR JACKSON. This administration has also abolished the NSC Planning Board. How do the departments and agencies work together in doing the kind of things that were performed by the old Planning Board?

MR. BELL. Again, your question puts me a little at a loss because I don't know much about the old Planning Board. If I understand it correctly, it had at least two metamorphoses. At one point, it was regarded as a group of people who met together to make sure that appropriate planning was being carried out. It was not a planning board itself, but a group of people who made sure that planning was being done where it was supposed to be done. Later on, I gather, it was transformed gradually into a group that met virtually constantly, and it was supposed to be doing the planning, preparing papers for the Council, and so on.

If I am correct in my understanding of the past, the present system is not unlike the former idea. It is very unlike the latter.

There is now no group of people designated as a planning board. The planning for different problems is done either through the normal processes—as when the President asks the Secretary of Defense to prepare plans for alternative contingencies in a given situation, the planning machinery of the Department of Defense is available and is used, and the appropriate coordination is achieved with the State Department and others who are involved—or, when the President wants a complete review of what the United States is doing in relation to a particular country, say, he may establish through the NSC a special task force, normally with an Assistant Secretary of State as chairman, to prepare an analysis and plan of what the United States should be doing, all aspects covered—information, military, economic, political, and so on. Under these circumstances, there will be a special planning effort on a one-time basis with people participating from the different agencies, and the product of this task force will be reviewed at the top level of each department concerned; it will come before the President and be debated, and he will decide what he wants done about it.

What I am saying is that this administration has used the regular planning machinery of the different departments and has also used special *ad hoc* task forces.

There is an effort on the part of the Special Assistant to the President for National Security Affairs, Mr. Bundy, and people with whom he works regularly in the different departments, to make sure that the planning machinery of government is looking ahead to the different problems that are going to be coming up. He is working on the problems, not only the immediate crises, but those we can see ahead down the road. There is an organized attempt under Mr. Bundy's leadership to make sure we are looking ahead and making appropriate plans for problems that are going to confront us.

SENATOR JACKSON. Do you think the NSC as it now operates brings policy alternatives before the President in such a way that the sharp differences are adequately given to him? Is there sufficient staffing to back up the policy alternatives that are presented?

MR. BELL. Obviously, you don't want me to get into the substance of particular cases. It is appropriate and proper, I think, to say that there have been differences in the quality of the product in some instances and other instances. In some cases, the system has worked exactly as it should—namely, there has come to the President a very clear, definite analysis of the problem and an outline of a proposed policy that is specific, costed out, with all the elements included in a very nice presentation. This has been available to everybody concerned sufficiently in advance so that those who might differ with it have a chance to think about it and formulate their points of view. The matter was in a position to come to the President and be debated crisply on real issues. This is the way the system ought to work. There is no reason it can't work that way nearly every time. It is a little too much to ask of human institutions that they work every time.

There have been cases in which the system hasn't worked perfectly. Perhaps the fellow who was the task-force chairman did not quite know what was expected of him. He may have come up with a lowest-common-denominator type of report, or the timetable may have been very short and the people concerned may not really have had a chance to get all the issues staffed out.

We have had a very brief experience. I think it is clear that understanding of what the President wants, and of how he wants the system to work, is becoming much more widespread.

SENATOR JACKSON. Are you getting clear-cut guidance to the departments?

MR. BELL. I am sure that they have not always felt this to be the case. I am sure it has not always been the case—particularly in the early period. Everyone had tied his procedures to this previous machinery; it was suddenly abandoned and nobody knew where to look next. I am sure there has been a considerable uncertainty in many parts of the government.

As an observer from the Executive Office, it now seems to me that the machinery permits the President's instructions to departments to be quite clear and definite, and that in any case in which there is doubt, it is very simple to bring the matter up and get it clarified. The system is flexible, simple, and can be fast-moving.

SENATOR JACKSON. It is very important, I would think, to make sure that all these decisions are in writing, so that the departments and those responsible know what their duties are.

MR. BELL. This, as in the past, is a responsibility that rests on Mr. Bundy, the Special Assistant for National Security Affairs.

SENATOR JACKSON. And there is a follow-through, so that those responsible understand, first of all, in writing what they are supposed to do? Mr. Bundy monitors what is going on and reports to the President, I take it, so that he will know what the story is?

MR. BELL. That is right.

SENATOR JACKSON. How is the budgetary process related to the NSC? At what point do you enter the picture? In other words, you have price tags on a lot of these things. Mr. Stans has referred to the financial appendixes.

MR. BELL. The present system does not necessarily involve a financial appendix. The figures may appear in the body of the document—it depends on the subject. But the essential point is that the cost of doing the things that are proposed is expected to be a part of the presentation, part of the consideration of the merits of the issue. At every stage the benefits and costs are supposed to be and are typically included in the staff work that precedes the President's consideration.

Now, the Budget Bureau, as an institution, does not have to participate in every stage of every piece of staff work. However, the relations we have worked out with Mr. Bundy's office are so close that we have participated in every case in which we wanted to participate. We have been in a position to make sure that the financial, budgetary aspects were included and not just rely on the system to make sure of it.

SENATOR JACKSON. In view of the present method of using the NSC, I would think that the President would want to place major reliance on the budgetary process for monitoring and coordinating various matters that have to be decided.

MR. BELL. I think this is correct, in the sense that he is using the Budget Bureau as a general staff-support agency, much as Mr. Truman used to do. I don't know to what extent this was done under President Eisenhower. I think President Kennedy, like Mr. Truman, whom I knew, wants to be sure that the budget does not, of itself, determine the answer to a given problem. I don't want to give the impression that cost considerations settle issues by themselves. What I have tried to say is that cost and budget considerations have been appropriately integrated into the procedure, and that the President and everybody else who considers a given policy decision is aware of what the alternative actions would cost and also can be aware of the benefits that might be expected from whichever action was chosen.

SENATOR JACKSON. Are the NSC meetings limited to those directly involved in a matter, in order to encourage completely frank and open discussion?

MR. BELL. The NSC meetings vary greatly in size.

SENATOR JACKSON. But when it is larger, it is due to the necessity of the situation?

MR. BELL. That is right. In other words, the President varies the attendance list depending on who ought to be there to have an appropriate discussion or to hear the President's judgment and decisions. When it is a matter of exceptional security classification, the President will keep the session quite small—that is, quite small for an NSC meeting. You can't have an NSC meeting with much under a dozen people because of the statutory requirements and the President's desire to have people there from his own staff.

SENATOR JACKSON. You are speaking of a formal NSC meeting. As the President uses the NSC process——

MR. BELL. He holds many, many meetings——

SENATOR JACKSON. Of the subordinate groups within the NSC structure?

MR. BELL. That is right. You could call them subcommittee meetings, if you wish.

SENATOR JACKSON. Right. Is a task force expected to produce a paper making specific recommendations, in order to achieve precise discussion and decision?

MR. BELL. Yes, sir.

SENATOR JACKSON. They are held to that?

MR. BELL. Yes, sir, they are held to that. The President and those who work with him are very impatient if a paper comes up with the pros and cons neatly labeled but with no recommendation, no conclusions, nothing to chew on.

SENATOR JACKSON. As I understand it, you are trying to make sure that the President gets sharp alternatives and that the departments' views are clearly expressed.

One of the great reforms Winston Churchill introduced into the Imperial Defense Council was to require that all decisions be put in writing. From what you have said, it is my understanding this is being done and that it is primarily Mr. Bundy's responsibility.

MR. BELL. That is right.

SENATOR JACKSON. Testifying before the Subcommittee in 1960, Mr. Robert Lovett said, "The authority of the individual executive must be restored." You have alluded to this in your earlier remarks. First, do you believe the authority of the individual executive is now being restored, and, second, what steps are being taken specifically in the NSC process to assure this?

MR. BELL. As I have indicated, I think this is an underlying element in the President's administrative philosophy in which he has exactly the point of view that Mr. Lovett expressed in 1960.

SENATOR JACKSON. Mr. Lovett spoke about "the derogation of the authority of the individual in government, and the exaltation of the anonymous mass." You feel quite strongly that, under present procedures, the individual is being emphasized and held responsible?

MR. BELL. I think this is very characteristic of this President. I can testify to it from my personal experience.

SENATOR JACKSON. What do you think are the most important as yet not satisfactorily solved problems in the present mode of operating the NSC? In other words, in what areas do you feel you can make some adjustments and changes that would be helpful?

MR. BELL. If you will permit me to speak broadly, I think that none of us would be satisfied with the basic system for appreciating, analyzing, and proposing solutions to the biggest questions we face in the national security area. These are problems that concern primarily the State and Defense Departments. I have already alluded to that. It is an enormous task to infuse the State Department with the ability and the attitude to do the imaginative, accurate sizing-up of the situation and preparing of recommendations that are needed. This is something Secretary Rusk understands very well and is working very hard to achieve. It is a matter of leadership, and of being sure that everybody understands exactly what is expected of him. To some extent, it is a matter of restaffing, to some extent a matter of organization, of the relative roles of the Policy Planning Staff, the Office of the Deputy Under Secretary for Political Affairs, the offices of the different geographical regional Assistant Secretaries, the Office of the Under Secretary for Economic Affairs. Each of these parts of the Department is responsible for contributing to the product of national policy. All this is being worked on to improve the State Department's capacity to contribute to national security policy-making.

Similarly, there is much work under way to improve the policy-making capability of the Defense Department. As far as the National Security Council is concerned, I think it has been evolving, and people have been finding out what kind of papers make the best discussion papers for this President and this NSC.

To me, the most impressive aspects of the system under the new administration are, first of all, the attitude the President has toward assigning individual responsibility; and, second, the degree to which a kind of intellectual interchange among departments is building up—with the White House and with the Executive Office staffs—which makes for understanding, quick communications, assurance that all sides of an issue are looked at.

SENATOR JACKSON. Is this true between State and Defense, too? Do you gather that their relationship is becoming closer in dealing with problems?

MR. BELL. Yes, sir. There is a long way to go on that, but both Mr. McNamara and Mr. Rusk are keen on improving it. There is now a new exchange system for assigning officers back and forth on an experimental basis. The first officers have been assigned.

SENATOR JACKSON. Mr. Bell, the public gets the idea sometimes that the National Security Council is an agency separate and apart from the departments. Actually, in one sense, we have always had a National Security Council in our Government. From the founding of the Republic, we had the War Department and we had the Department of State. Now, as a codification of our World War II experience, we have brought together the key national security departments and have worked out a system which each President can adapt to help him get the information he needs. In all of this, it seems to us on the committee that the Secretary of State has a primary role. We believe very strongly in the primacy of the Secretary of State in advising the President on the full range of national security problems. I just wondered what your approach or philosophy is in that regard.

MR. BELL. The same as yours, sir, the same as the committee's. I think that is the same way the President feels, the same way I know Mr. Bundy feels. We all look to the Secretary of State, just as you say, as the leader in the development of national security policy in its broad sense.

I think this President has given evidence, by the actions I have described—eliminating the OCB and changing the reliance on interdepartmental committees—that he wants to give to the Secretary of State this responsibility. This places a tremendous burden on the Department of State, and gives it a role it has not had for years. It requires reforms to be undertaken in internal management, personnel staffing, and so on, which the Department is in the process of making.

SENATOR JACKSON. I think the conclusions we arrived at can be stated rather simply—to utilize and to strengthen the traditional Departments.

MR. BELL. There is a problem that Mr. Lovett referred to that is far from solved in this respect, and that is how to enable the Secretary of State to carry out this role in view of the enormous burden on him for negotiations. As long as foreign secretaries in other countries regard it as demeaning to deal with anybody but the Secretary of State, this really presents a situation that no one man can handle. Obviously, any Secretary handles it only by skimping on something. You would hope, and I would agree, that he would handle it by skimping on the negotiating and by placing heavy emphasis on the policy-making, which is very difficult to do.

SENATOR JACKSON. It is quite clear from this approach to the development and execution of national security policy that the Department of State needs all the support it can get. It needs all the assistance it can properly obtain to do the job that goes with primacy in national security affairs.

MR. BELL. That is right.

The Secretary of Defense*

ROBERT S. McNAMARA

Robert S. McNamara, Secretary of Defense, came to his post from a business career. From 1940 until 1943 he was Assistant Professor of Business Administration, Harvard University. During World War II, he served as a lieutenant colonel in the U. S. Army Air Corps. He was continuously associated with the Ford Motor Company from 1946 to 1961, first as comptroller, then assistant general manager of the Ford Division; as vice president and general manager of the Ford Division; as group president of the car division; as company director, and, finally, as company president.

Mr. Chairman, it is indeed a pleasure to have been given this opportunity to appear before your committee to discuss various aspects of national security policy machinery. Your committee is making a major contribution to national security. I was aware of the committee's work prior to being appointed Secretary of Defense. Since assuming office, I have asked several of my assistants to consider the deliberations and findings of the committee in their research on Defense Department management and organizational problems and their relationship to other governmental agencies.

Through the candid testimony of the witnesses whom you have invited to appear and through the findings contained in your committee reports, an unusual collection of invaluable material on national security policy machinery is being assembled.

Members of the executive and legislative branches of our government, students of the political process, and a great number of public-spirited citizens, are being provided a reservoir of information to assist them in their studies on governmental administration.

* Testimony delivered to the Subcommittee on National Policy Machinery, August 7, 1961.

As a result, a more complete understanding is being provided of various alternative procedures and organizations that may be used to meet the challenges which face our national government.

In my opinion, however, it is extremely important to keep in mind that national policy machinery is not an end in itself but, rather, a means to an end. National policies, in the last analysis must be determined by the Congress and the President acting together. Under our system of government, it is the President who has the ultimate authority in the executive branch. He occupies the pivotal position in the government and has a direct responsibility to the entire electorate. As your committee has underscored in its reports, each President must determine for himself how he can best use the policy machinery of Government. Of course, the top machinery of Government is closely tied to the manner in which the President works with his Cabinet officers and his other agency heads.

Relations with the State Department

In the planning and management of national security policy, two executive departments are predominant, the Department of State, and the Department of Defense. Your committee has referred to this as "the central partnership" in national policy machinery. I agree entirely with your evaluation.

There are few great issues of military policy and over-all military posture that are not inextricably wed to the responsibilities of the Secretary of State in the field of foreign policy. And I am confident that the Secretary of State, Mr. Rusk, will assure you that the converse is essentially true.

It is for this reason that I believe the Secretary of State and I have a mutual responsibility to insure that our partnership is effective, harmonious, and completely responsive to the over-all requirements of the President and to his personal direction.

For my part, I consider that the personal and official relationships between myself and the Secretary of State are of the highest order. But this relationship must, and does, extend deeply into our two departments. Among the regular points of contact between the two departments are weekly meetings at the Executive Office of the President, which are attended by, among others, the Under Secretary of State or his deputy and the Deputy Secretary of Defense. Many of the matters taken up at these meetings are of mutual concern to State and Defense, and these sessions are helpful in keeping officials of the two departments in close touch.

When specific national security problems arise, they are often assigned for study and recommendation to interdepartmental task forces. The Defense Department is, without exception, represented. There are frequent meetings in the Pentagon between the Joint Chiefs of Staff and representatives of the Department of State, at which topics on an agenda suggested by both departments are considered. The Assistant Secretary of Defense for International Security Affairs attends these meetings. The State Department is represented by the Deputy Under Secretary of State for Political Affairs.

However, these are the more formalized channels of communications. There are innumerable, less formalized, but no less important points of contact between State and Defense. Informal contacts, which facilitate the exchange and sifting of ideas at working levels, take place on a continuous day-to-day basis between opposite numbers in both departments. For example, representatives of the Office of the Assistant Secretary of Defense for International Security Affairs, who are most concerned with those military matters involving foreign policy, work closely and harmoniously with their counterparts in the State Department. Regular meetings, also attended by representatives from other interested governmental agencies, are held to discuss matters of policy planning and operations coordination, such as those which were formerly dealt with by the National Security Council Planning Board and Operations Coordinating Board structure.

I must also bring you up to date on the State-Defense exchange program, in which this Subcommittee has expressed such a strong interest and which was discussed with you by Secretaries Herter and Gates.

The program is now well under way: a second group of exchange officers was welcomed by representatives of the two departments a few weeks ago. Under this program, Foreign Service officers are detailed to politico-military offices in the Office of the Secretary of Defense, the service staffs, and the Joint Staff; and military officers and Defense civilians serve tours of duty in various offices of the State Department. The exchange officers are not liaison officers or observers; they are full working staff members, or action officers, within the departments to which they are assigned.

The program currently consists of eleven officers from each department on loan to the other. Although it is still early for a definitive evaluation, the reactions to date of both the exchange officers and their "employers" have generally been enthusiastic.

In the professional training courses at the National War College, at the three military department war colleges, and at the Military Assistance Institute, emphasis is placed upon the interrelation of political, economic, and military facts in our security policies.

State Department personnel and representatives from other executive departments and agencies regularly attend the several war colleges. Similarly, military officers and Department of Defense civilians are attending various courses offered by the Department of State's Foreign Service Institute.

On balance, in my opinion, Mr. Rusk and I and our principal assistants are working today toward the closest coordination and cooperation between the Department of Defense and the Department of State at all levels of decisional authority and staff action.

The Organization of the Defense Department

To be an effective partner in the State-Defense team, however, the Department of Defense must have its own house in order.

I should like to turn now to the measures which we are taking within the Department of Defense to make more effective our contributions to the national security policy process.

Your committee has suggested a number of areas in which the Secretary of Defense could improve the operation of the Department.* I agree wholeheartedly with your judgment that one must guard against seeking organizational solutions for problems that are not merely organizational in origin.

Your committee report suggested the possibility of "more vigorous employment of the broad authority already vested in the Secretary of Defense." One change, which I believe will improve my ability to make sound decisions in matters affecting national policies, is the new planning-programing-budgeting process within the Department of Defense. Under this new process, the Secretary of Defense for the first time will have an integrated financial management system specifically oriented to the manner in which he is to make decisions by program, in relation to over-all Department of Defense military missions.

I am fully aware that the National Security Act of 1947, as amended, has given the Secretary of Defense the ability to make

* See above, "Super-Cabinet Officers and Super-Staffs," pp. 27-28.

substantial management improvements on his own authority. Upon studying the scope of this authority, it came to my attention that there was no single office in the Department of Defense charged with the continuous responsibility of organizational and management planning for the Department of Defense as a whole. I learned that the work that had been done on broad administrative, organizational, and management problems of the Department had been generally accomplished on an *ad hoc* basis by the military services and not under auspices of the Department of Defense itself.

Upon assuming office, I therefore established an Office of Organizational and Management Planning Studies under the General Counsel of the Department. I assigned responsibility to this new office to conduct systematic research to provide effective solutions to over-all Department of Defense management and organizational problems. I might say it is working very satisfactorily.

We have already been able to make some changes in organization that I regard as distinct improvements. One such change has been the decision, announced last Tuesday, to establish a Defense Intelligence Agency (DIA). Our principal objectives in establishing this agency are to obtain unity of effort among all components of the Department of Defense in developing military intelligence and to achieve a strengthened over-all capacity in the Department for the collection, production, and dissemination of defense intelligence information. The organization will also achieve a more efficient allocation of intelligence resources, more effective management of all Department of Defense intelligence activities, and elimination of duplicating intelligence facilities, organization, and tasks.

I consider that the DIA will permit the Department of Defense to make a more effective contribution to many aspects of the national policy process. The establishment of the DIA was fully endorsed by the President's Foreign Intelligence Advisory Board and the Joint Chiefs of Staff.

Your subcommittee also highlighted the possibility of improvement through "more active participation of the Secretary of Defense in the deliberations of the Joint Chiefs of Staff." As you know, my predecessor, Mr. Gates, made effective use of this management technique by meeting weekly with the Joint Chiefs. I have attempted to expand upon this concept and have found it one of the most valuable means of obtaining the advice of my principal military advisers. I have found that by personally raising issues for discussion with the Joint Chiefs of Staff, I have been able to expedite the decision-making process.

Your committee also suggested the "possibility of increased reliance upon the Joint Staff for planning." I personally consider this to be a most worthwhile recommendation. The Joint Staff, being composed of experienced officers from all military services, has the potential of becoming a most valuable asset to the Department of Defense as a whole. I am attempting to realize this potential by strengthening the participation of the Joint Staff in Defense Department strategic deliberations.

Of the special studies I have initiated since taking office, thirty-five of the most important were assigned to the Joint Chiefs of Staff and thus to the Joint Staff for analysis. I intend to rely on the Joint Staff even more extensively in the future.

I will not attempt to comment in my statement on other suggestions your committee has made. I would like to underscore, however, the importance that I attach to your views that officials who are selected for top policy positions should be willing to remain in their posts as long as the President desires them to remain. Certainly, this is the policy of the present administration.

I would like to state that I am convinced that a great number of additional administrative, managerial, procedural, and organizational improvements can be made in the Department of Defense. I expect to study such improvements thoroughly and make whatever adjustments may be necessary. If I conclude that changes in basic defense legislation are necessary, I will not hesitate to recommend to the President that he request the Congress to act upon them.

Meanwhile, I welcome any suggestions that this committee, or its members, might have to improve the participation of the Department of Defense in the formulation and execution of national security policy.

The Defense Budget and Planning for the Future

SENATOR JACKSON. Mr. Secretary, would you indicate to us how you go about formulating the defense budget? I do not mean you should do this in great detail; I do not want to place that burden on you. But you might consider in general terms fiscal year 1963—what the procedures are, whether you have budget ceilings, guidelines, and so on.

SECRETARY McNAMARA. We start with the political objective,

the formulation of which is presented to us by the Secretary of State and upon which the President indicates his desires that we develop a military program that will support the political objective.

As you know, the President has stated that the defense budget is to be established without regard to arbitrary ceilings. We determine the force levels we believe are necessary to support the political objective, and then act to fulfill the President's second direction to us. He has indicated that we are to attain the specific force levels necessary to support the political objective at the lowest cost. Every effort is made to do that.

Now, further, I would say that the budget process in the full sense of the word will be a continuing one, that we expect to lay out a budget or operating plan, operating military program, covering a sufficiently long period of time so that the period covered by the plan or budget will equal or exceed the longest lead-time of the actions included in that budget. This means that the plan must cover at least five years.

We then propose to maintain that plan or budget up to date with monthly revisions to it, so that at any particular time that a budget for a special period, such as the fiscal year, is required, it can be abstracted from the continually modified and continually adjusted military program.

SENATOR JACKSON. All the large corporations, certainly, if they are exercising prudent judgment, have to plan ahead to know what the situation is going to be several years hence. Isn't that correct?

SECRETARY MCNAMARA. Yes. I think the difference between the two is that the large corporation can predict with greater accuracy the future it faces.

SENATOR JACKSON. The forces they deal with are rather different than the forces you have to reckon with.

SECRETARY MCNAMARA. Exactly. But the unpredictable nature of many of our situations does not by itself make planning unnecessary. Quite the contrary, I think it further emphasizes the need for planning and the need for constant readjustment of those plans.

Defense Department Committees

SENATOR JACKSON. Mr. Secretary, as you know, we have been greatly concerned during the course of our study with the number of committees in the Department of Defense alone.

SECRETARY MCNAMARA. I do not look with favor upon committees except when they perform a very limited function. Following

President Kennedy's inauguration, I examined the number of committees in the Department of Defense and they approached a total of 3,000. Between then and July 1, we dissolved more than 400, and we have scheduled for dissolution another 130, but that leaves 2,400 to continue to work on. These numbers, of course, somewhat exaggerate the situation because some of these committees are very small. They cover management of an officer's club, for example. But some of the others operate in very important fields.

As I say, I feel that committees can serve a useful purpose, but they cannot be considered substitutes for creative leadership and personal responsibility for such leadership. Nor, in my opinion, should they be thought of as decision-making bodies; rather, their function should be limited to that of a forum in which advice can be exchanged. In the latter role, they can play a very important part in our decision-making process, but I suspect in the past they have been relied upon for far more than that. Where we find that to be the case, we are dissolving them.

SENATOR JACKSON. Do you feel that in the operation of the committee system, more power should be vested in the chairman?

SECRETARY McNAMARA. I do not believe that a committee should hold a meeting unless the decision-maker is present. Normally, I believe, the decision-maker should function as chairman of the committee.

Availability of Professional Military Advice to Congress

SENATOR MUNDT. I read an article in The New York Times recently that may or may not be accurate, dealing with the guidance memo you have circulated through the services, which they quote: "After the President has established a policy or after appropriate officials of the Defense Department have established a policy, I expect no member of the Department, either civilian or military, will discuss that policy other than in a way to support it before the public." Now, is that the true sense of the guidance memo under which your associates operate?

SECRETARY McNAMARA. Yes, with one qualification. I expect that the representatives of the Department when appearing before Congress and asked to present their personal opinion will do so. The statement I made to the Department and also the specific written piece of paper that carries that guidance includes that qualification.

SENATOR MUNDT. I wanted to establish for the record here, which is more official than *The New York Times*, the fact that there were no new inhibitions, no changes in policy that would preclude your associates, from the lowest to the top, who are considered competent enough to be called before Congress for a hearing, to testify before us free from any guidance or any directive compelling them to maintain silence. Is that correct?

SECRETARY MCNAMARA. That is absolutely correct. I would add, further, however, that when an individual representing the Department appears before Congress and in answer to a question from the Congress as to his personal opinion on the matter, expresses that opinion, I would ask that he express a balanced opinion, that he indicate whether or not he has had an opportunity to express his opinion to the decision-maker before the decision was made, that he state that there are pros and cons, and that he list those pros and cons so that the Congress obtains a balanced view of the problem, and that he indicate further his acceptance of the decision. It is my belief that the Congress should be presented with the pros and cons even by the person recommending a particular course of action, giving more weight to the pros.

It is only in this way that we can properly fulfill our responsibility to Congress to inform it fully on the issues. None of these issues is clear cut, they are not black and white, they are mostly gray. It is my intention that we will present the grays and then state quite forcefully and clearly that recommendation.

Because that is to be done initially, it should be done in all discussions following on the same issue.

SENATOR JACKSON. Mr. Secretary, what you are doing is following the traditional rule that previous administrations have adhered to —namely, that when a policy has been agreed upon—when a decision has been reached—the people who are responsible in the executive branch of the government have the duty to carry it out.

Congress has a constitutional responsibility to provide money for the national defense, and if Congress is to act wisely and effectively, then it needs the professional advice of our top military leaders. I take it from your statement, that you have made it very clear that any officer is free and, in fact, has a duty to respond to any question that a Member of Congress should ask concerning his personal views on, we will say, a given weapons system. You honor that right and your directive covers it?

SECRETARY MCNAMARA. My directive is very specific on that point.

There is no question in my mind, and I do not believe that there is any question in the mind of any member of the Department.

The National Security Council*

SENATOR JACKSON. Mr. Secretary, Mr. Lovett emphasized to our Subcommittee in 1960 the need for "constant, close, and sympathetic cooperation" between the Departments of State and Defense. He said, "The tone of the cooperation must be set by the two Secretaries." Would you tell the Subcommittee what you are doing to strengthen the State-Defense partnership, particularly in relation to the NSC? You have mentioned your close working relationship with Secretary of State Rusk. Would you now discuss this in connection with the National Security Council?

SECRETARY MCNAMARA. Yes. I think the relations of the departments to the National Security Council are simply an extension of the relation I mentioned earlier, which is carried out (a) by a close personal relationship between Dean Rusk and myself and a feeling of mutual respect between us and (b) by each of us stating to all the personnel in our departments that we expect each of them to work with their counterparts within the limits of our approved Department of State and Department of Defense policies to the closest degree possible, and to make whatever decisions need to be made on their respective affairs within those limits of policy.

Now, this evidently is a change from what has existed in times past. There are no curtains—iron curtains, paper curtains, or any other kind of curtain—between the departments on any echelon. On a day-to-day basis, this results in expeditious action, and I believe an entirely satisfactory working relationship at all echelons.

As it relates specifically to National Security Council affairs, it is simply an extension of this day-to-day process. There are times when the President assigns to either the Secretary of State or the Secretary of Defense a particular project for that officer to develop and bring back to the President for discussion before the National Security Council. Even prior to the time the President makes a decision on the recommendations, such projects frequently involve the other department.

It is Mr. Rusk's practice in the development of recommendations, as it is mine, to solicit the recommendations and advice of the other parties affected. In this particular case, I would solicit the

---

* Testimony delivered to the Subcommittee on National Policy Machinery in executive session, August 7, 1961.

views of Mr. Rusk or his designee. He, in turn, if the project were assigned to him, would solicit my views or the views of my associates.

SENATOR JACKSON. So that there is a close working relationship not only at the secretarial level but also below?

SECRETARY McNAMARA. Yes. We would bottleneck our affairs were we to insist that the working relation between the two departments flow through us. We realize that, and, therefore, even before we were formally appointed, we agreed we would foster and sponsor a close relationship at all echelons, and that we have done.

SENATOR JACKSON. In addition to the formal NSC meetings, do you have panel or subcommittee meetings of the NSC with the President and the Secretary of State?

SECRETARY McNAMARA. Yes. There are frequent meetings of the President with the Secretary of Defense and the Secretary of State and their key associates, frequently the Chairman of the Joint Chiefs or other personnel from the Department of Defense and similar personnel from the Department of State.

SENATOR JACKSON. You find that this method is helpful in dealing with certain types of national security problems? Can you deal with a lot of problems that perhaps you would not want to bring before the entire NSC?

SECRETARY McNAMARA Yes. I wanted to emphasize that frequently it is wiser and more practical to deal with a matter in a small group than in a larger group. These meetings between the President and the Secretaries of State and Defense serve that purpose.

SENATOR JACKSON. Do you feel that Defense and the services are now getting adequate political guidance from State?

SECRETARY McNAMARA. Yes, I do. I would qualify that statement by saying that political guidance in the world in which we live is a shifting guidance and must be so. It is extremely difficult for State or any other Department to predict with any accuracy the situation we will face a year or two or five years from now. We in Defense recognize that and are quite willing to adjust our plans as the guidance changes, as it must.

SENATOR JACKSON. This administration has eliminated the NSC Planning Board. How does Defense now work with the other departments and agencies in preparing the position papers and in staffing out the papers, in doing the sort of thing that was done by the old Planning Board?

SECRETARY McNAMARA. The President assigns to a particular individual or department the responsibility for preparing a plan in relation to a particular requirement. That individual to whom the task has been assigned is responsible for obtaining the views of others in the government who are affected by the plan. If he assigns to me a responsibility for preparing a plan in relation to a certain situation, I recognize the interest of the State Department in that matter and solicit from Dean Rusk his views on my plan. If he accepts the plan or if I accept his views and we therefore present to the President a unanimous position, it is so stated. If, on the other hand, his views differ from mine and I do not accept his views, I don't try to find a common denominator but rather I present to the President my recommendations and state that Mr. Rusk holds contrary views and they are these.

The specific approach depends on the matter at hand. In certain instances, Mr. Rusk or I will call a group together, present a proposal, obtain their views, modify the initial proposal in relation to those views, come to an agreement in our own minds as to the course of action to be followed, and then put the matter under discussion in writing.

Alternatively, if the matter is more complex and requires more study, we may assign the task to one of our subordinates and ask that the other department participate formally in the discussion by assigning an individual to work with our subordinate—in effect, setting up a small task force which studies the matter, presents in writing to Mr. Rusk and to me their recommendations, which we then either accept, reject, or modify.

SENATOR JACKSON. You mentioned a task force. This administration has made considerable use of task forces, both at the Presidential level and within the departments. I wonder if you would comment on the role and operation of task forces from the standpoint of the Department of Defense.

SECRETARY McNAMARA. They are a very useful, effective way of approaching a complicated problem and insuring that people with a variety of interests and points of view and experience bring to bear their experience upon that problem and upon its solution. They are effective if they are properly directed, if they operate as a working group with a director and a responsible leader. They are not effective if they turn into a leaderless committee-type organization. Some of them do, in which case they prove to be worthless.

SENATOR JACKSON. In other words, they can suffer from the failings of any other committee, especially those you alluded to earlier.

SECRETARY McNAMARA. Exactly.

SENATOR JACKSON. As the NSC is now operating, do you feel that the President is presented with the clear-cut choices he needs in order to exercise his constitutional responsibility? And are they adequately staffed out?

SECRETARY McNAMARA. Yes, I do. I would say this: to the extent that he isn't, the fault is not with the system but rather the particular individuals. We will always have failures of individuals in a particular assignment, and we sometimes do in the national government. But I attribute this to human frailty rather than weakness of the organizational structure.

It does not happen very often. When it does happen, I will say he is receptive and realizes it is happening and insists that it may be redone and other alternatives presented.

SENATOR JACKSON. This administration has abolished the Operations Coordinating Board. Do you feel, as Secretary of Defense, that satisfactory arrangements have been made, and are being made for policy follow-through?

SECRETARY McNAMARA. Yes. Here again I do not mean to say that all follow-through is perfect, but the arrangement of the organizational structure and organizational procedures are in my opinion entirely satisfactory. They are simply to assign to a particular individual specific responsibilities and then have the White House or NSC staff follow up on the action the individual takes to carry out that responsibility. To me that is the proper way of operating.

SENATOR JACKSON. What steps have you taken to insure that budget decisions will be properly related to policy decisions? If an agreed-upon policy is worked out at the NSC level, what follow-through is there to make sure that the Department of Defense will have the necessary ability to implement the decision?

SECRETARY McNAMARA. I consider the budget nothing more than and nothing less than the quantitative expression of a plan or a policy. So in developing the budget, I propose to start with the plan or the policy and translate it into quantitative terms, terms of benefit and cost. This you might contrast with a budget that starts without any specific policy or plan but is based on meeting a specific dollar ceiling.

We are not starting that way. We are starting with the policy or the plan, as the case may be, and developing a quantitative expression of that in terms of our military force levels and military requirements.

SENATOR JACKSON. What you are trying to do is work out a long-range strategic plan and to make sure that the budget decisions you make reflect the objectives in the plan.

SECRETARY McNAMARA. Yes, exactly so.

SENATOR JACKSON. What do you think are the most important as yet not satisfactorily solved problems in the present mode of operating the National Security Council? What are the areas where more needs to be done to improve the operation of the system?

SECRETARY McNAMARA. I think the passage of time will result in smoother operation within the limits of the present organizational structure and present procedures. As you might expect, a new administration with but six months' experience behind it frequently finds rough spots in the application of a particular procedure to policies.

Individuals may have failed clearly to understand their instructions or may not have had sufficient experience to carry them out. On the whole, it is my personal opinion that the present procedures and organizational structures are functioning very effectively, but I realize that occasionally, as is true in most organizations, particularly large organizations, there are gaps and omissions, resulting, as I say, primarily from failure on the part of particular individuals to carry out the task assigned to them. I don't believe the solution for that problem is a change in the procedure or the organizational structure, but rather either a replacement of the individual or a more careful training of that individual.

SENATOR JACKSON. Or a better formulation of the written decision that has been made or the instructions to the individual.

SECRETARY McNAMARA. Yes.

SENATOR MUNDT. As I interpret your explanation, Mr. Secretary, the main change in procedure that has come in with the new administration is a tendency to rely more upon interdepartmental coordination and task forces, as against hammering these decisions out at meetings of the National Security Council. Is that correct or incorrect?

SECRETARY McNAMARA. It is difficult for me to state the main change by comparing present and past practices, because I really am not very familiar with past practice, other than what I have read of them.

But I would say the main change is a reliance on individuals, specific individuals, rather than on groups of individuals, reliance on the individual to develop a plan and reliance on the individual to carry out that plan—in contrast to reliance on a committee to develop a plan or to monitor the action under the plan.

SENATOR MUNDT. But as the procedure has operated, has it not resulted in a substantially fewer number of National Security Council meetings over the passage of time than was previously true?

SECRETARY McNAMARA. Again, I cannot speak with authority on the number of meetings because I have not seen a quantitative comparison of the number of meetings during the first six months of this administration, for example, and some comparable period of past administrations.

The National Security Council meetings are now held frequently but irregularly, in the sense that they are scheduled to meet in connection with particular problems at particular times. Sometimes, there will be three meetings in a week and other times maybe only one meeting in two weeks. The President has spoken of the advisability of meeting at least once in two weeks. But how this compares with the past, I cannot really say.

SENATOR MUNDT. Are you sure under this system the President gets into the participation of these decisions as fully and as early as he would if he were confronted with differing points of view rather than a consolidation of a point of view between the different departments which has taken place before he gets into the discussion?

SECRETARY McNAMARA. It is my belief that, under this new system, he is confronted with more alternatives and more differences in points of view than under the old. Again, I am speaking in part from hearsay, but, under the old system, it was my impression in examining some of the papers that the committee system led to an attempt to achieve a unanimous position. In order to accomplish this, it was frequently necessary for particular parties to dilute their proposals and points of view down to what might be called the lowest common denominator, and this was presented to the President as an agreed-upon position.

In contrast to that, today, the responsibility is assigned to a specific individual, the Secretary of Defense or the Secretary of State or the Director of the CIA or some other specific party, who is responsible for preparing a recommendation, his own recommendation, and for reviewing that with the other parties concerned and obtaining from them either agreement to his position or alternatively, a statement of their position. In the latter case, the conflicting views are presented to the President.

Now, it seems to me that this system, therefore, presents the President with more choices and a better understanding of the differences of view than did the previous system. I qualify my remark by saying I can't speak with authority on the previous systems.

SENATOR MUNDT. When there are differences, is it at the National Security Council level that the differences are discussed?

SECRETARY MCNAMARA. Yes. They are discussed initially by the parties that differ, but then, presuming the parties don't change their views, those differences and views are discussed with the President at the National Security Council level or conceivably at what I believe the chairman referred to as the subcommittee level in the National Security Council, where some of the members of the National Security Council meet with the President and discuss the issue.

SENATOR MUNDT. When it is discussed at the National Security Council, you bring into focus not only the independent judgment of the President but I would assume also the views of other representatives who attend the National Security Council who did not participate in the task-force or interdepartmental operations?

SECRETARY MCNAMARA. Yes, that is true.

SENATOR MUNDT. So that you have more heads operating.

SECRETARY MCNAMARA. Yes.

SENATOR MUNDT. To me, this is one of the advantages of the National Security approach; we need the best judgment of the best people we can get. Sometimes, somebody not directly connected with Defense or with State, looking at it as an umpire or as a judge—or three, four, five, or six of those fellows—can give you a better chance of coming up with a composite judgment.

SECRETARY MCNAMARA. It seems to me that is right. It would seem to me you have a better chance when the views are presented to the Council instead of having the lowest common denominator hammered out by the Planning Board.

SENATOR STENNIS. When President Kennedy returns from an overseas trip, he is bound to have a lot of impressions. I am hopeful he would bounce them against your mind and you would bounce them back against his without the formality of staff or anything else. Does that happen—not at specific intervals, but on any major problems?

SECRETARY MCNAMARA. It happens on almost all major problems but in most cases, and I think quite properly so, the opinions are solicited and given only after thought has been devoted to the matter. These questions are so complex and so difficult that one's immediate reaction may not be the best. Therefore, while there might be a preliminary discussion, more often than not the preliminary discussions are followed by a final discussion with several days intervening between the two, to permit more thought and study to be given to the matter.

SENATOR STENNIS. When it comes time for action, the President alone can speak. I was once a trial judge: the worst part of it is you have no one to confer with; you make a decision that may take a man's home from him or some other part of his fortune, his life, his freedom.

SENATOR JACKSON. Your point is excellent, Senator Stennis. As a judge, you have a statutory and constitutional responsibility to make decisions. The President has a constitutional responsibility, and he alone must make certain decisions. But the NSC process, properly utilized, makes it possible for the President to weigh all the arguments. As a judge you have a chance to listen to the arguments in court but a lot of restrictions are placed on you. After you have completed the case, you might like to get the information that you can't get and it is too late, and you have to make a decision. But it seems to me that this NSC process, properly utilized, makes it possible for the President to get all the alternatives.

I take it that there have been quite a number of these informal meetings of portions of the NSC membership that have some right to be heard. The President, therefore, may not be calling as many formal NSC meetings with all the members provided for by law. But, as I see it, the NSC process is still at work when one or two or more Cabinet officers make presentations to the President and decisions are reached.

SECRETARY MCNAMARA. Yes. The parties primarily interested in all these decisions are the State Department, the Defense Department, CIA, the President, and the President's staff assisting him. Very frequently, a group composed of representatives such as I have outlined will meet to discuss an issue. The meeting might be called informal, but it is not informal in the sense that preparation did not precede it but informal only in the sense that it is not a statutory body. It is the President's view, as it is mine, that one should not express an offhand opinion on an issue of great national or international importance. Therefore the meetings that he holds are preceded by very careful preparation on the part of the people present who are advising him and recommending to him particular courses of action.

SENATOR MUNDT. Referring, Mr. Secretary, to the unfortunate Cuban situation; looking at it in retrospect, from the outside, it would appear that some place along the line, inadequate coordination, inadequate information must have been involved. Out of those experiences involving the whole Cuban procedure, have any changes been made that would tend to prevent or preclude that type of lack of fully coordinated effort, should some similar situation develop in some other place in the world? Have we learned anything procedurally as a consequence of the Cuban invasion?

SECRETARY MCNAMARA. I think it is clear that the President has appointed a military representative following the Cuban episode. In part, this is a recognition, I think, of the need for close day-to-day coordination between the affairs of the CIA and the Department of Defense and the Department of State.

The machinery for the National Security Council, however, I think is much the same today as it was then. As I have said, I believe it has functioned quite satisfactorily. I think that, as you might expect in any large operation, an organization and set of procedures will function more effectively with the passage of time. The longer the period of time that people have participated in them and are familiar with the operational procedures and working habits of one another, the more effectively they will operate together.

I think this committee has properly emphasized the importance of Presidential appointees remaining in their posts for as long a time as the President wishes them to do so. It is this, in my opinion, rather than any change in procedure, that will lead to the greatest effectiveness and efficiency on the part of governmental operations.

The Executive Office of the President*

DON K. PRICE, JR.

Don K. Price, Jr., teacher and author, is Dean of the Graduate School of Public Administration, Harvard University. He served as a member of President Eisenhower's Advisory Committee on Government Organization and as an adviser to President Kennedy on major issues affecting the structure and operations of government; and he has been an adviser to President Johnson on problems of government organization.

Your invitation to appear before this Subcommittee is a great compliment. Those of us in the academic world who are interested in the crucial problems you have been discussing have been learning a great deal from the published record of your hearings. It would be very hard to find similarly authoritative public information on the central policy-making processes of any other government. Speaking as a professor of political science—in which position I still feel a little out of character, after only three years in the academic world—I am most grateful to this Subcommittee for the production of a plentiful supply of raw material for my business.

At the same time, this makes it very hard for me to imagine just what I can say that would be of use to you, since I have the benefit of neither recent full-time experience within the executive branch, nor the first-hand observation that Capitol Hill provides. Perhaps my most useful role today would be to try to sum up the general theory regarding the Executive Office as it seems to me a number of official studies and actions have established it over a number of years. It seems like a long time to me, but that Office is still a relatively new institution as government agencies go. Since it has just about come of age, this is not a bad time to see whether there

* Testimony delivered to the Subcommittee on National Policy Machinery, August 17, 1961.

is a reasonable degree of agreement about what it was set up to do.

I am particularly glad that your Subcommittee's subject deals broadly with policy machinery. I don't find it very useful to try to think about security policy separately from other policy. The essence of the problem, I suppose, and the reason for the creation of the Executive Office, is that you cannot neatly parcel out assignments to different executive departments and expect their interests and purposes not to be mixed up with each other. It takes a lot of sophisticated effort to keep them from working at cross purposes, even with the best of intentions and with the most complete agreement on general political ideas.

At the same time, I don't think you can very usefully separate policy and administration except as ideal concepts. The major administrative controls are the President's most effective tools for directing the development of policy and for producing a program to lay before Congress for its consideration. The details of administration, and a share in the development of policy, the President and the Congress both have to delegate to the executive departments and agencies. While the President and the Congress obviously have certain jurisdictional conflicts, in the main I think we cannot get anywhere unless we think of them as having common interests in enforcing the responsibility of the executive agencies. The job is obviously now so tremendous that this function of the President is no longer one that he could, by the help of constitutional lawyers, defend against the Congress. By the exercise of its legislative procedures—by simply failing to give the President the institutional help he needs—the Congress could reduce the Presidency to little more than a symbolic office. It could, that is, if it wished to do so and if the public would let it. I am sure that neither is true.

General Theory of the Executive Office

The Executive Office of the President was established in 1939 on the basis of a theory that is very much in line with your main concern with policy. There were those who had long urged that such a Presidential office include all the managerial and housekeeping agencies of the Government, for the purpose of enforcing economy and efficiency, but already in 1939, as the President's Committee on Administrative Management believed, the government was too big for such centralization to work. Responsibility for efficiency must be imposed, in the main, on the operating agencies. It was wise then, and I think it is wise today, not to put in the Executive Office such functions as those of the General Services Administration, the National Archives, and similar agencies.

If, then, the Executive Office is to include the main staff agencies through which the President directs the central policies of the executive branch, should it have any different relation to the Congress from the other executive agencies? It seems to me extremely important to maintain such a distinction, in the interest of the Congress as well as of the President.

One of the first concerns of the Congress is, I suppose, to have as clear as possible a channel for enforcing the public accountability of executive agencies. Every department that is given public money to spend or government power to exercise in relation to the public should be publicly accountable for its actions. To enforce such responsibility, it is necessary by statute to set up the major departments, to define their powers and determine their appropriations, to put them under the control of officers confirmed by the Senate and politically responsible to the President, and to require them to account for their actions publicly before Members of the Congress. Both the Congress and the President in a very practical sense have to delegate very heavily to such political officers, who obviously receive a corresponding degree of independence of action. No matter how much the policies of one department head are related to another, it seems to me that the specific functions of his department—the power he exercises and the money he spends—should be granted as clearly and exclusively to him as possible, so that he can be held exclusively responsible for his mistakes. This is the general theory that led the authors of the Federalist Papers—for example, Hamilton, in No. 70—to argue for unity in the executive power, with no executive council or committee to disperse responsibility.

The nature of the Executive Office, it seems to me, should be entirely different. Its constituent units should not be given any powers at all. They come into existence because, in a government that is tremendously larger and more complex than the framers of the Constitution could have imagined, a considerable institutional machinery is needed to make it possible for the President to do what the Constitution expected him to do personally in a very small government. Every effort should be made, I think, to leave in the several departments and agencies the operations that can be defined and clearly assigned and to put in the Executive Office only such machinery as is necessary to help the President keep informed of the intricate interrelationships of their operations and their policies, and to develop the required degree of unity among them.

It seems to me fundamental that two channels of responsibility are not better than one. If the Secretary of an executive department is to be held responsible publicly for a certain function, nobody in the Executive Office other than the President himself should also be called publicly to account for that function. This is why it seems to me that we should, while giving the President all the institutional assistance he needs, do everything possible to make sure that we do not let that machinery begin to compete with the departments whose political heads are not only responsible to the President but in another sense accountable to the Congress and to the public.

For this reason, I do not think that it is supporting the interest of the President against the Congress, but equally in the interest of both of them, to say that the President should be given a very much greater degree of discretion with respect to the organization, the personnel, and the working procedures of his Executive Office than with respect to the executive departments and agencies. In the interest of the Congress, I think it would even be true to say that he should be forced to take such responsibility whether he wants it or not. For, if the Congress gives any part of the Executive Office an opportunity, in its own right, to influence a decision that a department head may be responsible for making, it will never be possible to fix responsibility clearly on the department head for the ultimate success or failure of an action. At the same time, with respect to the President, it needs to be said that any statutory prescription with respect to the way his Office works—even if it is exactly right at the time it is enacted—may soon be used against his interests as well as for them.

What I have been saying is no more than a summary of the general position that was taken first by the President's Committee on Administrative Management and later by the first Hoover Commission, and I consider it rather conventional theory and I must almost apologize to you for rehearsing it here.

The need for Presidential decision is all the greater because the Executive Office is no longer simply a collection of staff agencies. The new element that has been added, mainly since the war, is the interdepartmental committee. Some such committees are statutory and others informal; some work at the very highest levels and are in effect Cabinet subcommittees, while others work and are made up of subordinates; some are permanent and others are merely *ad hoc*. They were set up as people came to realize that national policy was too complex to be sliced up neatly and assigned to different departments, but that their interrelationships were too complicated and too fast-moving to be directed with the help of staff agencies alone; much interdepartmental business had to be handled under the President's direction by agreement around the table with his staff and representatives of the affected departments participating.

The interdepartmental committee was not first invented after World War II; I helped to set up a very elaborate one as a junior staff officer in the mid-1930's. But it certainly became fashionable after our staff officers learned a great deal from the more sophisticated techniques of the British during World War II, and some of them got a bit too enthusiastic about what they learned and tended to misapply it, to rely on it too much, or to give it a more independent role than it deserved. It was not until the first Hoover Commission made its report that the interdepartmental committees created by the National Security Act of 1947 were put in the Executive Office, where they belonged.

The limitation of both staff agencies and interdepartmental committees in helping the President deal with policy is a fundamental one. You can't slice policy up neatly among them, any more than among the executive departments. However you define their fields of interest, they overlap not only those of the executive departments they try to coordinate but those of each other. The Budget Bureau is in a broad sense not dealing with different things from the Council of Economic Advisers. Each tries to help the President by working over the same raw material in different ways. Similarly, there is no way in which you can say in advance just where the interests of the National Aeronautics and Space Council end and the Joint Chiefs of Staff begin, or how they relate to any other interdepartmental committee that may exist in the fields of economics, transportation, communication, manpower, education, science, or strategy. The multiple overlaps among such committees and the staff agencies of the Executive Office, and the fact that each of these overlaps also cuts across the assignments for which various executive departments are primarily accountable, means that it is not useful to try to define by statute the precise functions and responsibilities of the several parts of the Executive Office of the President. This is over and above the point that I think it would be fundamentally wrong to give any power to any one of them, since the only power in the Executive Office ought to be that of the President himself.

Yet this is a very great temptation. When I was working for the first Hoover Commission, I used to remark rather sourly that I had discovered a fundamental law of politics: every bureau or agency in the government wanted either to be absolutely independent of everybody else or to be established in the Executive Office of the President. Certainly, every major aspect of federal policy that cuts across departmental lines has earnest and public-spirited advocates who think that its problems can be straightened out only by a new piece of machinery in the Executive Office; obviously the more prestige it has the better, and this requires statutory status. I have been greatly tempted by my special interest in various of these aspects—for example, scientific research or education or international cultural relations—from time to time to join in one or another of these crusades. But I was usually rescued by being interested in more than one at a time and then finding it hopelessly impossible to define just where the interests of one began and the other ended.

So I conclude, sometimes regretfully, that once we have organized the executive departments as rationally as we can, we ought not to do anything to confuse the ability of the Congress and the President (in their several constitutional ways) to hold them publicly accountable. The way of the Congress is the legislative process, which inherently involves publicity and open debate. Hence, in the American constitutional structure, unlike those of parliamentary systems, specialized standing committees are necessary. They, too, get into jurisdictional problems, but fortunately that is not our subject today. The way of the executive branch, on the other hand, is one of discretionary executive action that must have in it a large element of flexibility and—if I may dare use the dirty word—secrecy, if it is to have the energy and achieve the unity of action that the Constitution intended and that we never needed more than we do today.

With an eye, then, on keeping the main channel of public responsibility through the heads of the executive departments quite clear and uncluttered, the Executive Office should be seen as a secondary problem. It ought to have in it only what the President needs to control the policies and the operations of the departments and agencies and thus should be a means of making his constitutional power effective, not a means of creating new powers or assigning new functions. For this reason, just as each House of Congress should be left free to determine the organization and the staffing of its committees, it seems to me that the President should be left free to determine the organization and staffing of his Executive Office. I do not think any part of it should be assigned powers in its own right, at least not beyond the power of the President to reorganize and transfer elsewhere in the Executive Office at his pleasure.

Similarly, it seems to me that the President's discretion in the selection of personnel for the Executive Office should not be subject to the same degree of restraint that is proper in the appointment of political officers to be held publicly responsible for the direction of departments. Whether this end should be attained by an informal tradition or whether it would be better to follow throughout the Executive Office the precedent of the Budget and Accounting Act, which made the Director of the Budget not subject to confirmation, seems to me a secondary matter. The status of the Budget Director is unusual even in the Executive Office, and the precedents are more on the side of Senate confirmation. The essential point, I think, is that the process of confirmation, which has a proper purpose with regard to an officer in whom powers and functions are vested by law, does not have that purpose in the case of one who has no legal authority in his own right but only an administrative function in support of the President's constitutional authority.

Finally, I am glad to see how frequently your Subcommittee has recognized the limitations on efforts to coordinate policy at the Executive Office level. There is first of all the problem of quantity; if you start by trying to settle all interdepartmental problems at that level, you will have so much business that the Executive Office will itself grow so large that it will be impossible to coordinate its several parts and it will begin to project its internal differences onto the departments. The only way to avoid this is to get more of the job of coordination done by the departments themselves. This leads, in national security policy, to a coordinating job of major importance and major difficulty for the Department of State.

The second limitation is that of personnel. Our national weakness, I think, is to try to make up by elaborate organization for the defects of the men on the job. Neither staff agencies nor committees can coordinate officials who are interested only in the programs of their several bureaus; or who are subject to the influence, on account of their temporary status, of the interests with which they have been or expect to be associated; or who are simply unaware of the complex ramifications of modern governmental problems.

This is, of course, a separate problem, which needs to be tackled both throughout government and in our universities. If I mention it to you, it is not to suggest that the machinery of policy coordination is unimportant, but only that improvements in machinery and personnel have to go along together if we are to get the results we want.

A First Secretary versus the State Department

SENATOR JACKSON. In view of what you have said about pinning responsibility on operating agencies and departments, I assume you would be somewhat skeptical about such proposals as a First Secretary of the Government, an official who would stand between the President and his department chiefs?

DEAN PRICE. That particular phrase was attached to several ideas with rather different meanings in the two or three years I heard it discussed. I had a certain degree of skepticism about all of them. If I am to comment at all, I would rather talk about a specific proposal. But as for one of these ideas—the notion that there should be set up by law an officer who would, under the President, have authority to make decisions that would be binding on the heads of the executive departments—this seems to me to be a profound mistake.

SENATOR JACKSON. Do you really think the State Department is now geared, particularly in terms of adequate staffing, to give the Secretary the help that he requires to be the President's first adviser in national security affairs?

DEAN PRICE. Senator Jackson, I think the obvious answer to that is and has to be no. I could say that with equal confidence if I had not known anything whatsoever about what was going on in the past year or so, and I do not know too much.

The situation we got into at the end of World War II was that a nation that in the 1920's and 1930's had managed to stay pretty isolationist and maintain a Foreign Service that was interested only in very restricted political functions had to take on a tremendous range of military and economic responsibilities and propaganda responsibilities all over the world. The Department of State was consequently not equipped in the slightest degree to take on the direction of those responsibilities.

I think this is what forced the creation by statute of interdepartmental machinery at the Cabinet level to deal with strategy and international security affairs. I think that the business of putting so much into the Executive Office, partly by statutory and partly by Presidential action, was an effort to make up for the fact that the State Department, not by doing anything specifically but rather by negative action, abdicated its primacy.

Winning that primacy back cannot be done simply by enunciating a principle or enacting a law; it will take years to build up the necessary personnel and institutional habits. It seems to me we have to try to do so, because the only other alternative is to put into the Executive Office itself such a tremendous and complicated bureaucracy that I do not believe it would be good for the President, the Executive Office, the Congress, or anybody else.

SENATOR JACKSON. This administration is trying to get more coordination done by the departments themselves rather than by interdepartmental committees at the White House level.

You say that, for national security affairs, this leads to a coordinating job of major importance and major difficulty for the Department of State. Could you discuss this further?

DEAN PRICE. I would be glad to, although I am not closely in touch either with the general things the administration has been doing in this respect or with what has been going on specifically in the State Department.

It seems to me that the most conspicuous development in the administration of foreign policy in the past twenty years has been the way in which every government department has gotten into the act. I think every executive department has a special staff or bureau now that deals mainly with its international interests. This is a development that is completely warranted. They really have to. Agriculture does have interests abroad, Labor does have international labor interests. I think the question then is, if you are looking at the politics of the trade unions internationally and thinking about their role in the cold war, do you simply let the Labor Department go off entirely on its own? Or, how do you relate it to our general foreign policy?

One solution, which is entirely too cumbersome, is having a special unit for each such subject in the Executive Office. The second thing one is tempted to try to set up is a formal interdepartmental committee, and to have every special problem of this nature brought before such a committee and more or less voted on. I think our temptation to do this was more or less an attempt to imitate the British Cabinet subcommittee system. Each of those approaches is justified in a few of the most important matters, but with the great bulk of business, I think it much more expeditious to handle it as an international matter by having some officer in the State Department responsible for following the international problems in each special field. Whether this is best done by basing that coordinating effort mainly on the geographical Assistant Secretaries with respect to their particular parts of the world, or whether that responsibility in some cases has to be based on the functional parts of the State Department, I think has to be worked out according to the needs of each individual problem.

It does seem to me that this is a job that has to be assumed by the State Department, if it is not to abdicate its primacy in the international field. From the point of view of the management theorists, it has been hard to take, because as a sort of article of faith it has been held that one department cannot be asked to coordinate another. This doctrine got going and was quite valid, in a way, at the time when the arguments came up about taking the Budget Bureau out of the Treasury where it had some real conflicts of interest. After all, even though the Budget Director was supposed to report to the President from his position in the Treasury Department, there were still troubles when it came to checking his nominal boss' budgets. But I do think that this doctrine, as valid as it is, in a broad sense cannot be pushed to its logical conclusion. You really have to have a system in which it is understood that in the normal conduct of business most of the coordination of a particular problem will be worked out across departmental lines under the leadership of a particular person in a particular executive department. If it gets to be an important issue on which departments have different interests, you then have to have a means of appeal up the line. In the most important instances, it has to go to the President.

Easing the Secretary of State's Burdens

SENATOR JACKSON. In his testimony before our Subcommittee, Mr. Lovett said that one important attribute of a Secretary of State was "availability in Washington," where he can be close to the President and run his Department. Apparently, Mr. Rusk has not had any more luck than his predecessors in this regard. Do you see anything that can be done to ease the Secretary's travel burdens?

DEAN PRICE. This was one of the main notions in one version of the First Secretary idea—that there be some sort of officer with high status and prestige available to go to big international meetings and, in addition, a man with equal rank who would be running the Department. In a way, I think this was a valid purpose to work toward. We are not very flexible or inventive in using titles in our government. The British manage to have a lot of ministers without portfolio who carry a lot of rank, and I do not believe we have learned how to do this very well. In a way, it is because we are too reasonable in our approach—we do not think high title and rank should be given unless a man has some specific responsibility to discharge. The notion that rank goes with statutory responsibility makes it very hard to avoid difficulty in this matter. This is acute at a time when there are many new nations of the world that are understandably sensitive about their protocol relations to the great powers. When they come to Washington they want to see the top man. I certainly do not have the answer to this problem.

SENATOR JACKSON. The top officials of foreign governments inevitably gravitate to the individual who does have the power, and creating another office will not satisfy them. Is this part of the problem, do you think?

DEAN PRICE. I think that is true. It might be possible to try to invent some additional title for a Second Secretary in the Department of State.

SENATOR JACKSON. What about the ambassador at large?

DEAN PRICE. Historically, going back to Colonel House, and others more recently, this man usually was thought of as representing the President, quite apart from the Secretary of State, and this caused more trouble than it was worth. I think that when the man is formally accredited as an ambassador at large, it is very much more responsible and very much more orderly.

The White House Staff

SENATOR MUSKIE. Should the President's White House staff be able to reach down into the departments to pick up problems that might not get to the White House at all except through action of a department head? Should they be able to reach down into departments to be able to get facts or judgments? Should they have this much flexibility? Should they be able to set up channels of communication that bypass Secretaries and Cabinet-level people?

DEAN PRICE. About all I can say about this is it seems to me to be a matter of balance. Certainly, that opportunity should not be denied the White House staff, and they should exercise it occasionally. If, in my own office, I tell my secretary how to keep her files and take her notes, I would not have a good secretary within a week or so; a good one would leave me. I would not like her to tell me I did not have the right to instruct her on how to get the files in order, but I would not want to try to do that too much.

I think this is a question essentially of proportion. In order to get some big policy decisions straightened out, occasionally a staff officer has to go down and work on some tiny management problem. He ought to be free to do so, but that can be done, I think, and should be done, without creating an intolerable degree of meddling or interference in all aspects of the department.

SENATOR MUSKIE. In the last analysis, he must be the judge as to whether he is going too far?

DEAN PRICE. I think that is true, although I would not say "in the last analysis." In the last analysis, I think, if he goes too far, the head of the department will appeal, and in the last analysis the President will have to decide whom to back up.

The Secretary of State*

DEAN RUSK

*Dean Rusk, Secretary of State, came to his position
with broad experience in the area of national security. During World War II, he served with the
U. S. Army and later as special assistant to the Secretary of War, 1946-47. In the State Department,
he held the posts of Director of the Office of United
Nations Affairs, 1947-49, and Deputy Under Secretary of State, 1949-51. He was President of the
Rockefeller Foundation, 1952-61. When the Council
on Foreign Relations in New York made the Jackson Subcommittee project the subject of one of its
study seminars in November, 1959, he served as
chairman of the meeting.*

Mr. Chairman and members of the committee, I greatly appreciate the opportunity of appearing before your Subcommittee.
Since its inception, I have followed closely your deliberations and
have read your reports with interest. I did not think, of course, when
I had the honor of participating in the meeting you held with the
Council on Foreign Relations in 1959, that I might be appearing before your group as Secretary of State.

I think I should observe at the outset that the philosophy embodied in your reports *Super-Cabinet Officers and Superstaffs* and
The Secretary of State and the American System has by and large
been adopted by President Kennedy's administration. This is particularly true with regard to freeing the national policy machinery
from overdependence on committees, with their attendant dull-
ing of issues and reduction of decisions to a least common denominator.

The corollary to this, in accordance with the recommendations

* Testimony delivered to the Subcommittee on National Policy Machinery,
August 24, 1961.

of your subcommittee, has been the upgrading of the role of the Department of State. Since the Department functions as the principal coordinating arm of the President in carrying out policies affecting our international relations, it is playing a daily role in developing, coordinating, and administering national security policy. It performs these tasks primarily through its operating bureaus, which have been assigned those national security responsibilities of concern to the Department that were previously held by interdepartmental committees.

Those of us concerned with the staffing and organization of the Department of State have therefore sought to make it fully responsive to its increased duties and to justify confidence on the part of the President, other agencies of government, and the American people. I might describe a few of the ways in which we have been working toward these ends.

State Department Staffing and Organization

In selection of personnel both in Washington and in the field, while relying heavily on the skilled professionals of the Foreign Service, we are also bringing in a number of outstanding men from private life and from other government agencies. All of these men have relevant previous experience and proven qualities of leadership. From the new and the old, I believe we are developing an effective team.

Fresh talents have been brought into planning as well as into operating jobs. Thus, the Policy Planning Council has been augmented and strengthened. By September, more than half its membership will be new, including three former ambassadors as well as men with distinguished records in pertinent professional fields. Planning advisers have also been assigned to most of the operating bureaus, to take the lead in developing regional and country planning formerly done by the National Security Council, as well as to maintain close working relations with the Policy Planning Council.

Thus, we are in the process of making a vigorous response to your verdict that "a better planning effort is needed in State." In addition to strengthening the specialized planners, we have markedly increased the participation of the operating bureaus, including the Assistant Secretaries personally, in the planning process.

As anticipated by the President's statement of February 19 abolishing the Operations Coordinating Board, I have been relying heavily on the Assistant Secretaries for interagency leadership in the implementation, as well as the planning, of policy. Coordination is achieved at both the working and policy levels in Washington, and likewise with the "country teams" in the field. The role of ambassadors in this regard has been strengthened by new instructions from the President, and they are regularly consulted in the stage of policy formulation as well as execution. Throughout these processes, the Department of State seeks to exercise initiative through teamwork with the other agencies of government, attained flexibly according to the problems in hand rather than rigidly under an elaborate committee mechanism.

Another way in which the Department has moved is in the creation of the Operations Center, which assists me in carrying out my responsibilities when a crisis or near-crisis situation exists, on a highly operational twenty-four-hour basis. This is done without disturbing the ordinary chain of command in the Department. Officers are especially assigned to the Operations Center to work with the geographic and functional bureaus and other agencies to develop operational plans, arrange for interdepartmental coordination through its regular liaison officers, and monitor the execution of operational decisions. The Department is thus able to act effectively with a speed that would be difficult to obtain otherwise and that will be further enhanced when communications equipment now being procured is installed.

I might mention one other important tool in the field of national security policy—the task force, a team selected to come up with the answer to particular problems, usually on a short-time basis. This is not a wholly new device but has perhaps been used more widely in this administration than previously. Its importance lies in the highly personalized and centralized basis of its assignment. Since the authority for the task force stems directly from the President or other high officials, there usually results added urgency and a more thorough consideration of the problem than would otherwise be possible.

In most cases, the head of a task force is that person, such as the Assistant Secretary of State in charge of the appropriate regional bureau, who would normally be responsible. Interdepartmental coordination is assured through the membership of representatives of other agencies involved. Task forces will continue to have a useful role; however, they can be costly in time and personnel and should not be used for ordinary operating problems.

Relations with the Defense Department

Although a number of other departments and agencies are concerned with national security policy, as is indicated by the statutory composition of the National Security Council itself, the other great department of government most intimately involved is, of course, the Department of Defense. In his excellent statement to your Subcommittee, the Secretary of Defense has given a thorough description of the cooperative relationship developed between the Departments of Defense and State. Perhaps the most important and from my standpoint the most pleasant aspect of this is the very satisfactory personal relationship I enjoy with Secretary McNamara. This makes it possible for us to discuss matters of common concern with the utmost frankness. As a result, I believe we are achieving a close coordination of foreign and defense policies.

As Mr. McNamara pointed out, there are frequent regular and *ad hoc* meetings between officials of the two Departments, including the Joint Chiefs of Staff, which give depth to this cooperation. On our side, we have created the Office of the Deputy Assistant Secretary for Politico-Military Affairs, to assist the supervisory level of the State Department in the management and conduct of all the Department's relations with the Defense Department, including the military establishment. It is intended to provide leadership on such matters within the State Department and thereby enable it more effectively to provide timely political guidance to other governmental agencies on politico-military matters.

With regard to broader training of personnel, Secretary McNamara told you of the present stage of the State-Defense exchange program, and I fully share his favorable preliminary impression of the results. In addition, State now has thirty-two officers on detail to the Department of Commerce, as well as some fifteen divided among other important agencies such as Treasury, Labor, CIA, USIA, and ICA. We are also reviewing the training courses for senior officers in the war colleges and our Foreign Service Institute with a view to better integration of training and matters of high-level concern.

Relations with Other Departments and Staffs

Mr. Bell's testimony dealt fully with the very important question of the relationship between the Department of State and the

Bureau of the Budget in matters affecting national policy. As he pointed out, arrangements have been made which assure that cost and budget considerations are worked into programs of military and economic aid, regional and country planning, and into task-force reports at an early stage in their development.

One of the most difficult and long-standing problems of the Department of State has been its complex pattern of relations with other departments and agencies of the Government on international economic, commercial, and financial matters. As you know, the President earlier this year abolished the Council on Foreign Economic Policy and emphasized the role of leadership the Department of State must play in the development and coordination of our foreign economic policies. This role involves contacts with other departments and agencies at almost every level, but the principal responsibility for exercising the Department's leadership in this field rests with the Under Secretary of Economic Affairs, George W. Ball. To assist him in dealing with issues that require high-level policy consideration, there has recently been established an arrangement whereby the Under Secretaries of the departments principally concerned with economic and trade matters hold regular meetings to discuss these issues.

Scheduling of matters for consideration by the National Security Council is normally arranged by the President's Special Assistant for National Security, McGeorge Bundy, working in close cooperation with the appropriate officers in the Department of State and other departments and agencies. Responsibility for presentation is assigned to the department chiefly concerned. An effort is made to present issues in breadth and depth and in terms of the alternate courses of action offered. Once a decision is taken by the President, clear responsibility is assigned to the appropriate agency, in most cases the Department of State, for the coordinated execution of the agreed policy. Thus, the principle of departmental responsibility, which was emphasized in the excellent presentation made to your Subcommittee by Don Price, is adhered to throughout.

In conclusion, I should like to say that in my judgment the present system goes a long way toward meeting the objectives recommended by your Subcommittee. But, at the same time, I do not wish to imply that we have no problems yet to resolve. We will continue to seek for ways of providing the President with ever greater flexibility in focusing his attention, and that of the Cabinet officers involved, on problems requiring high-level decision.

Tasks of the Secretary and Department of State

SENATOR JACKSON. Mr. Secretary, as you undoubtedly know, this committee and witnesses before it, and, of course, the President himself, have taken the position that the Secretary of State must be the President's first adviser in national strategy and national security affairs—in fact as well as theory. In other words, we see the job of the Secretary of State and his Department as going far beyond the limits of practicing diplomacy in the original sense of that word.

Dean Price has told us that the job of winning back the primacy of the Secretary of State in international affairs "cannot be done simply by enunciating a principle or enacting a law; it will take years to build up the necessary personnel and institutional habits." My question, Mr. Secretary, is this: what do you see as the toughest problem facing you and your Department in staffing and organizing yourself so that you can do the job the President has laid out for you?

SECRETARY RUSK. If I might make a preliminary comment as to just what the nature of this job is, it might set the framework for the specific reply to your question.

I think we need to bear in mind that the business of the Department of State or the substance of our national security policy is a world over which we ourselves do not have control. We are dealing with a hundred or more other sovereign governments in different parts of the world with different cultures, different national interests, different outlooks on the world scene. This world scene is in a stage of massive transformation, including great revolutionary movements—of nationalism, of rising expectations, of science and technology—not to mention the pressures Communist-bloc nations are putting behind their doctrine of the historical inevitability of this revolution.

All these things are producing a world that is in rapid change in a considerable amount of disarray. It is this world with which we have to deal.

Further, the United States has itself emerged in a new position of responsibility, simply because of the position it found itself in after World War II. In power and economic strength and in vitality, we have found ourselves in a position where what we do and what we do not do become in themselves important decisions that affect what is happening in the rest of the world.

Now we are in a rather special position, in the conduct of our foreign relations in this country. In a certain sense, influence on American policy is a primary target of any foreign office in the world. In a certain sense, if we do not act, we have already made a decision. We can shape the course of events by action or inaction, which imposes upon us sometimes a frightening responsibility. It involves us in questions that, taken together, may well be passing beyond the competence of the mind of man to handle, in the complexity and the pace of the matters with which we deal.

I would like to emphasize pace, because this has to do with some of our problems in the Department of State. The pace of events has itself been revolutionary—others have used the metaphor that we must lead with our sights in trying to work with the future if we are to come on the target of the present.

One of our problems is that we try to keep not just abreast but ahead of events in our approach to these surging world affairs.

Now, all of this means a transformation over a period of time of the role of the State Department and the United States in the world, and the demand made upon the State Department personnel. It means a revolutionary transformation of diplomacy itself. That is the task in front of us and our problem is to try to keep up with it.

That means professional staff in the Department who are involved in problems that contain almost every aspect of national life, problems that ramify into every part of the world. Any action taken on one important matter in one place sets off a chain reaction of effect on every other important problem with which we are dealing. It means that we need officers who understand these chain reactions, who not only can deal with the specific problem before them but can understand the effect of what we do upon every other problem before our nation. It means officers who not only are equipped on political matters but on scientific matters, economic matters, cultural matters; we are involved totally in the network of our relations with other countries. It now means more and more management. An ambassador of an embassy in an important country has a first-class management problem on his hands. It also means making a desperate effort to try to anticipate, to look ahead, so that if we do not act, we do not act on purpose; so that if we delay, it is intentional delay. Everything we do has something to do with what happens in the rest of the world.

I would say that one of our most important tasks is to train and prepare the personnel of the State Department to think as a government, to try to imagine themselves in the position of the President, and to think broadly about the world scene and what we are trying to do, so that the immediate decisions that they make become a part of a consistent pattern of national policy. In doing so, we must also be sure that we are talking about national policy as it is reflected in the actions of other agencies and departments of the government. This is a very large task involving comprehensiveness of thinking as well as a pace of thinking. If I might say so, it takes the best team we can possibly put together. We have not achieved yet what we hope to achieve, but it is an endless task toward which we are constantly working.

State-Defense Problems

SENATOR JACKSON. I was very much interested in your statement of your relations with Mr. McNamara on State-Defense problems.

Do you have the opportunity from time to time really to sit down together and discuss these problems, which are at the heart of our national security task?

SECRETARY RUSK. Yes, Mr. Chairman, I must say that one of the most heartening things about the responsibility which I bear is the relationship with the Secretary of Defense. I have served almost as much time in the Pentagon as I have in the Department of State over the years, and I have, myself, a strong awareness of the need for the close relationship and coordination between those two Departments. It must start at the top.

Secretary McNamara and I do see each other with great frequency in my office or at the White House or at Cabinet meetings or in special meetings to consider specific questions which we might wish to talk over with the President—in a variety of ways. I have on occasion gone over to meet with him and the Joint Chiefs of Staff in his building. This personal contact at the top not only is important in giving the two individuals concerned a better understanding of the problems each of us might have, but also sets the tone and atmosphere for contacts down the line.

Secretary McNamara and I agreed at the very beginning that we would not look upon our own offices as the channel of contact between our two departments, but that we would encourage our colleagues at all levels to establish contact with their counterparts. There would be, then, a continual exchange of ideas between the two departments as a part of this great problem of coordinating foreign and defense policy in a national policy. I think that the relationship between the two departments is good. I think the spirit of that relationship is good; we are pulling in the same direction.

SENATOR JACKSON. Do you feel that we are making progress with this attitude and philosophy in the depth of the departments as well, so that the people down below understand there should be greater exchange?

SECRETARY RUSK. I do, and I am convinced that this is of great importance. I can look back to the time when I was a relatively junior officer on the general staff and remember how important it was to keep in touch with relatively junior officers in the Department of State. To squeeze these relationships into a single, narrow, stilted channel, I think would be a great mistake. It is important for people who are handling vital matters to know their colleagues in the other department.

Today, because of the pace of business, relatively junior officers in the Department of State are sending out telegrams on matters that, before World War II, might well have gone to the Secretary himself. Our business could not be handled in any other way. We have to give broad policy guidance, but we also have to let our junior colleagues act because not to act itself is a decision. If a deputy director has a responsibility—and we believe this in the Department of State—for insuring that the interests of the other departments are fully taken into account, then he must be in direct touch with his colleagues in the other departments. That means that there is a range of contact that I think is inevitable and essential.

The Secretary of State and Congress

SENATOR JACKSON. Mr. Secretary, roughly how many appearances have you made before congressional committees this year?

SECRETARY RUSK. I would think, sir, that the number would approximate twenty.

SENATOR JACKSON. Some of us feel quite strongly, you know, that this is a great drain on your time. I wonder if you have any suggestions to meet this problem?

SECRETARY RUSK. Mr. Chairman, if I appear to make an admission against interest, perhaps you will forgive me.

I, myself, do not regret the time I spend with important committees of the Congress. There are occasions when joint consultation would be more convenient and would help in reducing the pressures on the Secretary's time. On the other hand, this is a country that moves by consent. It moves through the cooperation of the executive and legislative branches. I have found that in these consultations with the committees of the Senate and House of Representatives, the exchange of ideas, particularly those that can occur in executive session, are a very important part of the process of forming national policy.

Some of the most experienced individuals in public life, who have been dealing with foreign-policy matters for long periods of time, are found in these committees.

My own thought would be that if there were other ways to save time, that is fine, but this consultation between the executive branch and the Congress is time very well spent.

SENATOR JACKSON. I agree that much good can come from an exchange of ideas, but I think a lot of effort is duplicated on the Hill. We complain about duplication in the executive branch, but I think we have room for improvement up here.

It took the executive branch to come up with the National Security Act of 1947 which, by its very enactment, forced the amalgamation of the Military Affairs and Naval Affairs committees into one committee, the Armed Services Committee. Maybe some executive prodding will force us to get our own house in order.

SECRETARY RUSK. There have been occasions when it is possible to draw leaders of different committees together for consultation on a very informal basis. I must confess, there are times when it does appear to be a bit strenuous to appear on the same subject before four different committees and try to say the same thing in four different ways.

Easing the Burdens of the Secretary of State

SENATOR JACKSON. Mr. Lovett told us that one important attribute of the Secretary of State was his availability in Washington where he can be near the President and give leadership to his Department. Have you given any thought to possible approaches that might ease your travel burden?

SECRETARY RUSK. I do think that a Secretary should try his best to occupy his post in Washington to the maximum extent possible. However, I do not believe that he can make it a matter of dogma. He has to be able and willing and ready to do what has to be done to support the national interest.

This is not just a problem for the Secretary of State. It is a problem for all foreign ministers. The burdens of schedule upon them are getting to be very heavy indeed.

I have discussed this problem with my colleagues, the other foreign ministers. There is a gentle effort going on among a number of them to organize a trade-union of foreign ministers to create more tolerable working conditions.

One of the advantages we do have, which is convenient to the Secretary of State for geographical reasons, results from the fact that foreign ministers are in the habit of attending, more and more frequently, the first portion of the General Assembly of the United Nations. I think that where they are together, various groupings of them can consult each other, and individuals can see each other, which may serve to take the place of at least some of the travel.

SENATOR JACKSON. Mr. Lovett suggested before our committee —and Mr. Herter, then Secretary of State, endorsed the idea— that an international conference be held to revise present protocol practices and come up with some sensible procedures. Have you given any thought to that or has anything been done in that area?

SECRETARY RUSK. There have been some steps taken to simplify protocol itself, but I think there are more measures that could be taken to reduce the formality in the conduct of intergovernmental relations without damagining its uses in preserving a dispassionate and impersonal exchange among states. I think we need to review internationally the procedures by which we conduct intergovernmental business. We should try to get a common agreement among governments that questions of prestige will not become attached to the channels of intergovernmental communication—so we can simplify, expedite, and clarify these intergovernmental relationships. I think it would be an unfortunate thing if, when governments speak to each other, too much special importance is attached to the channel through which they speak, because, after all, it is governments who are speaking.

This is a matter which does need further study; perhaps it could only be dealt with eventually by systematic international consultation.

SENATOR JACKSON. What about the use of ambassadors at large? Do you find this can be helpful in easing some of the burdens of your Office?

SECRETARY RUSK. This helps some; indeed, ambassadors at large can fulfill a very important role. As a matter of fact, Ambassador

Philip Jessup was appointed ambassador at large with the thought that he might take the place of the Secretary of State in certain international meetings and negotiations. This did not work out quite as expected, because other governments would not look upon a substitute as the equivalent of a foreign minister. But, nonetheless, a special ambassador, such as Ambassador Averell Harriman, can play a very important role as the personal representative of the President or the Secretary of State in *ad hoc* special consultations with the heads of other governments.

A Super-staff for National Security?

SENATOR JAVITS. There has been considerable discussion about the need for some super-board that will tie in all elements of our governmental apparatus in order more effectively to carry on the "cold war." What do you think about that?

SECRETARY RUSK. Let me say that the cold war is nothing less than the determination by the Sino-Soviet bloc to press their doctrine of the historic inevitability of world communism into action in all parts of the world, and it has manifested itself in many forms. We did not, ourselves, start or declare the cold war. This came about when it became clear, immediately after World War II, that the Soviet Union was not going to join the United Nations and help build the decent kind of world order we were all looking for. They have, in later years, been pressing in a great variety of ways—not just the military pressures of Mr. Stalin, but all sorts of techniques of economic, cultural, and other forms of penetration, and guerrillas and techniques of that sort.

The cold war, therefore, necessarily involves almost every aspect of our foreign policy—whether we are working with international organizations to get certain parts of the world's daily work organized across national frontiers, whether we are in a sharp debate in the United Nations, or whether we are in direct confrontation in some troubled spot somewhere in the world. In the broadest sense, I do not believe there is any one board that can take on the elements of the cold war in all of its ramifications. This is deeply and intimately involved with many, many aspects of what the great departments of government are working on.

SENATOR JAVITS. Though it may not have been so designed, was it not the purpose of the National Security Council to have at least one place where the President had a sounding board in which all these threads were gathered together?

SECRETARY RUSK. That is one of the places where this could occur. It also occurs, of course, at Cabinet meetings and in meetings which are called specially to deal with certain aspects of a problem.

SENATOR JAVITS. And all three techniques are employed by this administration?

SECRETARY RUSK. That is correct, sir.

SENATOR JAVITS. So far you have found no collision of operation in the fact that they are all concerned?

SECRETARY RUSK. No, sir, because in the three techniques to which I refer the principal department heads are all involved, and they can translate the conclusions that might be reached in any one of these into the direct operations of their department.

The National Security Council*

SENATOR JACKSON. As one of its first acts the new administration abolished the Operations Coordinating Board. Will you comment on why this was done?

SECRETARY RUSK. The principal reason was to identify the responsibility of departments, and within departments of individuals, for following through on decisions of the President or, in our case, of the Secretary of State.

Over a period of time—and this goes back to World War II days when I was on the general staff—we felt that much of the committee machinery left dangling, hidden vetoes all over town and that this tended to slow down operations rather considerably.

Now under the present situation we get policy guidance from the President on an agreed basis. Operational responsibility is assigned to a department. That department has the responsibility for keeping in touch with other departments and agencies that are interested, but not necessarily on a veto basis. If an important question does come up or if another department or agency raises a point to which it attaches great importance, then, of course, that point has to be brought up to the policy level for determination.

We have also found that we must speed up the processing of papers among departments—that the action people have to be in a position to act promptly.

The decision to shift operating responsibility to the Department away from the Operations Coordinating Board was in the interest

* Testimony delivered to the Subcommittee on National Policy Machinery in executive session, August 24, 1961.

of having a man who knew it was his job to see that things moved.

SENATOR JACKSON. Emphasizing individual responsibility.

SECRETARY RUSK. That is correct.

SENATOR JACKSON. So that you rely on the traditional departments to follow through or on an action officer who will carry it out.

SECRETARY RUSK. That is right.

SENATOR JACKSON. Along this same line, Robert Lovett told us, "The idea seems to have got around that just because some decision may affect your activities, you automatically have a right to take part in making it. . . . There is some reason to feel that the doctrine may be getting out of hand and that what was designed to act as a policeman may, in fact, become a jailor." Mr. Lovett called this the foul-up factor in our methods. Do you have any comment on that?

SECRETARY RUSK. Mr. Lovett and I, over the years, have talked about this problem. I called it a potential Parkinson's law, that "everyone who is affected by a decision must participate in making it." Now, this is a great burden upon policy formulation and action, but on the other hand our present system throws a very large responsibility on the department primarily concerned to insure it does in fact take into account these other interests.

In other words, a particular decision may involve five or six departments of government. It may not be desirable to have all of those sit in on the entire policy-making procedure, but it is of critical importance that those who make the policy fully understand what the interest of the Department of Labor, the Department of Commerce, or the Space Agency, might be in a particular decision. At times, that means that you do in fact draw them in, but you don't set up a machinery which gives them a veto.

SENATOR JACKSON. What was the reason for abolishing the Planning Board? Do you think the new system of policy planning and development will work better than the old Planning Board system?

SECRETARY RUSK. I think one of the reasons for abolishing it was to put stronger emphasis on planning within each of the departments. This tended to leave the wrong impression—there was a tendency to think that if there is a planning board in the NSC, then it will be doing the planning and the rest of us need only consider the operational side. This is not a partisan criticism; this goes back a long way.

At the present time, the departments are responsible for assuring that there is a planning orientation at all levels. This was, I think, one feature. Secondly, we felt that general planning was not of too great utility. It was important in terms of the education of those who were to make policy decisions and for the background, alternatives, and general orientation of policy. The most effective planning, however, is focused rather particularly on a situation or on a developing crisis or any idea on foreign policy. We have used as a planning technique the task-force arrangement, by which, under the leadership of a known individual, people are drawn from the affected agencies to sit down and think in a concentrated fashion about one particular problem or set of problems.

I think this applies not only to planning but to operations. The interdepartmental task force is preferable in many instances, I think, to a professional interdepartmental planning board, because it can call upon those from each of the departments who have not only the deepest background of the group in the particular problem, but also who will have a heavy responsibility for it when the planning is over.

One of the most effective task-force exercises was the practically one-man task force that John Foster Dulles constituted in getting the Japanese Peace Treaty. I think that had we tried to handle that problem on an interdepartmental committee basis, we could never have gotten that peace treaty negotiated and ratified. He simply took it on with a two-page letter from the President, saying, "Dear Mr. Dulles: I want you to get a peace treaty of this sort with Japan." On the basis of that, he could cut away the stacks of materials that had developed over the years in the departments. He concentrated on a simple treaty of reconciliation. My job then, as Assistant Secretary of Far Eastern Affairs, was not only to support him, but to block off interference from all the other agencies. They knew that if they wanted to interfere they had to go to the President, and this was difficult to do. The task-force technique provides the President and the Secretary with an instrument with which they can concentrate on a job and move in on it without unnecessary interference that might come from around the fringes.

SENATOR JACKSON. Mr. Secretary, one of the many problems any administration faces is a proper division of labor and responsibility between the Secretary of State and the President's own foreign-policy and defense aides in the White House and Executive Office. Would you describe briefly the division of responsibility?

SECRETARY RUSK. The chief role which the advisers in the White House play is that of liaison and of assistance in the preparation of papers and agenda of meetings. They do not operate as independent policy-makers. They are in very close touch with us through two or three channels. We also constitute special groups when the President wants to talk to a few people on an *ad hoc* basis about a particular problem.

The NSC staff has on it a number of people of considerable competence. When we have an interdepartmental task force on a particular problem, we ask one or another White House staff member to sit in on that task force.

SENATOR JACKSON. We mentioned earlier the view of many of us on the committee and of witnesses before the committee and of the President himself regarding the necessity of reestablishing the primacy of the State Department in foreign-policy matters. Do you find that you are getting good cooperation from the other departments in doing this job?

SECRETARY RUSK. I literally don't feel any interdepartmental resistance, shall I say, on a bureaucratic basis. I think the attitude of the heads of those departments is all one could ask for, and that that attitude is making itself felt right down inside the departments. It is perfectly obvious, and indeed desirable, that from time to time there would be differences of view or emphasis between departments on particular questions and these are talked out between the Secretaries and, if necessary, with the President. But the general attitude of cooperation, I think, is very well established.

There is a certain feeling of jealousy in the lower echelons of departments. I know that there is a problem at times, whether I see it or not. We are constantly working to get a more complete exchange of information and ideas right down through the whole machinery.

SENATOR JACKSON. You mentioned the *ad hoc* informal groups for policy-making. Some people say that maybe we have gone too far in this direction, that the system becomes a bit too casual at times. Do you have any comments on that?

SECRETARY RUSK. I think we might draw a distinction between certain groups that were put together at the very beginning of the new administration, and what I would call a task force as I discussed it a little earlier. When the President took office, there were certain things that had to be done straight away and with some urgency. For example, we had to meet a deadline on negotiations on nuclear test bans; we had to get a program up to the Congress quickly on problems arising out of the Act of Bogotá—on the $500 million social development plan; we had to get our foreign-aid program whipped into shape. These matters were handled by special task forces specifically drawn in to get a job done at a pace at which the normal machinery could not be expected to operate. Now, the foreign-aid task force has gone out of existence; the Latin American task force has been disbanded and the Assistant Secretary has taken on there.

From now on, when task forces are put together for a particular problem, the Assistant Secretary or his deputy will be placed in charge, so responsibility will remain within the geographic bureau.

Task forces are serviced by the Operations Center on a twenty-four-hour alert basis. We discovered we need just that. But the task forces being serviced are a part of the Department's normal responsible bureau.

SENATOR JAVITS. I wondered about this Operations Center. Does this actually have a top-level man in charge of it every hour of the day and night?

SECRETARY RUSK. It has a responsible Foreign Service officer—not just a junior clerk—in charge throughout the day and night. Its communication setup will be rapidly improved. The center assures us that there is someone who can alert the Department and raise people for the necessary action at any time of the day or night.

Mr. Chairman, we are going to have to improve greatly our communications facilities in order to be ready for some of these crises which occur—

SENATOR MUNDT. You are talking about communications within the Department?

SECRETARY RUSK. No, international communications under U.S. control. I ran into this first when I was in Bangkok for the SEATO Conference. Any communications delay with Washington is something that the United States cannot afford these days. We will have proposals to try to improve this.

There are some extremely delicate technical problems which are causing us to revise basically some of our communications techniques. Again, with the large number of new countries to deal with and with this turbulence going on in the world, we have had to ask for fifty additional people to avoid a substantial backlog in the actual decoding of incoming telegrams. There are times when a few hours delay in receiving a telegram can make a very large difference when you are handling a situation.

SENATOR JACKSON. To get back to the *ad hoc* groups and the informal committees, are the decisions that have been arrived at put in writing so that there is a clear record, so that what is agreed upon is clearly understood and the follow-through will be carried out in accordance with decisions? The question arises whether some of these things get too casual and some of the understandings or agreements are misunderstood.

SECRETARY RUSK. Our present practice is to put these matters in writing so the responsible departments will better be able to follow up on the action to be taken. But some care has to be taken not to let these action papers get imprisoned, because those very pieces of paper themselves need constant monitoring to be sure they continue to be relevant to the situation. From time to time, we bring decisions back to the Secretary or President for adjustment in the light of changes in the situation. McGeorge Bundy, for example, after meeting at the White House, circulates a note to make clear to everybody exactly what was decided. If there are differences as to what was decided that is straightened out.

SENATOR JACKSON. Mr. Bell has told us that nobody in the administration is yet "satisfied with the basic system for appreciating, analyzing, and proposing solutions to the biggest questions we face in the national security area. These are problems that concern primarily the State and Defense Departments." Toward what type of basic system do you think the administration should move to do a better job than it now does?

SECRETARY RUSK. I don't myself believe that there is an organizational gimmick that will meet this problem. I would agree with Mr. Bell that we have not reached the point that we should like to reach in dealing with these matters, but we must keep in mind that these are problems of the most incredible complexity. When you think about the nature of modern weapons, the confrontation between the free world and the Soviet bloc, the problems of negotiating within the shadow of a nuclear exchange, the problems of really identifying the vital interest for which you must be prepared to use whatever force is necessary as an alternative to surrender on the vital issue—these are things that make pygmies of us all.

I don't think we will ever be able to say that we have fully got them under the kind of control we would like to have. But again, this is a matter of continual work to develop a situation in the world that makes these problems easier to handle. There is also the problem of developing people with a deeper and broader understanding of what the problem is and how it can be handled. I think the nation itself is learning as we go along. I was deeply encouraged, for example, to know that despite the costs of the additional military effort we had to make, both Houses of Congress gave the extent of financial support to the foreign-aid program which they did and did not take their eyes off the nature of the crisis right around the globe and say, "Build our defense at the expense of foreign aid." I think this is the kind of learning that we, as a nation, must seek in the years ahead.

SENATOR MUSKIE. With the elimination of the Planning Board and the Operations Coordinating Board, what is left of the NSC institutionally, other than a convenient label for a meeting of people who would probably meet anyway?

SECRETARY RUSK. It has, first, a small NSC staff headed by Mc-George Bundy, which provides excellent machinery for prompt and immediate liaison with the President or with any other members of the White House staff whose help is needed on a particular problem. Also, the staff is in turn a valuable aid to the President. They meet with him at the regular Presidential staff meetings, and they pass along to the departments requests for information or questions or suggestions that might be raised by the President himself.

Secondly, this staff also helps in preparing the necessary papers and agenda needed for meetings of the NSC or any groups related to it. I consider that the meetings of the NSC are themselves important; however, this is only a part of the process by which the President consults with his chief advisers—frequently with various combinations of members who might ordinarily be at an NSC meeting. The staff is valuable in passing on things that we know the President will be interested in or that will need his attention. The staff pulls matters together for presentation to the President at the earliest opportunity, consistent with the President's own needs and his own schedules.

We would be greatly crippled if that staff were not there.

SENATOR MUSKIE. I hope the elimination of the Operations Coordinating Board as part of the structure does not eliminate the follow-through, which it seems to me was implicit in its existence, the follow-through on action by the operating department to implement decisions.

SECRETARY RUSK. The follow-through becomes a responsibility of the department concerned. The periodic reports submitted both to the Secretary and through the NSC staff to the President on the follow-through are an important disciplinary element.

SENATOR JACKSON. Mr. Secretary, it has been a marathon session. We are most grateful to you for giving us of your time and counsel.

SECRETARY RUSK. I want to express appreciation, not only for me personally as Secretary of State, but also for the Department, for the extraordinary help that this study has been in the conduct of our foreign relations and in dealing with these very difficult problems of national security policy. I don't know that there can be found anywhere a more thorough and penetrating look at this complicated problem than in the reports coming from this committee. We are grateful to you and your colleagues for having undertaken it.

SENATOR JACKSON. Thank you, sir.

The National Security Council in the 1960's

McGEORGE BUNDY

*McGeorge Bundy, Special Assistant to President
Kennedy for National Security Affairs, has continued
to serve President Johnson in this same capacity. He
came to his post from Harvard University where he
was Dean of the Faculty of Arts and Sciences,
1953-61, and Professor of Government, 1954-61.*

THE NATIONAL SECURITY COUNCIL
UNDER PRESIDENT KENNEDY*

I have thought hard about your letter of July 13, which asks for official memorandums that would be the current equivalent of memorandums submitted by the previous administration. I find that this is not easy to do, but let me try. The previous administration wrote out of many years of experience in which it had gradually developed a large and complex series of processes. This administration has been revising these arrangements to fit the needs of a new President, but the work of revision is far from done, and it is too soon for me to report with any finality upon the matters about which you ask. It seems to me preferable, at this early stage in our work, to give you an informal interim account in this letter.

Much of what you have been told in the reports of the previous administration about the legal framework and concept of the Council remains true today. There has been no recent change in the National Security Act of 1947. Nor has there been any change in the basic and decisive fact that the Council is advisory only. Decisions are made by the President. Finally, there has been no change in the basic proposition that, in the language of Robert

* Letter concerning the National Security Council to Senator Henry M. Jackson, September 4, 1961.

Cutler, "the Council is a vehicle for a President to use in accordance with its suitability to his plans for conducting his great office." As Mr. Cutler further remarked, "a peculiar virtue of the National Security Act is its flexibility," and "each President may use the Council as he finds most suitable at a given time." It is within the spirit of this doctrine that a new process of using the NSC is developing.

The specific changes that have occurred are three. First, the NSC meets less often than it did. There were sixteen meetings in the first six months of the Kennedy Administration. Much that used to flow routinely to the weekly meetings of the Council is now settled in other ways—by separate meetings with the President, by letters, by written memorandums, and at levels below that of the President. President Kennedy has preferred to call meetings of the NSC only after determining that a particular issue is ready for discussion in this particular forum.

I know you share my understanding that the National Security Council has never been and should never become the only instrument of counsel and decision available to the President in dealing with the problems of our national security. I believe this fact cannot be overemphasized. It is not easy for me to be sure of the procedures of earlier administrations, but I have the impression that many of the great episodes of the Truman and Eisenhower administrations were not dealt with in their most vital aspects through the machinery of the NSC. It was not in an NSC meeting that we got into the Korean war or made the Korean truce. The NSC was not, characteristically, the place of decision on specific major budgetary issues, which so often affect both policy and strategy. It was not the usual forum of diplomatic decision; it was not, for example, a major center of work on Berlin at any time before 1961. The National Security Council is one instrument among many; it must never be made an end in itself.

But for certain issues of great moment, the NSC is indeed valuable. President Kennedy has used it for discussion of basic national policy toward a number of countries. He has used it both for advice on particular pressing decisions and for recommendations on long-term policy. As new attitudes develop within the administration, and as new issues arise in the world, the NSC is likely to continue as a major channel through which broad issues of national security policy come forward for Presidential decision.

Meanwhile, the President continues to meet at very frequent intervals with the Secretary of State, the Secretary of Defense, and other officials closely concerned with problems of national security. Such meetings may be as large as an NSC meeting or as small as a face-to-face discussion with a single Cabinet officer. What they have in common is that a careful record is kept, in the appropriate way, whenever a decision is reached. Where primary responsibility falls clearly to a single Department, the primary record of such decisions will usually be made through that Department. Where the issue is broader, or where the action requires continued White House attention, the decision will be recorded through the process of the National Security Council. Thus the business of the National Security staff goes well beyond what is treated in formal meetings of the National Security Council. It is our purpose, in cooperation with other Presidential staff officers, to meet the President's staff needs throughout the national security area.

The second and more significant change in the administration of the National Security Council and its subordinate agencies is the abolition, by Executive Order 10920, of the Operations Coordinating Board. This change needs to be understood both for what it is and for what it is not. It is not in any sense a downgrading of the tasks of coordination and follow-up; neither is it an abandonment of Presidential responsibility for these tasks. It is rather a move to eliminate an instrument that does not match the style of operation and coordination of the current administration.

From the point of view of the new administration, the decisive difficulty in the OCB was that without unanimity it had no authority. No one of its eight members had authority over any other. It was never a truly Presidential instrument, and its practices were those of a group of able men attempting, at the second and third levels of government, to keep large departments in reasonable harmony with each other. Because of good will among its members, and unusual administrative skill in its secretariat, it did much useful work; it also had weaknesses. But its most serious weakness, for the new administration, was simply that neither the President himself nor the present administration as a whole conceives of operational coordination as a task for a large committee in which no one man has authority. It was and is our belief that there is much to be done that the OCB could not do, and that the things it did do can be done as well or better in other ways.

The most important of these other ways is an increased reliance on the leadership of the Department of State. It would not be appropriate for me to describe in detail the changes the Department of State has begun to execute in meeting the large responsibilities that fall to it under this concept of administration. It is enough if I say that the President has made it very clear that he does not want a large separate organization between him and his Secretary of State. Neither does he wish any question to arise as to the clear authority and responsibility of the Secretary of State, not only in his own Department, and not only in such large-scale related areas as foreign aid and information policy, but also as the agent of coordination in all our major policies toward other nations.

The third change in the affairs of the NSC grows out of the first two and has a similar purpose. We have deliberately rubbed out the distinction between planning and operation that governed the administrative structure of the NSC staff in the last administration. This distinction, real enough at the extremes of the daily cable traffic and long-range assessment of future possibilities, breaks down in most of the business of decision and action. This is especially true at the level of Presidential action. Thus it seems to us best that the NSC staff, which is essentially a Presidential instrument, should be composed of men who can serve equally well in the process of planning and in that of operational follow-up. Already it has been made plain, in a number of cases, that the President's interests and purposes can be better served if the staff officer who keeps in daily touch with operations in a given area is also the officer who acts for the White House staff in related planning activities.

Let me turn briefly, in closing, to the role of the Presidential staff as a whole, in national security affairs. This staff is smaller than it was in the last administration, and it is more closely knit. The President uses in these areas a number of officers holding White House appointment, and a number of others holding appointments in the National Security Council staff. He also uses extensively the staff of the Bureau of the Budget. These men are all staff officers. Their job is to help the President, not to supersede or supplement any of the high officials who hold line responsibilities in the executive departments and agencies. Their task is that of all staff officers: to extend the range and enlarge the direct effectiveness of the man they serve. Heavy responsibilities for operation, for coordination, and for diplomatic relations can be and are delegated to the Department of State. Full use of all the powers of leadership can be and is expected in other departments and agencies. There remains a crushing burden of responsibility, and of sheer work, on the President himself; there remains also the steady flow of questions, of ideas, of executive energy which a strong

President will give off like sparks. If his Cabinet officers are to be free to do their own work, the President's work must be done—to the extent that he cannot do it himself—by staff officers under his direct oversight. But this is, I repeat, something entirely different from the interposition of such a staff between the President and his Cabinet officers.

I hope this rather general exposition may be helpful to you. I have been conscious, in writing it, of the limits which are imposed upon me by the need to avoid classified questions, and still more by the requirement that the President's own business be treated in confidence. Within those limits I have tried to tell you clearly how we are trying to do our job.

THE NATIONAL SECURITY COUNCIL
UNDER PRESIDENT JOHNSON*

In response to your request, I am bringing up to date my letter to you of September 4, 1961, concerning the National Security Council. In almost every particular, the principles and procedures set forth in the 1961 letter have governed the work of the Council under both President Kennedy and President Johnson.

The National Security Council continues to operate as an advisory body to the President as provided by the National Security Act of 1947. It meets whenever the President has decided that an issue is ready for discussion in this forum. Other business in the national security area is settled by separate meetings with the President, by letters, by written memorandums, or at levels below that of the President.

Experience has proved the validity of the premise that the NSC should not be the only instrument of counsel available to the President in dealing with problems of national security. But in the past four years, the Council has been used frequently by both President Kennedy and President Johnson for advice on particular pressing decisions and for recommendations on policy.

President Johnson meets at frequent intervals with the Secretary of State, the Secretary of Defense, and other officials closely concerned with problems of national security. A record is kept of Presidential decisions. The Council staff participates in the preparations for such meetings and follows the execution of resulting Presidential decisions.

The increased reliance placed on the leadership of the Depart-

* Letter to Senator Henry M. Jackson, January 28, 1965.

ment of State from 1961 on has been fully maintained. No question has arisen during the past four years as to the clear authority and responsibility of the Secretary of State not only in such large-scale related areas as foreign aid and information policy but also as the agent of coordination in all our major policies toward other nations.

In bringing my earlier letter up to date I have again been reminded of the need to avoid classified questions and of the requirement that the President's own business be treated in confidence.

Staffing the Presidency*

RICHARD E. NEUSTADT

Richard E. Neustadt, student of the "new Presidency" and author of Presidential Power, *served on President Truman's White House staff and as consultant to President-elect Kennedy during the transition of 1960-61 and thereafter. He is now a special consultant to President Johnson and Associate Dean of the Graduate School of Public Administration and Professor of Government at Harvard University.*

An Office of National Security Affairs?

Let me put it as candidly as possible: I don't like the thought that we may have to come to another fairly large-scale institutionalized office in the President's own neighborhood. I think we ought to avoid it if we can. I am not prepared to come here and say to you, "It can be avoided." I don't know if it can be.

Let me simply say that staff facilities around the Presidency are not an unmixed blessing for the President. The man needs the kind of flexibility and reach which that staff is supposed to give him, the kind of balanced advice which that staff is supposed to be able to procure for him—by careful watching and airing of difficulties and differences, grievances and information that may not appear upon the surface of advice from the departments. But staff itself can all too quickly become another "department," another complicating echelon in a very complex system.

There are two ways one could build up the staff in the President's neighborhood; both ways have disadvantages. The first way is markedly to enlarge the office of the Special Assistant for National Security Affairs, Mr. Bundy. But the more one does that,

* This discussion is comprised of comments by Professor Neustadt during the question period, Subcommittee on National Security Staffing and Operations, March 25, 1963.

the more one threatens Mr. Bundy's utility as a personal aide. He is pushed toward the troubles that your predecessor subcommittee treated in its report on "Super-Cabinet Officers and Super-Staffs," the troubles Mr. Rockefeller evidently found himself in eight years ago—or Mr. Stassen and others—when their personal service, their ability to be personal agents, to move quickly, to keep abreast of the President's mind—in short, their intimacy—was compromised by all the second-level work their staffs were doing and all the fights their staffs were getting into. The personal assistant begins to bog down as a personal watchdog and intimate servant once he starts to preside over fifty, eighty, or one hundred subordinates.

A second method would be to create an Office of National Security Affairs detached from the Special Assistant's office, manned by careerists across the street, like the Budget Bureau. We may come to this in time. But in doing so, we must remember that we are adding another echelon, another level for clearances, another level for negotiations, another set of career officials who have to relate every day with Pentagon and the State Department and the domestic economic agencies. To a degree, we are throwing more pressure on the White House for personal staff work to protect the President's interest in these new interagency relations. My feeling is we should resist this as long as we can.

One asks, why hope for anything from the Secretary of State's office—only one Cabinet office among others? What can it do? Well, I think you will find some grounds for hope in some of the efforts now being made there. Some of the planning and research efforts strike me as particularly interesting. I have the impression that a deliberate effort is being made not to treat planning papers as ends in themselves but as means to get a broader kind of thinking done by operating offices throughout the national security complex. Planning and research exercises now seem to be aimed at getting everybody gradually accustomed to think in three dimensions at once—economic, military, and political—regardless of organizational placement.

I think it is worth inquiring whether, over a period of several years, efforts of this sort may not actually change some of the ways people think, whether it may not build into the State Department a broader frame of reference for the operating officers—hopefully, broad enough to sustain staff work from the Secretary's Office which supports and supplements the work of White House aides. The more one can do that, the less is the need for towering staff structures up above. I certainly would want to see all such experiments furthered before we start building new structures.

There is one other difficulty; it underlies my caution.

In my experience, the most effective kind of staff organization is built around what I would call an action-forcing process, by which I mean a steady stream of actionable issues, concrete issues, that have to be attended to, where something has to be done, a decision has to be reached.

In national security affairs, you have a number of these processes: the budget process, with its statutory deadline, is one; action cables coming from embassies abroad requesting answers and instructions are another; requests for instructions from military assistance groups, the flow through International Security Affairs is another. In wartime, the conduct of hostilities creates still others.

Wherever you build a staff, you ought to try to do so around one or another of these streams of action issues that have to be attended to. Otherwise, you just get planners floating in a void. Now, most of these action streams do flow through the departments. The action cables come through the State Department or, if the military are involved, through the Pentagon. One reason why the Bureau of the Budget as an institution is stronger and has lasted longer than others at the Presidential level is that it is built around just such a stream of actions—budget deadlines, apportionment deadlines—which belong to no department but are imposed routinely and directly on the President himself. If you compare the strength of this entity with the strength of the Council of Economic Advisers, which has much less of an action orientation, I think you will see the difference.

One of the reasons that I keep backing away from an Office of National Security Affairs is that if the staff work there were to be effective, it seems to me you would have to lift up to the President's level, on a routine basis, a great part of the action issues and the action officers now located in Pentagon and State. Otherwise, it would be a kibitzer, another echelon of planner-kibitzers, on the day-by-day business of the two Secretaries and their subordinates. If we build the new office and then try to insure its success, we tend to pull away from the two Secretaries a lot of relatively routine action-taking, decision-taking before we are done. If we don't pull it away, we run the risk that we just have this other layer, this waffle layer of planners and kibitzers operating in a void. If we do pull it away, what have we done to the President?

This is very tricky, in my opinion, and it is the underlying reason why I would like to see the preparatory staff work and the follow-up on everything the White House now can't handle kept down as close to the present operators as possible.

I grant you that if we took the new Office of Science and Technology, instead of the Budget Bureau, as the model for a staff above the departments, the case for an Office of National Security Affairs might look better, at least on the surface. Jerome Wiesner, the President's Scientific Advisory Committee, and the Office of Science and Technology taken together have made quite an impact, even though they aren't organized around an action-forcing process they can call their own. But I think this is partly because their full-time staff is still rather small. I don't think I would want to be in Mr. Wiesner's shoes when his staff gets big, as it will surely tend to do. More importantly, he and his associates have been able, up to now, to reach out and hook onto action-issues in other people's bailiwicks for a rather special reason: his office has been able to claim special expertise, because it can lay hands on technical resources and judgments better or more readily or more confidently than they can. An Office of National Security Affairs could never hope to be in such a good position vis-à-vis the expert claims and confidence of others, especially not others like the Pentagon, or CIA, or State—or Treasury and even Commerce, for that matter, if you want to talk about economics. This is part of the problem of the Council of Economic Advisers.

If you are going to have a strong Office of National Security Affairs, you have to build it around actions. You have to build it around the process of receiving and answering requests for instructions from diplomatic and military missions abroad. There is something solid, a solid core of work to build a staff around. If you build it around that, what have you done to the work of the Office of the Secretary of Defense and the Office of the Secretary of State?

If we can't make this thing work without another echelon, then I think we have to face the fact and establish one. This question has been with us since 1947; with all the experimenting since then, it is still with us.

I know a number of very able career officials in the Executive Office of the President who have been convinced for years that in the long run we shall have to come to an Office of National Security Affairs and an Executive Office staff for national security affairs, that the State Department cannot be at once a department and then something more. I think this is a perfectly tenable position.

It is only out of conservatism that I urge us not to hasten toward this without making every effort to do it the other way.

A Secretary of State's Priorities

I think a Secretary of State, unless he is hired specifically for a different purpose, as Mr. Stettinius was, will and should try to put first his role as senior adviser to the President. I think he must put immediately after that, really as part of it, the role of collegial relations with that other senior adviser, the Secretary of Defense.

If a Secretary of State takes seriously his mandate, as expressed by Mr. Bundy's letter to Senator Jackson of September, 1961, then he would have to put next the attempt to stand at the center of the group of Cabinet officers concerned with national security affairs, while attempting to act as agent of coordination.

This would leave him very little time for all the roles assigned and demanded of him within his own organization. But it seems to me that a Secretary who started off to be a Presidential adviser has to put ahead of department management these other obligations.

A buddy-buddy relationship with the Secretary of Defense, while getting at the heart of the task of coordination, will not automatically take care of two other aspects of his job. One is within his departmental mandate: coordinating with the traditional bureaus those autonomous units—AID, ACDA, USIA—which take policy advice from him. This is really a matter of interagency relations, even though in form some of these agencies are within the Department. The other aspect involves the Secretary of the Treasury. Treasury is our third Foreign Office. I think, in these times, as long as the balance-of-payments problem and all it represents is with us, and as long as the Secretary of the Treasury, in his internal job of debt financing, is heavily and delicately involved in a host of external relations (among others, the banking community's interrelations around the world), one can never afford to regard Treasury as a marginal agency in the national security sphere. On some issues, the State-Treasury relationship will be as crucial as State-Defense is all the time.

I personally doubt that one can ever hope to build inside of the State Department all the specialties it needs. I think it is probably a mistake to try. What one does need to build in State is great generalist capability combined with great competence in political analysis. Political analysis is supposed to be its stock-in-trade. We need to add great skill in dealing with, interpreting, other analytical specialties. But all the other specialists don't have to be in State. We couldn't get them in there if we tried.

Speaking of political analysis, I don't think there is always present in the State Department sufficient appreciation for the difference between politics as diplomacy and politics as politics, not only at home but abroad. State always claims for itself the political advisory role, by which is ordinarily meant the role of diplomatic advice, diplomatic judgment. But one of the difficulties I sense from the outside, in some recent situations, is inadequate consideration for, or perhaps argument for, aspects arising out of social trends and party trends and bureaucratic politics in Britain, to say nothing of palace and other sorts of politics in France. Sensitive advice on things like these is as important as the other kind of political advice, diplomatic advice. We look to State for both kinds, whether we get them or not.

This is a lot to ask, but beyond this I think we have a right—and a chance—to ask for competence in seeking and in using other sorts of expertise found elsewhere: military, scientific, specialized economic, and so forth. All these don't have to be put into the State Department if there are good generalists who can tap outside experts and combine their concerns with its own. This takes familiarity with other specialties and some in-house capability, but not, I should think, great masses of specialized staffs. To try to go beyond that—well, I think that is asking too much.

The State Department—A Super-Agency?

One aspect of the various super-Cabinet proposals is the "czardom" concept of coordination, the "court-of-first-resort" role. I see nothing of the sort for the State Department. The task here is not to decide, but to channel, to funnel, to sharpen, to make sure that other experts are consulted and that conflicts are rendered plain and decidable. That is the essence of preparatory staff work. This requires that an agency with its own expertise have great self-restraint, great generalist capability, if it is going to weigh its own perspectives against the perspectives of other people.

My hope is merely that we can get generalist skill in the State Department to do this kind of channeling and weighing with appropriate restraint. We ought to be able to get it more nearly from a department that specializes in diplomatic judgments than from experts who specialize in hardware judgments: it is easier to visualize it coming from the State Department than from the Defense Department.

It may be that the perspective which stems from the State Department's primary daily work—to take in diplomatic cables and to get them out, to deal with foreign offices and other diplomats—simply overwhelms the effort to serve also as generalist coordinator of contending perspectives. Yet this combination is what I think we have to try to achieve in the upper reaches of the State Department.

The Secretary of Defense is unlikely to be a shrinking violet; neither is the Secretary of the Treasury. I can't make promises about personalities in the future, but their institutional positions are such that they will be able to make their voices heard and their subordinates will have strong rights and will push to get them exercised. As for the White House, I am most doubtful that it would depend on the staff in the Secretary of State's Office to bring up all the papers, that the President's aides would merely scan them for proper form and then have the President sign. This seems to me a most unlikely eventuality.

All one really wants from State is this: on issues that the Special Assistant's office cannot handle because they aren't at the top of the President's own list, or because the President shifts off to something else after a decision has been made while such issues must be tidied up and tended to—all one wants is that the staff in the Secretary's Office will, conscientiously and carefully, with a sense of serving the whole government, make sure that all the people with a right to know, a right to be involved and to express opinions, will get a crack at the right time and place. This is asking a lot, but this is all I am asking. The better the State Department is able to do this, the more confidence will develop in the Pentagon and in the Treasury. The more effective this begins to be, the less will be the tendencies to hide information.

If other agencies find the State Department staff a good resource for them, a good avenue for them, they will use it. In the best of all possible worlds, this is still a far cry from czardom or from a "single" or "sole" source of advice. This is merely a means of getting the preparatory work done, putting everybody's advice in shape, getting the follow-up work done, passing the word, checking on what has been done, getting both kinds of work better handled beyond the range where White House staffers can do it themselves on an *ad hoc* basis.

Countering Parochial Perspectives

I think that most career officials are very conscientious in attempting faithfully to represent their superiors' needs. Narrowness of perspective is bound to creep in.

I think we have to try more to counteract this in certain key echelons, by all kinds of devices: exchanges of staff, an ever more imaginative use of War College methods of mingling military and civilian officials, an ever more imaginative use of our new situation overseas—making sure that younger officers in the national security complex out in the field, who are close to one another's business in a way they never were before, have every chance to interchange their roles and work wherever possible.

Ideally—and this is a bigger ideal than I care to spend much money on or tie myself to the stake for—we should be able over the next decade to broaden in considerable measure the career development of both Foreign Service officers and military officers headed for Pentagon work or field assignments at high levels. If we mix them up enough, in their work in the field as well as at home, in operations as well as in training, we are doing much to counter parochial tendencies.

We will never do away with these tendencies, but the mere fact that we have become accustomed over the last decade to interrelations that Secretary of Defense Johnson found rather abominable gives me some hope. If we really start building these interrelations into career development, we can gain—at least with respect to the crucial combination of Defense and State—not an identity of interests or experience or work but sensitivity about the other man's perspective and work to a degree we have never had before. If we start with a young enough Foreign Service or military officer, and many of our younger officers are extremely able, I should think that by 1975 we ought to have a civil service quite adequate for the problems of 1963, and that is progress.

THREE:

OFFICIAL DOCUMENTS

Excerpts from the Eberstadt Report

The Unification of the War and Navy Departments and Postwar Organization for National Security: Conclusions and Recommendations*

Summary of Conclusions

. . . *What changes in the present relationships of the military services and departments has our war experience indicated as desirable to improve our national security?*

Experience in the late war has revealed serious weaknesses in our present organizational set-up—weaknesses between and within the services, as well as in their relationships to other important elements concerned with our national security.

Mostly they were defects of coordination. Gaps between foreign and military policy—between the State Department and the Military Establishments. Gaps between strategic planning and its logistic implementation—between the Joint Chiefs of Staff and the military and civilian agencies responsible for industrial mobilization. Gaps between and within the military services—principally in the field of procurement and logistics. Gaps in information and intelligence—between the executive and legislative branches of our Government, between the several departments, and between Government and the people.

We have concluded that these faults were due principally to lack of appropriate and seasoned mechanisms and of adequate plans, policies, and procedures for coordination; lack of clear understanding and appreciation by one group or individual of the relation of others to the over-all job. These ills are susceptible of cure without dangerous experiments with our present set-up.

In our recommendations, we have indicated the form of military

* Excerpts from a report of Ferdinand Eberstadt for Secretary of the Navy James Forrestal, September 25, 1945.

organization which we think best adapted to dealing with the problems that face us, viz., a coordinate one having three departments— War, Navy, and Air—each headed by a civilian secretary of Cabinet rank and tied together by strong ligaments of coordination expressed by formal interorganizational links.

Obviously, neither the coordinate nor the unified form will equally advance all desirable objectives of postwar military policy. Our conclusion is that the coordinate form appears better adapted to advance those policies which seem more important.

This form would, in our opinion, foster civilian and Congressional influence and control over the military departments. It would, among other advantages, favor sound and efficient balance in the development of each arm of the service; it would furnish a broader basis for considerations of military and foreign policy and would be more responsive to new developments in the scientific field.

We thus come to your final question.

What form of postwar organization should be established and maintained to enable the military services and other Government departments and agencies most effectively to provide for and protect our national security?

The question of the form of organization of our military forces must be viewed in its proper perspective as only one part of a much larger picture encompassing many elements, military and civilian, governmental and private, which contribute to our national security and defense. It is obviously impossible to unify all these elements under one command, short of the President.

Our goal should be to bind them together in such a way as to achieve the most productive and harmonious whole. This calls for coordination as well as command, for parallel as well as subordinated effort. Where to use one and where to use the other are questions of balanced judgment and adjustment to be determined by the principles and traditions of our form of government, the lessons of experience, and the basic policies and objectives to be achieved.

The necessity of integrating all these elements into an alert, smoothly working, and efficient machine is more important now than ever before. Such integration is compelled by our present world commitments and risks, by the tremendously increased scope and tempo of modern warfare, and by the epochal scientific discoveries culminating in the atomic bomb.

This will involve, among others, organizational ties between the Department of State and the military departments, ties between the military departments in strategy and logistics, ties between the military departments and the agencies responsible for planning and carrying out mobilization of our industrial and human resources, between the gathering of information and intelligence and its dissemination and use, between scientific advances and their military application.

The next war will probably break out with little or no warning and will almost immediately achieve its maximum tempo of violence and destruction. Contrasting with the shortened opportunity for defensive preparation is the increased length of time necessary to prepare the complicated offensive and defensive weapons and organizational structure essential to modern warfare.

The nation not fully prepared will be at a greater disadvantage than ever before.

The great need, therefore, is that we be prepared always and all along the line, not simply to defend ourselves after an attack, but through all available political, military, and economic means to forestall any such attack. The knowledge that we are so prepared and alert will in itself be a great influence for world peace.

Much has been said about the importance of waging peace, as well as war. We have tried to suggest an organizational structure adapted to both purposes. . . .

Our specific recommendations follow. . . .

Creation of a National Security Council

To afford a permanent vehicle for maintaining active, close, and continuous contact between the departments and agencies of our Government responsible, respectively, for our foreign and military policies and their implementation, we recommend the establishment of a National Security Council.

The National Security Council would be the keystone of our organizational structure for national security.

It should be charged with the duty (1) of formulating and co-ordinating over-all policies in the political and military fields, (2) of assessing and appraising our foreign objectives, commitments and risks, and (3) of keeping these in balance with our military power, in being and potential.

It would be a policy-forming and advisory, not an executive, body.

Its membership should consist of the Secretaries of State, War, Navy, and Air, and the Chairman of the National Security Resources Board. . . . Provision should be made for such additions to its membership as the President may from time to time deem proper.

The President should be its Chairman. In his absence, the Vice President, being next in Presidential succession, or the senior member of the Cabinet, the Secretary of State, would act in this capacity.

The National Security Council should have a permanent secretariat, headed by a full-time executive, charged with preparing its agenda, providing data essential to its deliberations, and distributing its conclusions to the departments and agencies concerned for information and appropriate action.

The Joint Chiefs of Staff should be a part of, and meet with, the Council.

The National Security Council should take over the functions at present performed by the State-War-Navy Coordinating Committee.

The Central Intelligence Agency . . . should be a part of, and report to, the National Security Council. Its product is an important part of the grist of the Council's mill.

The Council should also control the policies and activities of the organizations responsible for the conduct of psychological and economic warfare and should maintain close relations with the civilian agency set up to coordinate military and civilian scientific research and development. . . .

It should review, and advise the President on, the combined military budget.

The Council should render annual reports to the President and to Congress. To the extent that national security does not absolutely require secrecy, its reports should be published. Thus the public would be kept posted on these vital matters by an authoritative and dependable source. In this way, the Council could aid in building up public support for clear-cut, consistent, and effective foreign and military policies.

In time of war, combination of the National Security Council with appropriate elements of the National Security Resources Board . . . would constitute the basis of a war cabinet.

Excerpt from the National Security Act of 1947, as Amended

Declaration of Policy

SECTION 2. In enacting this legislation, it is the intent of Congress to provide a comprehensive program for the future security of the United States; to provide for the establishment of integrated policies and procedures for the departments, agencies, and functions of the Government relating to the national security; to provide a Department of Defense, including the three military Departments of the Army, the Navy (including naval aviation and the United States Marine Corps), and the Air Force under the direction, authority, and control of the Secretary of Defense; to provide that each military department shall be separately organized under its own Secretary and shall function under the direction, authority, and control of the Secretary of Defense; to provide for their unified direction under civilian control of the Secretary of Defense but not to merge these departments or services; to provide for the establishment of unified or specified combatant commands, and a clear and direct line of command to such commands; to eliminate unnecessary duplication in the Department of Defense, and particularly in the field of research and engineering by vesting its over-all direction and control in the Secretary of Defense; to provide more effective, efficient, and economical administration in the Department of Defense; to provide for the unified strategic direction of the combatant forces, for their operation under unified command, and for their integration into an efficient team of land, naval, and air forces but not to establish a single Chief of Staff over the armed forces nor an overall armed forces general staff.[1]

[1] Amended by Section 2, Public Law 216, 81st Congress, August 10, 1949 (63 Stat. 578), further amended to read as indicated by Section 2 of Department of Defense Reorganization Act of 1958, August 6, 1958 (72 Stat. 514); 50 U.S.C. 401.

TITLE I—COORDINATION FOR NATIONAL SECURITY

National Security Council

SECTION 101. (*a*) There is hereby established a council to be known as the National Security Council (hereinafter in this section referred to as the "Council").

The President of the United States shall preside over meetings of the Council: *Provided*, That in his absence he may designate a member of the Council to preside in his place.

The function of the Council shall be to advise the President with respect to the integration of domestic, foreign, and military policies relating to the national security so as to enable the military services and the other departments and agencies of the Government to cooperate more effectively in matters involving the national security.

The Council shall be composed of—

(1) the President;
(2) the Vice President;
(3) the Secretary of State;
(4) the Secretary of Defense;
(5) [2]

---

[2] Reorganization Plan 7 of 1953, effective August 6, 1953, abolished the Mutual Security Administration and established the Foreign Operations Administration:

SEC. 2. TRANSFER OF FUNCTIONS TO THE DIRECTOR.—There are hereby transferred to the Director:

(a) All functions vested by the Mutual Security Act of 1951, as amended, or by any other statute in the Director for Mutual Security provided for in section 501 of that Act, or in the Mutual Security Agency created by that Act, or in any official or office of that Agency, including the functions of the Director for Mutual Security as a member of the National Security Council.

Pursuant to the provisions of sections 521 and 525 of the Mutual Security Act of 1954, Public Law 665, 83d Congress (68 Stat. 855, 856), and Executive Order 10610 of June 30, 1955, all functions (with certain specified exceptions) of the Director of the Foreign Operations Administration, and the Foreign Operations Administration, were transferred to the International Cooperation Administration in the State Department, to be headed by a Director. Pursuant to section 303 (a) and (b) of the Executive Order, the office of the Director of the Foreign Operations Administration and the membership of the Director of the Foreign Operations Administration together with the functions of the Director in his capacity as a member of the National Security Council were abolished.

(6) the Director of the Office of Emergency Planning;[3]

(7) the Secretaries and Under Secretaries of other executive departments and of the military departments, when appointed by the President by and with the advice and consent of the Senate, to serve at his pleasure.[4]

(b) In addition to performing such other functions as the President may direct, for the purpose of more effectively coordinating the policies and functions of the departments and agencies of the Government relating to the national security, it shall, subject to the direction of the President, be the duty of the Council—

(1) to assess and appraise the objectives, commitments, and risks of the United States in relation to our actual and potential military power, in the interest of national security, for the purpose of making recommendations to the President in connection therewith; and

(2) to consider policies on matters of common interest to the departments and agencies of the Government concerned with the national security, and to make recommendations to the President in connection therewith.

(c) The Council shall have a staff to be headed by a civilian executive secretary who shall be appointed by the President, and who shall receive compensation at the rate of [$10,000] [$15,000] $20,000 a year.[5] The executive secretary, subject to the direction of

[3] Reorganization Plan 3 (sec. 6) abolished the National Security Resources Board. Section 2 transferred to the Director of the Office of Defense Mobilization all functions of the Chairman of the National Security Resources Board (excluding those abolished by section 5), including his functions as a member of the National Security Council. Section 4 of Reorganization Plan 1 of 1958, effective July 1, 1958, as amended by Public Law 85-763, transferred the functions with respect to being a member of the National Security Council to the Director of the Office of Civil Defense and Defense Mobilization.

Public Law 296, 87th Congress (75 Stat. 630) changed the name of the Office of Civil and Defense Mobilization to the Office of Emergency Planning. Executive Order 11051, of September 27, 1962, continued in the Director of the Office of Emergency Planning the performance of certain national security functions already vested in the Director by statute or by prior Executive Order, including his functions as a member of the National Security Council.

[4] Reference to Chairman of Munitions Board, and Chairman of Research and Development Board deleted by Reorganization Plan 6, 1953 (sec. 2[b]) which abolished the offices of the Chairman of the Munitions Board and Chairman of the Research and Development Board and transferred their functions to the Secretary of Defense.

[5] Subsection (a) amended by section 3, Public Law 216, August 10, 1949 (63 Stat. 578), as amended by section 501 (e), Public Law 165, 82d Con-

the Council, is hereby authorized, subject to the civil-service laws and the Classification Act of 1923, as amended, to appoint and fix the compensation of such personnel as may be necessary to perform such duties as may be prescribed by the Council in connection with the performance of its functions.

(d) The Council shall, from time to time, make such recommendations, and such other reports to the President as it deems appropriate or as the President may require.

---

gress, October 10, 1951: subsection (c) supplemented by section 2 (a), Public Law 359, 81st Congress, October 15, 1949 (63 Stat. 880), under which authority the President fixed the salary of the Executive Secretary at $15,000 per annum: subsections (b) and (d) from section 101, Public Law 253, July 26, 1947 (61 Stat. 495). Pursuant to section 109, Public Law 854, 84th Congress, the President fixed the salary of the Executive Secretary at $20,000 per annum effective July 1, 1956.

Section 304(b), Public Law 426, 88th Congress, August 14, 1964, refers to the President's authority to fix the compensation of his administrative assistants, the NSC Executive Secretary, etc., at rates of basic compensation not to exceed level II of the Federal Executive Salary Schedule.

Executive Order 10700 by President Eisenhower, Further Providing for the Operations Coordinating Board, February 27, 1957

By virtue of the authority vested in me by the Constitution and statutes, and as President of the United States, it is hereby ordered as follows:

SECTION 1. (*a*) In order to assist in the effective coordination among certain agencies of certain functions relating to the national security and to provide for the integrated implementation of national security policies by the said agencies, there is hereby established within the structure of the National Security Council the Operations Coordinating Board, hereinafter referred to as the Board, which shall report to the National Security Council.

(*b*) The Board shall have as members the following: (1) the Under Secretary of State, who shall represent the Secretary of State, (2) the Deputy Secretary of Defense, who shall represent the Secretary of Defense, (3) the Director of Central Intelligence, (4) the Director of the United States Information Agency, (5) the Director of the International Cooperation Administration, and (6) one or more representatives of the President to be designated by the President. The Board shall have a chairman and a vice chairman, each of whom shall be designated by the President from among its members. Each head of agency referred to in items 1 to 5, inclusive, in this subsection may provide for an alternate member who shall serve as a member of the Board in lieu of the regular member representing the agency concerned whenever such regular member is, for reasons beyond his control, unable to attend any meeting of the Board.

(*c*) The head of any agency (other than any agency represented under section 1(*b*) hereof) to which the President from time to time assigns responsibilities for the implementation of national security policies shall assign a representative to serve on the Board when the Board is dealing with subjects bearing directly upon the responsibilities of such head. Each such representative shall be an Under Secretary or corresponding official. Each such head may provide for an alternate representative of his agency who shall attend any meeting of the Board, requiring representation of such agency, in lieu of the representative when the latter is, for reasons beyond his control, unable to attend.

(d) Any alternate members of the Board serving under section 1(b) of this order, and any representative or alternate representative serving under section 1(c) of this order, shall, while so serving, have in all respects the same status on the Board as the members of the Board provided for in section 1(b) hereof.

SECTION 2. The President having approved any national security policy after receiving the advice of the National Security Council thereon, the Board shall (1) whenever the President shall hereafter so direct, advise with the agencies concerned as to (a) their detailed operational planning responsibilities respecting such policy, (b) the coordination of the interdepartmental aspects of the detailed operational plans developed by the agencies to carry out such policy, (c) the timely and coordinated execution of such policy and plans, and (d) the execution of each security action or project so that it shall make its full contribution to the attainment of national security objectives and to the particular climate of opinion the United States is seeking to achieve in the world, and (2) initiate new proposals for action within the framework of national security policies in response to opportunity and changes in the situation. The Board shall perform such other advisory functions as the President may assign to it and shall from time to time make reports to the National Security Council with respect to the carrying out of this order.

SECTION 3. Subject to the provisions of section 101(c) of the National Security Act of 1947, as amended (50 U.S.C. 402 (c)):

(a) (1) The Board shall have, within the staff of the National Security Council, such staff as may be necessary to assist the Board in the performance of its functions, (2) the said staff of the Board shall be headed by an executive officer of the Board, and (3) employees of agencies may, consonant with law, be detailed to the aforesaid staff of the Board.

(b) Members of the staff of the Operations Coordinating Board provided for in Executive Order No. 10483, as amended, who are immediately prior to the taking effect of this order receiving compensation directly out of funds available to the said Board shall be transferred to the staff of the Board referred to in paragraph (a) of this section as of the effective date of this order. The said transfers shall be accomplished in consonance with applicable law, including the last proviso of section 12 of the Veterans Preference Act of 1944, as amended (5 U.S.C. 861).

(c) Appropriate arrangements may be made for the detail to the staff of the Board referred to in paragraph (a) of this section of employees of agencies who are immediately prior to the taking effect of the provisions of this order detailed to the staff of the Operations Coordinating Board provided for in Executive Order No. 10483, as amended.

SECTION 4. As used herein, the word "agency" may be construed to mean any instrumentality of the executive branch of the Government, including any executive department.

SECTION 5. Nothing in this order shall be construed either to confer upon the Board any function with respect to internal security or to abrogate or restrict in any manner any function vested by law in, or assigned pursuant to law to, any agency or head of agency (including the Office of Defense Mobilization and the Director of the Office of Defense Mobilization).

SECTION 6. The order supersedes Executive Order No. 10483 of September 2, 1953, and provisions amendatory thereof contained in other Executive orders (including, to the extent that it relates to the Operations Coordinating Board provided for in Executive Order No. 10483, the proviso of section 303(b) of Executive Order No. 10610 of May 9, 1955). Subject to the provisions of this order (including the limitations imposed by section 3 hereof), the Board may be deemed to be a continuation of the Operations Coordinating Board provided for in Executive Order No. 10483, as amended.

SECTION 7. The foregoing provisions of this order shall become effective on July 1, 1957, except that if funds appropriated for the National Security Council shall not have become available on that date for the support of the Board in consonance with this order, the said provisions shall become effective on such later date as funds so appropriated become so available.

DWIGHT D. EISENHOWER

THE WHITE HOUSE
February 25, 1957

Announcement by President-elect Kennedy of the Appointment of McGeorge Bundy as Special Assistant to the President, January 1, 1961

From: Press Office of
SENATOR JOHN F. KENNEDY
Palm Beach, Florida
For Release: Sunday,
January 1, 1961

President-elect John F. Kennedy today announced the appointment of McGeorge Bundy as Special Assistant to the President. Mr. Bundy will work in the field of national security affairs and will direct the staffs associated with the Council. Mr. Bundy succeeds Mr. Gordon Gray, President Eisenhower's Assistant for National Security Affairs.

Mr. Kennedy indicated that his appointment of Mr. Bundy represented a first step toward streamlining the National Security Council staff organization and simplifying NSC procedures.

The President-elect stated:

I intend to consolidate under Mr. Bundy's direction the present National Security Council secretariat, the staff and functions of the Operations Coordinating Board, and the continuing functions of a number of special projects staffs within the White House. I have asked Mr. Bundy to review with care existing staff organization and arrangements, and to simplify them wherever possible toward the end that we may have a single, small, but strongly organized staff unit to assist me in obtaining advice from, and coordinating operations of, the government agencies concerned with national security affairs.

Mr. Bundy will serve as my personal assistant on these matters and as director of whatever staff we find is needed for the purpose. It will be part of his assignment to facilitate the work of the National Security Council as a body advisory to the President. I intend to seek advice from the members of the Council, both collectively and individually, and it is my hope to use the National Security Council and its machinery more flexibly than in the past. I have been much impressed with the constructive criticism contained in the recent staff report by Senator Jackson's Subcommittee on National Policy Machinery. The Subcommittee's study provides a useful starting point for the work that Mr. Bundy will undertake in helping me to strengthen and to simplify the operations of the National Security Council.

Statement by President Kennedy Abolishing the Operations Coordinating Board, February 19, 1961

I am today issuing an Executive Order abolishing the Operations Coordinating Board. This Board was used in the last administration for work which we now plan to do in other ways. This action is part of our program for strengthening the responsibility of the individual departments.

First, we will center responsibility for much of the Board's work in the Secretary of State. He expects to rely particularly on the Assistant Secretaries in charge of regional bureaus, and they in turn will consult closely with other departments and agencies. This will be our ordinary rule for continuing coordination of our work in relation to a country or area.

Second, insofar as the OCB—as a descendant of the old Psychological Strategy Board—was concerned with the impact of our actions on foreign opinion—our "image" abroad—we expect its work to be done in a number of ways: in my own office, in the State Department, under Mr. Murrow of USIA, and by all who are concerned with the spirit and meaning of our actions in foreign policy. We believe that appropriate coordination can be assured here without extensive formal machinery.

Third, insofar as the OCB served as an instrument for ensuring action at the President's direction, we plan to continue its work by maintaining direct communication with the responsible agencies, so that everyone will know what I have decided, while I in turn keep fully informed of the actions taken to carry out decisions. We of course expect that the policy of the White House will be the policy of the executive branch as a whole, and we shall take such steps as are needed to ensure this result.

I expect that the senior officials who served as formal members of OCB will still keep in close and informal touch with each other on problems of common interest. Mr. Bromley Smith, who has been the executive officer of the OCB, will continue to work with my special assistant, Mr. McGeorge Bundy, in following up on White House decisions in the area of national security. In these varied ways we intend that the net result shall be a strengthening of the process by which our policies are effectively coordinated and carried out, throughout the executive branch.

Executive Order 10920
Revoking Executive Order No. 10700
of February 25, 1957, As Amended

By virtue of the authority vested in me by the Constitution and statutes, and as President of the United States, it is ordered that Executive Order No. 10700 of February 25, 1957, entitled "Further Providing for the Operations Coordinating Board," as amended, be, and it is hereby, revoked.

JOHN F. KENNEDY

THE WHITE HOUSE
February 18, 1961

Resolution Expressing the Concern of the Senate Over Turnover in Policy-making Posts

86th Congress, 2d Session, S. Res. 338*

Whereas the unprecedented challenge of the cold war has placed heavy demands on the energies and abilities of high Government officials; and

Whereas the requirements for policy planning and decision-making in the national security field have placed a premium on knowledgeable, experienced excutives; and

Whereas the complexities and technicalities of national security problems have steadily increased the minimum period of Government experience required before responsibilities can be discharged effectively; and

Whereas brief tenure in office tends to have a harmful impact on the effective formulation and execution of national security policies while the Nation has been well served through continuity of service in office by other officials; and

Whereas the problem of turnover has not been confined in its effects to any one administration: Now, therefore, be it

Resolved, That it is the sense of the Senate that individuals appointed to administrative and policymaking posts should be willing to serve for a period long enough to permit them to contribute effectively in their assigned tasks; and be it further

Resolved, That it is the sense of the Senate that nominees appearing before its committees shall indicate their willingness to serve so long as the President desires.

---

* On June 20, 1960, Mr. JACKSON (for himself, Mr. HUMPHREY, Mr. MUSKIE, Mr. MUNDT, and Mr. JAVITS) submitted the following resolution; it was referred to the Committee on Government Operations. On JUNE 28, 1960, the resolution was reported by Mr. JACKSON, with an amendment. On JULY 2, 1960, the resolution was considered, amended, and agreed to.

Index*

* Figures in boldface refer to pages on which the actual testimony of the person referred to, or the actual text of the listed document, appears.